A CELEBRATION OF POETS

ATLANTIC
GRADES 4-12
FALL 2010

creativeCOMMUNICATION
A CELEBRATION OF TODAY'S WRITERS

A CELEBRATION OF POETS
ATLANTIC
GRADES 4-12
FALL 2010

AN ANTHOLOGY COMPILED BY CREATIVE COMMUNICATION, INC.

Publishec by:

creativeCOMMUNICATION
A CELEBRATION OF TODAY'S WRITERS

1488 NORTH 200 WEST · LOGAN, UTAH 84341
TEL. 435-713-4411 · WWW.POETICPOWER.COM

Authors are responsible for the originality of the writing submitted.

ISBN: 978-1-60050-401-3

FOREWORD

As we start our nineteenth year of working with student writers across the US and Canada, I think back on the positive effects created by our contests and anthologies. Each year I receive hundreds of letters from students who state that being accepted to be published created a spark that brightened their educational experience. Years later, after these students have graduated, I have other letters that report back on successes after high school. These letters are from students who credited Creative Communication as the start of their writing career and have now published their first book of poems or a novel.

These letters help us to know the importance of what we do. I always tell our judges that behind the entries are students whose lives can be changed. I tell them that Creative Communication doesn't publish poems and essays, we publish hopes and dreams.

So here we are, another contest completed and more "hopes and dreams" being published. We hope that these entries fulfill their purpose of entertaining you and helping these student authors know that they have met a milestone in their lives. The poems in this book represent the best and brightest of today's student writers. Enjoy, and realize that the Hemmingways, Plaths or Frosts of tomorrow may be published today, between these pages.

Sincerely,

Thomas Worthen, Ph.D.
Editor
Creative Communication

WRITING CONTESTS!

Enter our next POETRY contest!

Enter our next ESSAY contest!

Why should I enter?
Win prizes and get published! Each year thousands of dollars in prizes are awarded throughout North America. The top writers in each division receive a monetary award and a free book that includes their published poem or essay. Entries of merit are also selected to be published in our anthology.

Who may enter?
There are four divisions in the poetry contest. The poetry divisions are grades K-3, 4-6, 7-9, and 10-12. There are three divisions in the essay contest. The essay divisions are grades 3-6, 7-9, and 10-12.

What is needed to enter the contest?
To enter the poetry contest send in one original poem, 21 lines or less. To enter the essay contest send in one original non-fiction essay, 250 words or less, on any topic. Please submit each poem and essay with a title, and the following information clearly printed: the writer's name, current grade, home address (optional), school name, school address, teacher's name and teacher's email address (optional). Contact information will only be used to provide information about the contest. For complete contest information go to www.poeticpower.com.

How do I enter?
Enter a poem online at:
www.poeticpower.com
or
Mail your poem to:
Poetry Contest
1488 North 200 West
Logan, UT 84341

Enter an essay online at:
www.poeticpower.com
or
Mail your essay to:
Essay Contest
1488 North 200 West
Logan, UT 84341

When is the deadline?
Poetry contest deadlines are August 16th, December 6th, and April 5th. Essay contest deadlines are July 19th, October 18th and February 15th. Students can enter one poem and one essay for each spring, summer, and fall contest deadline.

Are there benefits for my school?
Yes. We award $12,500 each year in grants to help with Language Arts programs. Schools qualify to apply for a grant by having 15 or more accepted entries.

Are there benefits for my teacher?
Yes. Teachers with five or more students published receive a free anthology that includes their students' writing.

For more information please go to our website at **www.poeticpower.com**, email us at editor@poeticpower.com or call 435-713-4411.

TABLE OF CONTENTS

STATES INCLUDED IN THIS EDITION:

DELAWARE
DISTRICT OF COLUMBIA
MARYLAND
RHODE ISLAND
VIRGINIA

Fall 2010
Poetic Achievement
Honor Schools

*Teachers who had fifteen or more poets accepted to be published

The following schools are recognized as receiving a "Poetic Achievement Award." This award is given to schools who have a large number of entries of which over fifty percent are accepted for publication. With hundreds of schools entering our contest, only a small percent of these schools are honored with this award. The purpose of this award is to recognize schools with excellent Language Arts programs. This award qualifies these schools to receive a complimentary copy of this anthology. In addition, these schools are eligible to apply for a Creative Communication Language Arts Grant. Grants of two hundred and fifty dollars each are awarded to further develop writing in our schools.

Bensley Elementary School
Richmond, VA
Carolyn Booth
Amanda Collins
Christy Frear
Katie Griffin
Maria T. MacLaughlin*
Satonya Perry

Bishop Walsh Middle High School
Cumberland, MD
Ann Workmeister*

Blackrock School
Coventry, RI
Michaela L. Wells*

Blue Ridge Middle School
Purcellville, VA
Ms. Brower
Virginia Walker*

Boonsboro Elementary School
Boonsboro, MD
Suzanne Sullivan
Jeremy White

Brandywine Springs School
Wilmington, DE
Lisa Davis
Margaret Johns*
Jill Szymanski

Chickahominy Middle School
Mechanicsville, VA
Holly Angelidis
Kimberly Harrell
Melissa Ingram-Crouch
Crystal Owens
Carol H. Valentine
Suzanne Zulauf

Covenant Life School
Gaithersburg, MD
Denise Griney*

Delaware Military Academy
Wilmington, DE
Brittany Carson*
Tara Dick
Najma Landis

Dinwiddie High School
Dinwiddie, VA
Scott Brockwell*

Eleanor Roosevelt High School
Greenbelt, MD
Danielle Sinclitico*

Floyd T Binns Middle School
Culpeper, VA
Cathleen Beachboard*
Charissa Hollyfield*
Lindsay McFarland*
Miss Shaffer
Cathleen Stocktill

Forestville Military Academy
Forestville, MD
Loretta Adih*
Faye Johnson

Graham Middle School
Bluefield, VA
John Crist*
Sandra Kegley*
Angela McClure
Karen Sluss

Homeschool Plus
Norfolk, VA
Carol Martin Gregory*

Immaculate Conception Catholic Regional
School
Cranston, RI
Judy McCusker*

Kilmer Middle School
Vienna, VA
Mary Kay Folk*
Joseph McElveen
Taheerah Stewart

Lafayette Winona Middle School
Norfolk, VA
Katina Dunbar*
Monica McDonald

Marshall Middle School
The Plains, VA
Sandra P. Simpson*

Mary Walter Elementary School
Bealeton, VA
Patricia Baker*

Parkdale High School
Riverdale, MD
Neville Adams*

Paul L Dunbar Middle School for Innovation
Lynchburg, VA
April Cutsail
Tracy Foster
Amy Hart
Contessa Johnson
Susan McLawhorn
Michael Potts
Meg Smith*

Pemberton Elementary School
Richmond, VA
Ann M. Ballinger
Kay Faries
Katie Schmid

Rosemont Forest Elementary School
Virginia Beach, VA
Beverly Wooddell*

Sacred Heart School
Glyndon, MD
Kathleen Gower
Lynda Rodgers
Donna Russell*

Sanford School
Hockessin, DE
Christine Yasik*

St Bartholomew School
Bethesda, MD
Sr. Nena Larocco*

St Jane De Chantal School
Bethesda, MD
Shannon Cron*

St Joseph School-Fullerton
Baltimore, MD
Trish Garing*
J. Delores Keefer*
Bonnie Myszowski
Peggy Radziminski*

St Rocco School
Johnston, RI
Judy Carroccio*

Tasker Middle School
Bowie, MD
Linda Lewis*
Natiqua Riley

Woodbridge Sr High School
Woodbridge, VA
Keiranne Barnicle
Mrs. Catherine
Mary Cavallaro
Jean Ellerbe
Nicole Etienne
Vanessa Gardiner
Susan Guidry
Catherine Hailey
Deborah Kelly
Vitali Kopylov
Ashley Lamb
Cynthia Lazo
Andrew McCarthy
Joseph Potente
Brittany Powell
Ann Ragsdale
Zita Stumhoher
Erin Wetzel

Language Arts
Grant Recipients
2010-2011

After receiving a "Poetic Achievement Award" schools are encouraged to apply for a Creative Communication Language Arts Grant. The following is a list of schools who received a two hundred and fifty dollar grant for the 2010-2011 school year.

Adolph Schreiber Hebrew Academy, Monsey, NY
August Boeger Middle School, San Jose, CA
Bedford Road School, Pleasantville, NY
Benton Central Jr/Sr High School, Oxford, IN
Birchwood School, Cleveland, OH
Blue Ball Elementary School, Blue Ball, PA
Bonneville High School, Idaho Falls, ID
Cedar Ridge High School, Newark, AR
Corpus Christi School, San Francisco, CA
Crestwood Elementary School, Rockford, MI
Dodson Elementary School, Canton, MI
Dr Howard K Conley Elementary School, Chandler, AZ
Eastport Elementary School, Eastport, ME
Emmanuel-St Michael Lutheran School, Fort Wayne, IN
Fannin County Middle School, Blue Ridge, GA
Fort Recovery Elementary School, Fort Recovery, OH
Frank Ohl Intermediate School, Youngstown, OH
Frenship Middle School, Wolfforth, TX
Gateway Pointe Elementary School, Gilbert, AZ
Greencastle-Antrim Middle School, Greencastle, PA
Greenville High School, Greenville, AL
Hancock County High School, Sneedville, TN
Holy Child Academy, Drexel Hill, PA
Holy Cross High School, Delran, NJ
Holy Family Catholic School, Granite City, IL
Interboro GATE Program, Prospect Park, PA
John E Riley Elementary School, South Plainfield, NJ
Joseph M Simas Elementary School, Hanford, CA
Lee A Tolbert Community Academy, Kansas City, MO
Malvern Middle School, Malvern, OH
Merritt Central Elementary School, Merritt, BC
Metcalf School, Exeter, RI
Norfolk Christian Middle School, Norfolk, VA

Language Arts Grant Winners cont.

Pioneer Career & Technology Center, Shelby, OH
Providence Hall, Herriman, UT
Ramsay School, Ramsay, MT
Reuben Johnson Elementary School, McKinney, TX
Round Lake High School, Round Lake, MN
Sacred Heart School, Oxford, PA
Selwyn College Preparatory School, Denton, TX
Shadowlawn Elementary School, Green Cove Springs, FL
St Elizabeth Catholic School, Rockville, MD
St Lorenz Lutheran School, Frankenmuth, MI
The Oakridge School, Arlington, TX
Tomlin Middle School, Plant City, FL
Vista Fundamental School, Simi Valley, CA
Walsh Elementary School, Walsh, CO
Washington County Union School, Roper, NC
Woodland Intermediate School, Gurnee, IL
Woodward Granger High School, Woodward, IA

Grades 10-11-12 Top Ten Winners

List of Top Ten Winners for Grades 10-12; listed alphabetically

Emily Alexander, Grade 11
Moscow Sr High School, ID

Yuliya Astapova, Grade 10
Paul D. Schreiber High School, NY

Lauren Bigelow, Grade 12
Marymount Academy, ON

Madison Corbett, Grade 11
Roswell High School, GA

Melissa Crow, Grade 11
Rifle High School, CO

Michaela Cunningham, Grade 10
Hilliard Davidson High School, OH

Beth Mader, Grade 11
Montgomery-Lonsdale High School, MN

Ferin Neff, Grade 11
St Joseph Central Catholic High School, WV

Jake Schwartz, Grade 12
William Mason High School, OH

Courtney Thompson, Grade 12
Lake Braddock Secondary School, VA

All Top Ten Poems can be read at www.poeticpower.com

Note: The Top Ten poems were finalized through an online voting system. Creative Communication's judges first picked out the top poems. These poems were then posted online. The final step involved thousands of students and teachers who registered as the online judges and voted for the Top Ten poems. We hope you enjoy these selections.

9-11

The fire is burning
Everybody watching is mourning
The fire is everywhere
There's no place to hide
A lot of bodies are burning up inside.

9-11 was the most tragic day
One minute they were there
The next day gone away
All anybody could do was cry
There was nothing much to say.

Survivors were burying their loved ones away
When you think about it, It must have hurt
Seeing ashes, laying on the dirt
Not knowing who they were.

It was sad, in a split second the whole world was turned bad
All the victims families could do was cry
And no one could even comfort them and explain to them why.

Julia Perkins, Grade 10
Thomas Jefferson Center, VA

The Short Pier

A blind man took a walk
He had no idea he was being stalked
He didn't know his life was going tick-tock, tick-tock
He fell off the pier
His life was ended like a deer
Because he put his faith in wooden piers

He should have listen to who was near
But now we fear
That dreadful pier
His life was ended
And it can't be mended
So young he was

We are the blind man
Putting our faith in the piers

Jor-El Sanchez, Grade 11
Leonardtown High School, MD

Pop-Pop

There he lies in his bed for eternity
Everyone is in tears
As they know we are going to the cemetery
This is not the greatest part of his life
As he looks above his children when they cry
All the memories of him were fun
But now there is no more pain
No more surgery
No more suffering

Bryan Merrill, Grade 10
Delaware Military Academy, DE

Get Off My Big Mac!!!!

I know you're staring at me
Every time I look at you
Turning your head each time
You pretend not to see me
Rubbing your hairy vomit covered hands together
Like you are actually doing something
But I don't want you near me
Find another to stare at
We had our moment
Stop staring!!!
Do you really not get it!?!?
I swing to send the message
But you come back again
And again
And again!!!!
Till finally
Swat!!!
It's over.
I hate flies.

Donald Ingram, Grade 12
Tunstall High School, VA

Tide

You are like a running tide,
Coming towards me, but pulling away.
Coming with a mighty force or a gentle touch.
Though you are reliable, you come every day.
I come to meet you when you come in, and
I chase after you when you run out.
If I get too close, you pull me under.
You take me away with your magnetic pull.
But you keep me calm with your pulsing rhythm,
It's a lullaby that lays me to sleep.
I can't resist you, you call me to you.
Your vast expanses draw me close.
I'm not afraid; you are a gentle giant,
You are like a running tide.

Shaune Young, Grade 10
Harford Christian School, MD

Missing You

All though I'm missing you, I'll find a way to get through living without you. You are my baby, my best friend, my strength, and my pride only God may know why but still I'll get by. Who would have known that you had to go so suddenly so fast, and how could it be that a sweet memory would be all that I'd have left? But now you're gone and every day I go on though life is just not the same but I'll try, I'll try to face the pain. You dried all my tears and calmed all my fears. I love you and you love me, when we are together it seems like it's meant to be. But the question is "Are you happy?" All though I'll be missing you I'll find a way to get through living without you. You are my baby, my best friend, my strength, and my pride only God may know why but still I'll get by.

Armethia White, Grade 11
Forestville Military Academy, MD

Self Portrait

Wrapped up in a blanket of self-loathing,
while swept away by superiority.
Self conscious; selfish
with an air of confidence.
A recluse with a
longing to be surrounded by friends.
A yawning conscience
and a giving heart.
Living in a fairytale and
reminding everyone of the reality.
Ready to go and
afraid to leave.
Fishing for compliments and
waiting for an empty hook to surface and disappoint.
Wholeheartedly caring
with a separate agenda.
Keeping everyone at arm's length and
secretly longing to let them in.
Contradictions.
Me.

Rachel Harman, Grade 12
Dinwiddie High School, VA

Fall or Fly

From God we come and to God we return.
Will I return to the light or fall below and burn?
These decisions I make now, they come at a price.
I can choose to fall from grace, or fly to paradise.
Earth is the nest, in reality a giant test.
Eventually we must leave the nest,
if we fly we did what's best, we passed the test.
And if we fall it is because we failed to learn God's words,
I don't know what I'm doing. Whether I'll fly with the birds
or be pulled down by Earthly gravity and the pleasures of today,
and push difficult thoughts of tomorrow away.
But tomorrow is always closer than it seems.
If life is balance, one day I'll fall off the beam.
One day I will leave the nest, one day I will die,
and back to God I will fall or fly.
From God we come and to God we return.

Ayesha Zafar, Grade 11
Gar-Field High School, VA

Jessica

I could say you're beautiful if I wanted to
but you're so much more
beautiful just looks good on you
your body spells angel from head to floor
you stand there and you never knew how hard I fell for you
I stand here thinking of what to say
wanting you to say you love me too
but it's hard to talk when you take my breath away
so don't break my heart as I hand it to you
and let's love life no matter what we do

Anthony Mikulskis, Grade 10
Johnston Sr High School, RI

Pieces

The world is a puzzle, to which we're the pieces,
That can't be completed if one piece releases.
No matter the shape, size big or small,
Each piece alone makes no sense at all.

Much like a bird that's lost from a flock,
Or one missing gear that stops a whole clock.
It takes several links to make up a chain
And there can't be a beach with only one grain.

You can't start a fire with only one stick,
Or assemble a wall with only one brick.
A slender rope is likely to shred
If it doesn't consist of more than one thread.
Decisions are based off multiple votes
And music is made with a sequence of notes.

Every part plays a definite role,
That work as a team for a mutual goal.
It's not the steps but the combination,
Each a star in life's constellation.

Courtney Thompson, Grade 12
Lake Braddock Secondary School, VA

Fall

Fall is here
Fall is near
Fall time is everywhere
As changes occur we all observe
Wondering what is taking place
Looking at how beautiful things are
Smelling the vivid scents
Enjoying every breath we take
Every day get up knowing fall is coming to a close
Oh fall please don't go
Winter hold off the snow
Give me another day with these parades of colors
I got my wish I'm outside playing in the leaves
Wow how I love to breathe
I never want fall to leave
Now November is here and fall is slipping out of my reach
I'm scared to go to sleep and wake up
I know fall is going to leave me
I go to sleep, wake up, same thing the next day
I woke up saddened
Finally fall went away

Ronesha Sockwell, Grade 10
Forestville Military Academy, MD

The Recollection

Sometimes I think back to that day;
my memory sparkles as it recalls the emotions.
Happiness brings tears, glistening within my eyes.
My heart aches at the remembrance of such compassion.

Amanda Wassenberg, Grade 11
Woodbridge Sr High School, VA

Winter

The leaves fall all around the Earth and sky.
She drinks away a glass of water. The
chill creeps up and bites. Why does it seem like
time is lost? There are no more pigments, just
white. Minds begin to wander mem'ries of
the warmth. The weather retells one of his
life. Tests and battles make him stronger in
the mind and frozen objects linger to
the side. Complex views will depart, just a
trace of the simple will remain. Hearts still
warm, they beat longer, deeper. Loving as
one piece, the world's content and hopes to see
the new light. People pass by and see the
change. It takes their breath up, away and lifts
it to the sky. Revived and pure, it says
to us goodbye. It makes way for new life,
old and cold has died and fresh new scents please
and bring delight. Smiles greet the warmth again
and the chill hides behind its coat once more.

Carla Schrader, Grade 11
Walsingham Academy Upper School, VA

Your Promise

Trying to go out of the past
and find someone new is hard.
You have to rebuild trust and honesty
With someone new.
But if you find the right someone
the past hurt will disappear.
Lucky for me I found that right someone.
You made it so easy for me
to forget my past.
You picked up the pieces of my heart
That were broken, and put them back with care.
You let me know you will always be there
for me and never hurt me.
That's why I am making this promise
never stop loving you no matter what
happens!

Gabrielle DeJesus, Grade 12
Delaware Military Academy, DE

Just Because

Just because I go to the Delaware Military Academy
Doesn't mean I love the military
Or that I'm a hardcore tank at pushups and sit ups
Or that I love wearing a Navy uniform every day
Or that I love putting on pins and ribbons every morning
Just because I'm in the NJROTC
Doesn't mean I love to march
Or that I like to rifle drill
Or that I like saying "yes sir" or "yes ma'am"
Just because I go to a military academy
Doesn't mean I love the military

Andrew Gebhart, Grade 10
Delaware Military Academy, DE

Normality

The sun in the sky hit the side of my face,
I knew I was in a far away place.
The trees were blue and the sky was green,
But somehow it felt normal as weird as it seemed.

The water was yellow and the grass was blue,
The sand was purple and the people were too.
I looked at myself and I wasn't what I seemed,
Then all of a sudden I awoke from my dream.

I awoke to find normality,
And I was back at home.
I went to look at myself,
And I was my normal skin tone.

My eyes were brown,
And my hair's back the same.
But what if my dream was our normal,
Things would not be the same.

Jacqueline Sweeney, Grade 12
Lighthouse Christian Academy, MD

I Am Not of This World

Life builds its walls around me
Trapping me in a prison of its design
My mind cannot be beaten into submission
I can soar past the walls
To worlds of my imagination
Different planets formed in my mind
With their own people, living their own lives
Struggling, loving, laughing, dying
In the dim streets of a lamp-lit city or the wilds of a forest
Always arriving at a happy ending, and ground to dirt
But my mind is always free, breathing and strong
Living lives I cannot
Joyous when my life is not
Free when I am not
I live in the world of daydreams
So that my life is not a nightmare

Rebecca Thayer, Grade 12
Bishop Walsh Middle High School, MD

Going Back

Going back to the chi,
Just me, myself, and I
Heading back I'll miss you all
Just wanted ya'll to know I had a ball
I'll keep you in my heart
Ya'll like my blood family
Close like my mommy and my daddy
I feel I've known ya'll since I was able to crawl
I feel like you people been there every time I fall
So enough with all the mushy stuff I just want to say *Bye*
I just hope I'll see ya'll again before I *Die*

Shomari Dowdy, Grade 11
Forestville Military Academy, MD

The Second Generation

They accumulate one by one,
About a year apart.
Too much for a mother to handle.
She seeks help.
Though illegitimate,
The mother still apathetic.
She handles them all
Like their donor.
Number one's donor was built
Of liquor, rather than blood.
She serves the offspring
Like his donor.
Number two's donor had powerful force.
To his advantage he used it.
She treats the offspring
Like his donor.
Number three's donor loved another.
Unloving and never present.
She rejects the offspring
Like his donor.
The second generation now becomes the first.

Ashley Turnbull, Grade 12
Bishop Walsh Middle/High School, MD

More Than Skin Deep

It can make people feel a negative way.
People look at the media and for it they will pay.
People go to a plastic surgeon and get operations left and right,
just so they can look acceptable in other people's sight.
Girls look at the supermodels and stars and are green with envy.
But they don't know how these people used to be.
If only they saw how these people looked back in the day.
If only they knew that beauty can be shown in more than one way.
It can be shown by your wit or personality,
which can be shown by the way you look at reality.
It can be shown by your intelligence and character too,
which can be shown by the way you go through.
It can be shown by your creativity or inner strength as well,
because people notice how you act when things aren't going so well.
So, remember this when you think that you can't take it no more
and the hill seems too steep,
true beauty is more than skin deep.

Amber Gardner, Grade 10
Warwick High School, VA

Christmas

I wake up on Christmas day
I open all gifts
I go back to sleep
I eat ham and green beans and sweet potato pie with cool whip
I am happy about Christmas

Cori Green, Grade 10
Woodbridge Sr High School, VA

2012

The ground is wet;
Dark patches of water fill up the concrete that was once light.
All of this based around a bet,
This bet had an intensity of much height.

The Sun doesn't shine, but clouds cover the sky.
Clouds of smoke, clouds of death, clouds that hide.
Buildings destroyed, the world kissing the universe goodbye.
Death instead of life, now it will abide.

No people move, no people can be seen.
No animals, no plants, no life.
Scientists, now on their theory, can lean,
But no one can hear their complaints; their heartache and strife.

It has now happened, just like they said it would.
Is it because of lack of faith and hope?
Has God come down and gotten us like we knew he could?
Or is this just another way that we humans could never cope?

When they said it would happen, some didn't believe.
They are now up in heaven, living without a care.
But many stayed in the burning flames that deceive,
This is the punishment that they will bear.

Benton Evans, Grade 11
Christiansburg High School, VA

How the Storms Change

At six,
Fear shook me
The imagined fist hit the house as the wind rattled windows
There were rivers from the sky
Mountain springs down my cheeks because I could not swim

My mother's stories of giants dancing, twirling,
Stomping
Above the clouds, never left me calm
Never kept me from running,
From the light
The flash
The boom

At Sixteen,
The boom excites me
Like the drum solo of my favorite song
The white cracks in the dark sky
Igniting air
The rain turns up
Adding new melodies
Ping! Patter Patter
And the wind and I sway together

Charis Pannell, Grade 11
Eleanor Roosevelt High School, MD

What Dance Means to Me

Dance it's one word, it's 5 letters
It means so much to me
Like you have no idea
Live your life, my life is dance
I eat breathe and sleep dance other than school and homework and everything else
Why dance you wonder well for me
I love the feelings it stirs in me, all the emotions that comes leaping out of me
I love performing I love choreography I love practice I love everything about dance. I love glitter and sparkles
Practice truly does make perfect
Dance why dance you ask?. I dance for everything
I dance for joy, I dance for tears, I dance because it amazes me
I dance and still believe, I dance for the world stops or at least it does for me. That's how I feel
Dance is passion, dance to heal hurt, dance to heal rejection
Dance under the rainbow, dance under the stars
Dance when no one is watching, dance when everyone is watching.
Dance Why dance? Good question
If I didn't dance I would cry every day. I have.
When you feel pain dance. When you want to cry dance.
For me everything is solved by dance. I just wish I could live dance
But you cannot always do what you want to
But I love doing other stuff too.

Eva Moffat, Grade 12
St Margaret's School, VA

Fall Season

Leaves fall delicately,
Each a different color of auburns and yellows,
Riding the wind, up the sky, to the ground.
Skies blue and winds crisp,
Breathing in the cool air
Breathing out the stress of yesteryear.
Children walking home from long days of knowledge for possible futures.
The sound of loud laughter and the sound of small cries,
Future adults ready to take on the world.
Here I am, sitting on the side
Watching God's paintbrush paint the sky the magnificent colors of the sunset,
Having a cup of warm goodness slide down my throat,
Letting my tongue enjoy the smooth tingling sensation of apple and cinnamon.
I watch time walk by me, changing, letting the bright day turn into a cool night.
I watch as He let His paintbrush stroke freely.
Create a masterpiece,
As I try to steal this image for my own and slap its majesty onto my own canvas.
I can never again let the glories of God escape my grasps because of the feelings that I have for it.
Above all, I believe this is His greatest creation that he is willing to share with us
And I, a lowly form of man, am able to see it, this beauty, the beautiful season of fall.

Morgan Richardson, Grade 10
Woodbridge Sr High School, VA

A Fall Breath

A breeze of a bittersweet summer blows a strand of freedom across the ground. The leaves change slowly and fall to the earth.
The smell of fresh air and the last few days summer sinks into the deep pores of earth.
The faithfulness of the leaves giving into temptation weakens the tree's soul.
The days grow shorter and the forest loses her only memory of those forgiving eyes of the cool creeks mud.
It's no escaping that what forever seems like a cold kiss from the morning air.

Kelsey Newcomb, Grade 11
Dinwiddie High School, VA

Tin Love

My shiny shell of tin,
The image of a knight in armor
Yet I'm hollow and haunted
By nightmares of love.

Love is just a word now
Which echoes in vast emptiness
Where my heart, my soul,
Where you used to be cradled.

The hands that once caressed your cheek
Are now rusted and flaking
From when I placed them over my face
To hide the tears that wouldn't stop.

I was once loved by you but the simple truth
Is now I'm only empty tin
My love, my faith, my confidence,
Was drained by you but it won't happen again.

April Teale, Grade 10
Woodbridge Sr High School, VA

Asperger's Syndrome

Wires twisted in my head,
swirls of cables,
electric.
A DIY, minus instructions
on how to put it together,
A to B and C to D.
So, the inventor decides to wing it,
see what happens.
I happened.
My shell is no more flawed than any other, but inside,
I am different,
unique.
Is that good, bad, or ugly?
I am still finding out,
day by day by day by day…

Sydney Anderson, Grade 10
Woodbridge Sr High School, VA

Muse

Pen to paper, ready to write
Where has my muse ran off to tonight?
I've checked through the drawers and TV stand
I've looked in the closet, the "no-man's land"
I dug through my pockets, just to see
If even a small idea would appear to me
But alas, I found nothing and continued to look
Searching my room, every cranny and nook
And just when it seemed, all hope had run out
I turned around, startled, and gave a small shout
I stared at my paper and what did I see?
I wrote all these words, my muse had found me!

Mary Tadlock, Grade 12
Turner Ashby High School, VA

Words

Words…
Always spoken, embedded in creation
Uttered by actions, jumbled throughout our inner-being
On the tip of our tongue, describing who we are
Not meant to hurt, yet the cause most often
Major contribution to advancement, depicted in all things,
Starting out as intelligence, and ending up stupid
Identifying humans, piercing to the heart
Made for worship, yet the cause of our fall
Infesting our hearts, consuming our being
Eternally beautiful, yet a recurring cause of death
Words are magic, they envelop voice.
Words are the dust on a rag,
Untied from one, yet tied to another
Words can be innocuous,
Yet so often leave profound ruts in a road
Shattering to the soul they may be,
Yet they create smiles that last a lifetime,
And eyes brighter than the sun

Abigail Dowell, Grade 10
James River High School, VA

1920s flapper, I wish I knew

half full jar of peppermint patties
comfortable on the antique side table
no more than six inches away from
that ugly blue lazi-boy

on your bed,
stripped of linen
your vanity mirror rejects my wide-eyed face —
it's not the porcelain doll in the red fringe dress

i feel robbed
sitting on your aged recliner,
next to the now emptied jar
of peppermint patties,
not yet dusty.

Anne Doyle, Grade 10
Eleanor Roosevelt High School, MD

Irreplaceable

I swear on everything above,
You're the one I truly love.

I lie to you not,
No one can take your spot.

Heart to heart,
Face to face,
You, I can never replace.

Because from the very start,
You were permanently tattooed across my heart.

Ka'Deazha Weeks, Grade 11
Norview High School, VA

Their Eyes Represent Hunger

The infant's mother looks into
His eyes and sees hunger
The infant does not have enough
To eat nor does his brother, sister,
Or mother
His mother cannot find a job
And his father is dead
His hunger pains define
Him and his family
They define them as impoverished
People
Their eyes represent hunger
And so do their thin bodies
Every night his mother prays
For a better life and every
Morning she wakes up to find
Things are the same
She does not give up hope
She has faith one day things will be better

Celestine Etterich, Grade 12
Delaware Military Academy, DE

Thorns

When I met you off the ocean
You had roses to sell.
Said — "Take it easy, don't you worry" —
Let go of yourself.

We ran into the valley
And make a necklace from the trees.
Don't know where to go now —
"Fly this conscience," a breeze.

We lay with the grapevine
Your smile a constant irk
"Love is never a folly" —
It whispered with your smirk.

We had plummeted off the mountain.
I heard the tolling of the bell.
Showed me true color beneath you —
You had roses to sell.

Charlotte Thomas, Grade 12
Bishop Walsh Middle High School, MD

Perfection

To fulfill an ultimate achievement,
And finish with great attainment.
Great accomplishment is the result,
The drive to be ideal is at fault.
It is the climax of your work.
Culmination is the aftermath,
To finish with paragon, such wrath.

Warren Purnell, Grade 12
Woodbridge Sr High School, VA

Roller Coaster Ride

Up and down the roller coaster goes. Exposing the fear and pain she shows,
Higher than ever her temper explodes. All the anger she beholds.
She screams louder than thunder. When people see her they start to wonder,
Does she scream because of the attitude?
Or is it fear of her surroundings that are rude?
Is it love conflicts making her nervous?
Or problems she faces that make her curious?
And down the path the roller coaster starts,
With 10 other roller coaster carts.
Friends and family will always be there,
But to help you they do not dare.
If you fall off that coaster in a sudden accident,
Who will be there in recent movement?
Around and round, over and out,
And everyone starts to shout.
Deep emotions begin to burst,
Crazy and wild, it's a curse.
And through it all I am brave,
Coming out of this dark cage,
To have enough strength to move on,
Furthermore and beyond.

Jessica Lopez, Grade 10
Parkdale High School, MD

Just Because I'm Loud

Just Because I'm Loud…

Doesn't mean I'm not sensitive.
It doesn't mean I'm not shy,
It doesn't mean that I'm hiding something,
It doesn't mean…
   I don't have a care for the world,
   I don't set high standards for myself,
   I'm not self conscious,
   That I look in the mirror and actually like what I see.
Just because I'm loud doesn't mean that…
   I'm a bad person,
   I'm not a good friend,
   I'm not a good listener.
Just because I'm loud, or weird, or whatever you think I am,
doesn't mean that I disregard what you think; every opinion matters.

Joanna Scatasti, Grade 10
Delaware Military Academy, DE

Tears of Steam

A train is like a gray cloud.
It weeps as it speeds along,
Leaving behind a curtain of tears —
Its sorrow for the sights missed.

A train is like a gray cloud.
It weeps as it speeds along,
Unable to contain its elation
For the next experience.

Elizabeth Kelley, Grade 10
Maggie Walker Governor's School for Government and International Studies, VA

Death

Death awaits me
His eyes are simmering coals
As they stare deep into my soul
Waiting — and waiting still…

I feel his presence everywhere
But when I look…
He is nowhere to be seen
Disappearing in a flash

His Laughter echoes off my mind
As he races away…then…
He creeps closer…and closer…
I can feel his presence everywhere

A mere presence — more of a 6th sense
I try as hard as I can to ignore him
But no matter what I do…
He never leaves my subconscious mind…

Death awaits me and I can't avoid him…
Kyle Garbacz, Grade 10
Delaware Military Academy, DE

Summertime

Red, white and blue.
Cheers from me and you.
The summer sun beating down.
It won't be long now,
before you smell the grill
or feel that little chill
from jumping in the lake;
it takes your breath away.
I see it in your eyes,
the fireworks, they shine.
If we stay out much longer,
I'll start to get a hunger
for teenage love, it's a feeling
no matter what it's dealing.
Summer love is refreshing.
I'm falling for you, so catch me.
Nadine Pipes, Grade 10
Strasburg High School, VA

My American Friend

She listens to my stories,
she listens to my complaints
She helps me with my English,
and never makes me say;
I'm sorry.
She doesn't count my mistakes
but forgives them all
and that's why she is my friend,
she's my best friend above all.
Marjolein Braas, Grade 12
Woodbridge Sr High School, VA

Life as an Expression

Life is like the cycle of a butterfly.
You may start off life as an egg.
Next thing you know you sprout wings and let your future glide.

Life is one of God's talented wills.
We always become emotional.
But like a roller coaster we are always on the edge of thrill.

We all have our ups and downs.
As well as our breaks and falls.
Like a football game we make both good and bad calls.

Every day we seek a rush or a thrill.
At this rate, we are attempting to ring Heavens bell.

Life is about setting dreams and accomplishing goals.
We even take risks and chances.
Sometimes we make them or we find ourselves in a hole.

Life is not a game so we should take it for real.
Have you heard the expression "You don't know what you have until it's gone?"
Well if you haven't you should take this as serious as an alarm!
Xaiver Travers, Grade 10
Forestville Military Academy, MD

Acid Rain

The rainbow sherbet swells of the neon sea
Amplify.
Their swirls tumbling into one another,
Color over color,
As waves smash sand, the pastel foam
Ebbs out
Leaving a stained shore
Like oil leaked on asphalt
The neon reaches into sand, permeating it with its twisted fingers,
Seeping, soaking.
And the yellowed sidewalk sky
Crackles with violet electricity
The smell of hot summer rain on crumbled pavement drenching the ocean.
And the music swells, and its wavelengths
Tango through chokingly humid air,
Over the crashing medley of hues
While the khaki skyscraper hotels
Loom over ocean and beach,
Their balconies topped only by the sizzling sky.
As bass fades and grows,
Ebbs in and out like the neon waves.
Virginia Hadley, Grade 11
Maggie Walker Governor's School for Government and International Studies, VA

Land of the Free?

Welcome to America,
Land of the free?
Aren't we the ones
Cutting down trees?
Ignoring children's pleas.
Ruining the economy.
Bombing silent cities.
Warming the Atlantic,
Infecting the seas.
Spreading disease.
Scorning teen pregnancies.
What happened to democracy?

Welcome to America,
"In God We Trust."
The question is,
Should God trust us?
Natalie Merritts, Grade 10
Harford Technical High School, MD

Running Away

We all run away from love
We run away from the truth
They say the truth can be hurtful
But running away is the true demon
We run away from the hurt
And run away from the pain
We are scared that if we stand there
We will be put to shame
Put to death
Put at rest
Yet then we will be put at ease
So what do we want?
To stay
Or to rest
But whatever you choose
Make sure it's the best possible way
Whether it's to run or to stay
Shakema Williams, Grade 10
Forestville Military Academy, MD

The Incongruity of Fall

after only five days
of rain and wet
the weather's changed
and I walk the dog
wearing mother's winter coat,
two sizes too big and baggy.
flip-flops slip-slop in the grass;
winter jacket, sandals, dog
as the wind pursues the leaves.
don't you love it all,
the incongruity
of all this imagery?
Ruth Williams, Grade 12
Hampton Christian High School, VA

My Girl

Grandma. Such a meaningless name compared to what you mean to me,
Our memories will remain in my heart for eternity.

Your kindness and generosity may bring some a surprise,
But me, I know these pure traits well, they are what I idolize.

Your reoccurring smile when I arrive brings me much relief,
And shows me there is more in this cold world than just pain and grief.

Your sweet, country voice never fails to bring a smile to my face,
And the way you scold us when we say a word that's out of place.

Trips to the pool during summer, cards by the fire in winter,
Climbing that unique tree in the yard and getting a splinter.

Nathan and I, we love your many 'old timer sayings' so,
Though remained unsaid, our favorite trait of yours is the love shown.

For some a grandma is just a person, for me it's much more.
'My girl', my best friend, the companion I shall always adore.
Nikki Daniels, Grade 10
Dinwiddie High School, VA

The Iraq War

We watch as the bullets bounce closely past our head
My lieutenant yells, "hit the deck!" and we go diving
I see my friend hit; my heart quickly fills with awful dread
So far it had been nothing but driving
But now that we had affirmed our presence
The enemy gained the courage to make a fight
A counter attack here was of essence
Or we would be forced to stay the long, unruly night
This war had finally changed forever
It is our turn to strike the enemy back hard
Someday we will win this great endeavor
Even if it is only to get stared
There is no doubt that our army is mighty strong
But even we could make this turn out wrong

James White, Grade 10
Delaware Military Academy, DE

The Words That Carry

She tries and never succeeds,
She flies but doesn't believe.
Her doubts are holding her back,
Her skill she doesn't lack.
She throws her hands up and allows herself to cry,
Pain becomes visible no need for her to lie.
Her name is Repetition, hands burnt from the lessons she's learned.
Recognition earned for the troubles she's turned,
Into success, happiness abreast, after all she lays all her confusions to rest.
Her years have taught her, her tears have caught her.
But what she fails to receive is realization, celebration, and coordination.
So what I say to you, "Push on girl, push on, life is sure to make you strong."
Claudia Peters, Grade 12
Loch Raven High School, MD

I Sit and Wait

I sit here and wait, that's all I can do
Until the day I'm up there, too

I think about you, all the fun we had
I have no choice but to be sad

I will miss it all, oh so much
I know we'll all miss your loving touch

Then I think back to all our laughter
I didn't realize it then, only after

But it's easier now, to smile because
I do realize how lucky I was

We Love you Mommom, and always will
To have had you here, was a blessing and a thrill
Courtney Gross, Grade 10
Delaware Military Academy, DE

Colors Don't Matter

I painted a picture today.
Black, white, and beautiful gray.
I use a pencil and a black pen.
No need for markers, no need for crayons.
Just two colors, so simple and true.
No red, no green, no yellow, no blue.
It got me thinking about the world.
All brightly colored and wonderfully swirled.
If I don't need color on my art.
I don't need color in my heart.
I now see that the world is great.
I don't see black and white, therefore I don't see hate.
Cherry Shutler, Grade 10
Stone Bridge High School, VA

The Raven Mocks

I know you've had a raven
High perched upon that tree
I know your life is quite shaken
Stretched beyond that sea
I know that you've got Hades
Under your palms beneath the tree
But bet that you don't faze me
With every eye that I can see
Underneath the earth is where it's meant to be
And staring at the raven as it stares and mocks at me
Raven, oh raven, your eyes the fake black sky
Your world like the crashing sea that you ever so defy
Nhu-Phuong Duong, Grade 11
Benjamin Banneker Academic High School, DC

Choose

Yes or No?
No answer either way.
She just wants him to show
One day, just one day.
She or Her?
Of course go with the one who loves you more
How could you contemplate that? You must concur.
But since it's you you're never sure.

Dead or Alive?
You dredge along each day as a facade of a human
You must know you can survive!
Add spice to your life: paprika or even cumin,
And yet even still you can't decide.

Hello or Goodbye?
Before you have the chance,
She was quick to reply.
She said shortly but surely "No more of this one-sided romance."
And at last someone heard
A decision, even though it was slurred.
Chenoa Zais, Grade 12
Bishop Walsh Middle High School, MD

Muse

Seeing your disposition — a very painting.
I'm always taken aback that you
do muse me.
(My shame, you've yet to see)
Myself, on a great gone.
For a woman's story is always beyond.
Don't be provoked that between us is more than footsteps
that I bring odds to thee,
Thrown to sides,
the (secret)…prithee
Can you quit my sight?
Let the good night (carry on)
without the
Hearty
(Liar).
That venom invades my while,
Sweet remembrance…
Most play ignorant,
But one.
Aside the riddle and beside, he not illusions what has been,
Sure now (never) suits, (nor) will it ever.
Racquelle Contreras, Grade 11
Institute of Notre Dame, MD

My Best International Friend

Eyes the color of muddy green,
Mixed with her musical Dutch accent,
Her smile brightens my day
Like the sunshine in May.
Thao Huynh, Grade 11
Woodbridge Sr High School, VA

Her Name Was Autumn

My name is Autumn.
My eyes change color with my favored mood.
My hair lays dead, like everything else about me,
But they still call me beautiful.
The only exception is when my heart
Floods cold, bitter rains.
That is when no one loves me,
No one except for you.

You, with your loving embrace,
Coating bare skin like a comforting blanket.
Warm rivers flow through your veins.
They cannot wait to have you around.
They love you.
I love you.

My name is Autumn.
Your name is Summer.
And I will follow you whenever you go.

Natasha Pendergrass, Grade 12
Dinwiddie High School, VA

Ode to Pinecone: The Runt of the Tree

The seed sprouts.
You're looming up high.
A life of waiting. "Sigh."
All alone; a dying branch.
Tears look like rain.
No one would have thought you would have pain.
Teased for life, however long it may be.
Ashamed of what's not there,
But you shouldn't care.

Shaking in the breeze, but that's why.
Scared you might be picked on a whim,
And leave the comfort of your limb.
Finally, your time has come.
You're picked by a single, simple gust.
"Ground below or bust!"
Loneliness approaches yet again;
A single tear, but then you know,
That all your kids already fell below.

Brandon Coffrin, Grade 12
Dinwiddie High School, VA

Light of My Life

Crying in the arms of night
Running on a moonlit path
With shapes of blackness wanting to bite
And try to consume the moonlight
Enough to wonder about its wrath
I see my face in the darkness
As if it is me consuming
The light in my life

Manica Petty, Grade 11
Dinwiddie High School, VA

I Smile Through the Pain

I smile through the pain
To avoid questions being asked
Questions I wish not to answer
Because those things are of the past

I smile through the pain
To avoid showing my sorrow
I must live for today
Because I am not promised tomorrow

I smile through the pain
To avoid being hurt even more
Don't want to no longer experience this pain
Need to worry about mine and not yours

Finally I am relieved
No more pain I'm set free
Worry first about yourself
For a better life that's the key

Kierra Gwynn, Grade 12
Charles Herbert Flowers High School, MD

The Stage

Biting my nails as I sit and wait
Waiting impatiently, shaking my legs
My heart accelerating throughout my body
My hands covering my burning red face

Waiting impatiently, shaking my legs
My trembling legs walking towards the stage
My hands covering my burning red face
As I approach the center, all I hear is the silence

My trembling legs walking towards the stage
I look at the audience, but all I see are peering eyes
As I approach the center, all I hear is the silence
I close my eyes, cast my worries, and then I sing out my soul

My trembling legs walking towards the stage
My hands covering my burning red face
As I approach the center, all I hear is the silence
I close my eyes, cast my worries, and then I sing out my soul

Sungwoo Park, Grade 11
Poolesville High School, MD

My Best Friend

When the rain is falling on your face
And when the whole world is on your case
I could offer you my warm embrace
To make you feel my best friend
I would run across the sea for you
I would go up and down the avenue
I would do just about anything for you
Just to make you feel my best friend

Maritza Placido, Grade 10
Parkdale High School, MD

America

America, with
Your mountainous lands, valleys,
And plains — beautiful.

Defined by ocean,
Now sadly flecked with oil, yet
Most don't see the sea.

The farmlands, rivers,
The lakes, ponds, and caverns, too —
All are inspiring.

The people are one,
And yet, are not. We are called
"The Great Melting Pot."

How can a nation
Be so diverse? However:
"United we stand."

Connected by our
Ancestors' flights to freedom,
Our hardships, our woe.

O, America,
I hope we stay together,
Wherever I go.
Shannon O'Neill, Grade 11
Barrington Christian Academy, RI

The Key

A dark, thick mist coats my body
I watch in anticipation, eyes fixed
The mist begins to move up my body
It loosely wraps around my chest
It feels like the mist is trying to break me
I scream in agony

The mist digs throughout my body
As it digs a woman stands in front of me
Her arm outstretched towards my heart
Her hand, open, palm up
She closes her fist

I fall to my knees
Sweat dripping off the tip of my nose
I stand up
Only its not me
I can see, hear, feel, taste
But I do not control myself
I am a victim of my own mind
She kisses me
I am behind bars I made myself
She bears the key
Kyle Bauer, Grade 12
Meade Sr High School, MD

A Hypocrite's Folly

Far too many poets talk of beauty
And turn their minds from ugly things
Far too many speak of true love
And ignore what hatred brings

Poets like to play with pretty notions
As small children play with fire
And to give them an unsavory thought
Is to quickly draw their ire

Young poets put their pens to paper
To write of peace in dreams
And yet we forever know
That dreams are not what they seem

I speak so ill of poets
Who shall forever waste their time
But if they are so contemptuous
Why do I speak in rhyme?

It is truly my curse, alas
That I speak out against poets now
But as I put my thoughts to paper
Poetry was the only way I knew how...
Emily Fisher, Grade 11
Coventry High School, RI

Final Goodbye

There is so many things I need to say
Yet there is so many things I can't
So many things you need to hear
If you would just listen to my rant

There is no doubt, I was falling in love
Oh you had me going crazy
My heart was doing somersaults
And my mind was completely hazy

Before I knew it, you were gone
Nothing left but sweet memories
Now I'm stuck with a broken heart
Left alone, with no remedies

It's time for me to move on
I need to put you in my past
I need to start this healing process
And I need to do it fast

You've worn me down so much
But I'll try to keep my head held high
I'll try to keep these tears hidden
As I say my final goodbye
Jennifer Rush, Grade 12
Thomas Dale High School, VA

Lost and Never Found

Have you so easily forgotten me?
Through our empty years of separation,
Was I too distant and so unworthy?

Your presence was not played in fantasy,
We sculpted the world into a question,
Have you so easily forgotten me?

There is a limit to infinity,
A dense wave drowning ardent intentions,
Was I too distant and so unworthy?

Shyness buried hidden sincerity,
It is a plague inside my lost prison,
Have you so easily forgotten me?

Silent hearts speak only iniquity,
My thoughts were floating with apparitions,
Was I too distant and so unworthy?

Youth meanders in rapid harmony,
To lose is nothing but a harsh caution,
Have you so easily forgotten me?
Was I too distant and so unworthy?
Rebecca Rosenblatt, Grade 12
Madison County High School, VA

When the Rooster Crows

When the rooster crows
The Sun lights the sky
Morning's bright face shows

Frost tickles life's nose
The snores of night die
When the rooster crows

Brisk wind quickly blows
Darkness starts to shy
Morning's bright face shows

Visages expose
Some are not too spry
When the rooster crows

We still deeply doze
In our sleep we sigh
Morning's bright face shows

Time maintains its flows
The Moon starts to shy
When the rooster crows
Morning's bright face shows
Jacob Herrman, Grade 12
Madison County High School, VA

Contamination Today

There is a problem in today's world
It is not very hard to see
The problem is hurting people and planet
It even affects you and me

The problem is pollution
It is more common than you know
Everyone and everywhere is affected
From dry deserts to the mountains with snow

The environment is dying
Forests and creatures are dead
The planet may be unlivable
For the generations ahead

God made this wonderful Earth
All the plants, animals, and trees
However as humans we have destroyed it
Through our ever expanding needs

We must come together
Every religion, country and race
To right this terrible wrong in our world
And put it back to its right place
Austin Hooper, Grade 10
Archbishop Curley High School, MD

School Fridays

Racing the halls of critters and mice
Rushing through the thick forest with haste
Pushing past pests who wander about
A horde of lifeless zombies crowd the air
They are like ants to a picnic
Mindlessly marching

Diving past the music
Voices chirp cheerful tunes that echo as death cries
Violins scream the cries of sheet music
A guitarist shreds out his instrument's soul
And the pianist burns his fingers with a collage of chords

Scram to history class late
And it's World War Two again
Children fire their paper airplanes at one another
A ball is tossed in the air like a bomb
The troublemakers take cover in the shelter of desks

The chaos continues on from each class
One war zone to the next in this endless network
Fail a test or pass it, these matters are of life or death
The bell rings and school finally makes it's peace treaty
The troops at last go home and rest awaiting their next call of duty
Kavin P. Swami, Grade 11
Eleanor Roosevelt High School, MD

This Envision of Life

This world is my horizon
But, the moon is my destiny
The stars take me as far as this journey will lead
But only this heart takes time to breathe.
This heart of mine won't let time go
So I live every second, every minute every hour
Living for the future.

Holding time as if it were my best friend
Promising not to let go 'til the very end
With my horizon spread wide and far
Thunder breaks the sadness
Suffering from happiness is my only madness
The sun, moon and the stars are really far
But my destiny waits, for time's sake
The sun is my smile, it shines all around
The moon, bright but at its best when full
And the stars are my personality, never dim but always bright
Life is a mystery, a journey and heartache
But when life gives you the Big Bang
It reminds me I'm only as big as my fate.
Tiffany Wright, Grade 11
Grace Bible Baptist Christian School, MD

Untitled

Nothing was the same now that it was all said and done
Actions can't be undone, words unspoken
Think before you fire the gun
Once a mirror's shattered, it can't be unbroken
The past can't reoccur
No one knows who's to blame
Things can't go back to how they were
Now that nothing's the same
I'm sorry things ended this way
I'm sorry I can't hit rewind
It hurts too much to stay
It's stuck on replay in my mind
I wish there was no tragedy
There was no fork in the road
For a broken heart, there is no remedy
So, now I must go
Now that nothing's the same
Ashleigh Gephardt, Grade 10
Harford Technical High School, MD

2012

Junior year has rolled around,
Now starts the worry of being college bound.
But remember to enjoy these last years
Before becoming an adult brings new fears.
We're the class of 2012, so bring on the fun
The best years of our lives have just begun!
Sierra Encarnacion, Grade 11
Walsingham Academy Upper School, VA

Unraveled Words

The world
Is covered with
Unraveled words,
Wrapped up in
Paper flowers
And spread out across
Newspaper-covered skies.
Every moment
Of every day,
People
Walk,
Run,
Prance,
Crawl
Past these
Alienated words
Of mystery
Without thinking twice
Because they do not know
That these invisible words
Are mine.

Kyle Rhodes, Grade 12
Bishop Walsh Middle High School, MD

Beyond the Grave

The clock moves beyond the grave,
Sometimes there are those you cannot save.
It ticks and tocks,
Leading people away,
However,
There are memories that will stay.
Memories that bring us hope,
Memories that save us from what we know,
It seems hopeless first,
But this is the mission of memories at birth.
They are the things that keep us safe.
Memories,
Oh memories,
These are the things that keep us warm,
Even in the grave.

Kennedy Phillips, Grade 10
North Kingstown Sr High School, RI

Football Equals Life

FOOTBALL equals life
It can be dangerous as a knife
But if you have fun
Anything you do will be done
Every single minute of it
Is worth every hit
Every hike of the ball
Makes me recall
Of that one precious goal
That makes FOOTBALL my soul.

Javon Adams, Grade 10
Red Lion Christian Academy, DE

Fanatic in Love

I am a fan of yours because your music gets me through
I've been following your work a long time and adore how much you grew
The lyrics, your voice
I had no other choice
But there's something more I have to say
I can't do this any other way
You would tell me how you felt in your profession
So here's me doing the same, this is my confession
I love you so much, more than you'll ever know
Read my other poems and feel the feelings flow
My emotions for you have been pure admiration
Forgive me for not telling you, I was procrastinating
If you do not feel the same than that is okay
I'm just glad I showed you my heart this way
I admit it will hurt
and I'll feel like dirt
But at least my heart will now be free
Free for you or for someone else to love me.

Jessica Crudup, Grade 12
SH Clarke Community Academy, VA

I miss Liberia

My heart aches because I'm stuck in this deserted island.
Life here is gloom.
My future is dark and doomed.
I want to be out there in the world.
Stuck minded because my story is untold.
Hate the thought of me left here.
Need to wake up to reality and know I'm going nowhere.
I GUESS I can manage prefer not to.
Do I dare to dream of greater?
Or do I stay here and live life later?
The sweetness of sugar would be the tasting goodness of freedom.
Like kisses to a newborn from their mother.
She rests in the arms of family and feeds off the crumbs of a crumbling world
She sits and waits for her turn to climb the ladder but her time will soon come
NO RUSH
Just like being independent…

Joyce Darway, Grade 12
Parkdale High School, MD

Just Because I'm a Girl

Just because I'm a girl doesn't mean I'm organized and obsessed with arts and crafts.
I can't see the floor in my room and can barely draw stick figures.
Just because I'm a girl doesn't mean my hobbies are dress shopping and makeup.
I love my chapstick and favor the food court.
Just because I'm a girl doesn't mean you can chalk my grumpiness up to me pmsing.
It'd be nice if you asked me why I'm not smiling.
Just because I'm a girl doesn't mean I think you're adorable.
Okay — maybe it does "but"
Just because I'm a girl doesn't mean I couldn't beat you senseless.
You probably wouldn't even fight back…
Just because I'm a girl.

Madison Goebel, Grade 10
Delaware Military Academy, DE

Never Perfect

My goal was to be perfect
My life to be changed
I'd try as hard as I could
To not be considered deranged
The closer I got
The farther I'd feel
No longer loved
Out of zeal
I began to think
Was I crazy
Could I ever be perfect
Was it just hazy
Not meant to be reached
But just ruin me
Taking my old friends
They could see
I was different
Ruining myself
Trying to be
Someone else

Courtney Schultz, Grade 10
Harford Technical High School, MD

Winter Man

Frigid air bites like mosquitoes in summer.
Skin, now flamingo pink,
screams for warmth.
There is no sense of time.
The sun has left a blank page for a sky.
The deserted streets,
ice rinks.
The parks,
ice statues of swings and monkey bars.
People look out the window and say,
"Anyone who would go outside in this cold
has lost it"
Then they see him.
Pale,
blending in with wind.
He sticks out his tongue.
I feel the cold sensation
as the white fingerprints drift down,
landing lightly on his tongue
like skilled dancers.

Melinda M. Thomas, Grade 12
Eleanor Roosevelt High School, MD

English Breakfast

The hot amber
Meets chilled cream. Spinning
Liquid
Honey
Gold

Ansa Woo, Grade 12
Lake Braddock Secondary School, VA

Where God Lived

I heard you snoring at lunch
Your small TV set blasting Dr. Phil
I could barely concentrate
After your nap I could smell the sautéed peppers you love to eat
Green, red, yellow, and fiery orange
Sizzling in a frying pan
I've told you about chewing with your mouth open
It sounds like a shotgun aimed at the ocean
Like mountain avalanches
And autumn leaves falling from trees all at once
I was in the bathroom crying and I know you heard me
My lips were shaking
And for five minutes all the noise was gone from my body
I tried to tell them I wasn't talking to myself
And that God lived in my ear
I told them that you fed me with your thoughts so I was never hungry
I know you're here
I can feel your heartbeat
And your tiny footprints run all over my heart
Like the lines that make up my fingerprints
You belong to me

Terra Campbell, Grade 12
Ellington School of the Arts, DC

Adieu

Needless to say my illicit amour I pertain toward you
Is a dithering fight between freedom and fate
My life on the sadistic hands of foolishness. My heart in the existence of time
For what reason, my soul is connected to yours; I am ravished
Yet, for what purpose I am in forever more agony; I am complexed
My liberation eternally is to be the remedy to your broken spirit
If not here on this simple Earth then I will meet you in the golden vaults of Heaven
Terrified by the only word we ever known; adieu
Nullified by how this world articulates of our love; hate
By only a simple breath I confide within you; bliss
My heart in the existence of time

With every fleeting moment I have cherished
With the never ending love I have confessed
With our devoted deliverance forever kept secret
My liberation eternally is to be the remedy to your broken spirit

Devising my heart for the words to come
Remember my word is the beginning of our twilight's fume
I promise you. Now, hear my heart break.
For here is my adieu.

Brianna Vazquez, Grade 10
RI

The Homecoming

vibrant bodies move
smiles appear all over

music blasts
eardrums tighten

chaotic laughter
enlightens atmosphere

hands laced
bodies grasped
music notes
float

adrenaline heightens

forever dancing
youth flows through
our veins.

Jamaris Burns, Grade 12
Eleanor Roosevelt High School, MD

Mortal's Envy

Among the clouds
flying amongst the birds
angels soar high above
death and decay
caused by the
turmoil
from the traitorous souls
of the people below
abandoning them
leaving them
to wallow in pity
in favor of flying
among the clouds.

Sarah Ruddock, Grade 12
Dinwiddie High School, VA

Christmas

You only come once a year.
My favorite time of all
I can hear the jingles of bells in my ears
And children singing "deck the halls"
Hang your stockings on the chimney
Make sure you give Santa plenty!
All his gifts to you are free.
All the presents in a bundle
Make sure you don't peek.
You hear the reindeer in a rumble,
For your chimney they seek
A time to spend with family and friends
I hate when this holiday has to end.

Katie Coleman, Grade 10
Dinwiddie High School, VA

Precipitation at Its Finest

Ah, the raindrops…Crashing on the windowpane.
Stealing every bit of our dreams, yet healing our pain.
Scornfully terrorizing our minds, merely expressing their disdain.
Unwillingly, we forgive them for they are a part of God's ordain.
Those frivolous raindrops, releasing the animosity from our veins.
Listening to the thunder in the depths of our souls is driving us insane.

Yet we shall be forever committed to those waves, until death do us part.
Meanwhile they rummage through and cleanse the imperfections in our hearts,
damaging every fraction of happiness we've ever sought.
Instantly conquering our phobias accompanied by the lightning they've brought.

Rather than, wishing the rain would go away,
welcome its nature for it destroys the impurities torturing us by the day.

Never become beguiled by the sun's desire to bring "happiness" with its foolish lies.
Making a mockery out of those who wish to continue their cries.
Blinding us all with that sunshine we began to despise.
But through these raindrops… we are peering within the tears from our own eyes.

Lauryn Froneberger, Grade 10
Western High School, MD

Just Because I'm a Cheerleader

Just because I'm a cheerleader doesn't mean I am not an athlete.
Just because I'm a cheerleader doesn't mean I am dumb.
Just because I am a cheerleader doesn't mean I act ditsy.
Just because I am a cheerleader doesn't mean I am mean to other girls.
Just because I am a cheerleader doesn't mean I am 'easy' and get with all the guys.
Just because I am a cheerleader doesn't mean I am self-centered.
Just because I am a cheerleader doesn't mean I am always peppy.
Just because I am a cheerleader doesn't mean I do it just to be popular.
Just because I am a cheerleader doesn't mean I am better than you.
Just because I am a cheerleader doesn't mean I can't be taken seriously.
Just because I am a cheerleader doesn't mean I am 'a flirt in a skirt'.
Just because I am a cheerleader doesn't mean I have to look good all the time.
Just because I am a cheerleader doesn't mean I have to be outgoing.
Just because I am a cheerleader doesn't mean I have to be perfect.

Lauren Hahn, Grade 10
Delaware Military Academy, DE

My Twin Sister

Just because I have a twin sister, doesn't mean you can ask me if she is hot.
Just because I have a twin sister, doesn't mean I look like a girl.
Just because I have a twin sister, doesn't mean we fight all the time.

Just because I have a twin sister, doesn't mean we can read each other's minds.
Just because I have a twin sister, doesn't mean I get lonely when I'm not with her.

Just because I have a twin sister, doesn't mean we are identical twins, we're fraternal.
Just because I have a twin sister, doesn't mean she is older than me.
Just because I have a twin sister doesn't mean we go to the same school.

Just because I have a twin sister, doesn't mean we wore matching clothes when we were little.
Just because I have a twin sister, doesn't mean I won't always love her; I love my twin.

Zachary Hanley, Grade 10
Delaware Military Academy, DE

What Would God Think?

The eyelid of night lifts
And God is done blinking
The day begins once more
As the dawn sun rises

The bloodshot eye of our disappointed
Watching one fills the sky once again
Staring down at our blundering selves
Watching us disobey him once more

Why do we leave
What we know to be right
Why leave behind
All we hold close and dear

Why do we destroy ourselves
For those seconds of pleasure
And tear the hearts of those loved
With meant to be private sins
We know would find the light one day

So the being watches
Stares at his creations
Pondering every day
Mourning all his mistakes
Gabriel D. York, Grade 10
Eleanor Roosevelt High School, MD

Form

Rise. Bow. Junbi!
Entering the Do Jang
With the whoosh of wind
Adorned in bleached gi:
Not just some black belt,
Not just some guy.

He walks like he flies
with hair of autumn
in calm contemplation
centering himself.

Then from a standstill
He steps.

skinny limbs of a tree break —
from their upright positions,
overtaking space and time
are swift stances like leaves that scatter:
each modulating movement
like living water…

Every air strike
strikes also the mind
which is left in awe.
Marjorie Decamito, Grade 11
Eleanor Roosevelt High School, MD

At the End

an eternity passes
although it's only been minutes
since I've last seen you
I feel the distance creep on me
putting miles between our words
how many more nights must I suffer?
I think about you every night
when I fall asleep
you're always in my dream
but where is my happy ending?
forever passes by me slowly
I feel the time begin to speed up
placing light years between our bodies
where does the happiness go at night?
I think about you every night
when I fall asleep
you're always in my dreams
but, where is my happy ending?
the one that comes at the end of time?
the one that comes at the end of dreams?
Victoria Shuklis, Grade 11
Dinwiddie High School, VA

Directions

A shadow of evil
biting into fire to release
a pivotal share of cheshire grin

Bent quarters spilled as needles on the
arms of my cheap keyboard
wrapped in; upside down

They fell like a faucet whose heart
dripped nothing but clear shame
across the shelled keys

The velvet insides roared truths — bare
frost — leaves rotting new
forgiveness to a belt

May the riches applaud in empty staves
to the parked leather skin
in the sun's boarded kitchen
Cristal Mean, Grade 12
Woodbridge Sr High School, VA

From on High

From on high they come
Their approach hidden by the sun
From on high they deliver justice
Conquering just like Caesar Augustus
From on high they protect us
Facing the enemy fearlessly nonetheless
From on high the Airborne comes
Brock Trexler, Grade 10
Delaware Military Academy, DE

I Stand

Here I stand before you
Offering what I've got
Though I know it is not much
I know you're my best shot.

Looking in your eyes
Begging on one knee
Please accept my sorrow
Please accept my plea.

Here there is beauty
Here there is grace
Despite all my failures
My vices you erase.

So now I see you here
Before you still I bow
I've heard about your love
And I can feel it now.
Anna Crow, Grade 11
Allegany High School, MD

Sea of Faith

The sea is alive tonight,
waves crashing, pebbles flying.
Approaching, then taking flight,
the water comes to the shore.

The ocean's perfume, salty-sweet,
intoxicating to the mind.
Sadness is a foreign concept,
a deep breath fills the heart with peace.

Sea of Faith, bright and calming.
Bringing a tranquil feeling,
that envelopes you and me.
Dreams are as high as kites, tonight.
Victoria Hudson, Grade 10
Dinwiddie High School, VA

The Sidewalk

Decay crept a fraction of an inch
monthly,
on waves that frothed aggregate,
that mixed sawtooth and sine curves
as they carved into sidewalk.

Salt and corner-steppers
released the roiling, choppy water
one pebble at a time:
the sidewalk did not recognize
the acquisition
until the smooth sand
flooded with decay.
Madalena Noyes, Grade 12
Eleanor Roosevelt High School, MD

The Truth About Lies

Sweet sensations, senses renewed by
wealth, available at the flick of the tongue.
A sugar crystalline unreality, spun by my own words,
spoken hurriedly, quickly.

Mistakes thread the sticky web,
melting in the spotlight.
The structure is flawed; the web
collapses unto itself,
the sugar now bringing only maggots
and vermin.

But even filth cannot clean the
wreckage created.
Family, friends, flee;
nothing remains
after life is based on
lies.

Joanna Morelli, Grade 11
Walsingham Academy Upper School, VA

Passing Time

Oh how happy we are when we are young,
No contemplation; dancing together,
They do say, these are the best days to come,
But I pray not, wouldn't they grow better?

On to a world of sophistication,
Oh what we will wear, bland dresses and ties
When will we receive our invitation,
To this eternal party of stress and lies,

Forever to be children of the past,
Old enough to wonder on our travels,
Floating lonesome on our own cardboard raft,
Left alone with only our small paddles,

We say goodbye to fair weather on shore,
And hello to storms that we find unsure.

Samantha Cubbage, Grade 12
Madison County High School, VA

Knows, But Doesn't Care

Do they not know?
All the things we've been through
All the sacrifices
The lives that had been lost
People murdered, lynched, and degraded
This long way we have come as a race
How could we take it for granted?
Throw everything they've worked for away
Unbelievable
They have to know
They just don't care

Denasia Ross, Grade 10
Forestville Military Academy, MD

Dreams

in the night,
through the mists of sleep,
a child is born.

she awakes in a bed of flowers,
an endless field,
an endless sky.

in the moonlight,
she grows and dances,
decorating her long hair with flowers.

a rose behind her ear,
a lily caught in the wild tangles
of her night-painted man.

she makes a dress of tulips and daffodils,
faces the horizon;
adventures are waiting.

when the golden fire
again burns away the darkness,
you awake, and remember nothing.

the golden chariot passes through the sky,
and you smell sweet pollen.

a white petal falls from your hair.

Jeanette Brown, Grade 12
Eleanor Roosevelt High School, MD

Journey

He travels
Plants his feet
Slugs one after the other
Running away from
Cold, clashing, currents of wind
He moves from street signs to metro stops
The ragged glove dangles
While his filth covered hand stretches
For unwanted scavenge
Through arid, hungry days
He looks forward to the nights.

Cement and baggage
Transforms to comfort bedding
Shredded corduroy pants
Do their best to conceal warmth
And the stolen child sized blanket
Make the goose bumps disappear
The battered tarp protects his home
Eyes shut, deleting all of the past
And recognizing what he has to call
Home

Ebone' Thornton, Grade 12
Eleanor Roosevelt High School, MD

Just Wait

I stumble through life, I trip and fall
I can't always get up on my own
I call out to you, but you don't hear me
Do it yourself
it's all you ever tell me
I know you think you're helping
but you're just leaving me to drown
I try to do as you say, but I can't
You might be able to do it yourself
but not me
Don't you hear me cry at night
Do you just ignore it or do you pause for a minute to think it over
I can't keep up with you
never could
You're always outdistancing me
why can't you wait up just this once
I need you, don't leave me here
At least turn around and look at me, you can't always walk away
I can't follow you forever
So now I'm walking away from you
And I won't turn around

Laura Caputo, Grade 10
Delaware Military Academy, DE

Trust

There is a world full of people of which I am one;
We all work together, with a variety of talents, to get our jobs done.
My path has been wavy and scary at times;
But I must work hard to reach the finish line.
I learned the hard way that not all are true;
And the only person to depend on is you.
Trust can't be held or given or touched;
It only something to believe in hopefully not too much.
People will say and do whatever they choose;
They're playing with other's feelings, so what's there to lose.
Before you decide and affect someone's fate;
Think about their life and don't act in hate.
What you may think is nothing too bad;
Remember your actions can make others terribly sad.
You can cause pain without profit or gain
And crush another's soul like the wheels of a train.
Life teaches us lessons, both happy and sad
It's our choice to choose good over bad
Perhaps you didn't mean it, or thought it was fun,
But the moral of the story is to trust no one.

Brianna Marriott, Grade 10
Delaware Military Academy, DE

Shadows of Sunlight

Sunlight pours through everlasting green
And I see that gleam in your eyes
The mischief evident across the pages
The story is written upon your face
But a blooming sorrow
Roses of the dead ones gone
Alas the fate of the world
Upon thine own shoulders
Smiles glimpse a hidden past of pleasure
While song birds sing of ever-so-beautiful feathers
Earthwrite Papermate
Pencils long and yellow
Fall on down
Like a rain flooding the floors
Of the spirits of the world
Forever flying in the sky
My happiness
A scary thing
As sunlight pours through
This everlasting love of you

Laura Engel, Grade 10
Christiana High School, DE

That Way

Falling slow and falling fast
Do you think that it'll last
My mama told me not to stay
But then you looked at me that way

We're halfway in and halfway out
We're ready to scream and ready to shout
My mouth says no my eyes say yes
And our next plan is anyone's guess

We're laughing hard, we're crying loud
Your hand's in mine and I'm so proud
You're saying three words that I'm ready to say
You're holding me close on this fine day

Falling slow and falling fast
We now know that it will last
My mama told me not to stay
But then you looked at me that way

Emma Decowski, Grade 10
Madison County High School, VA

Silly Willy

His name is funny.
He's as sweet as honey.
Cheerful, Happy, and really funny.
He always want to sing.
He pushes you high on the swing,
Holds your hand when you're scared,
And most of all he is a friendly bear

Holly Berry, Grade 11
Dinwiddie High School, VA

VA Tech Massacre Through Nikki Geovanni's Eyes

I glanced up at those dark brown eyes
Filled with hatred and despise.
I quickly looked away unseen
Except for those eyes, that looked so mean.
I wondered why all the hatred and pain
Then it hit me as hard as a train.
I was the target of his evil plan
I could not believe this ungodly man.
His fingers tightened.
His gaze held strong.
I wondered if he knew right from wrong.
I quickly thought of possible ways to distract his demonic gaze.
Now hoping the bell would sound
I didn't want to be tortured another round.
After class I pulled him away
To talk about his uncomfortable stay.
I got right to the point and kicked him out.
With unsure feelings — that's no doubt.
A few weeks later more then thirty died.
But I'm thankful that I survived.

Kelly Barock, Grade 12
La Plata High School, MD

The Chronicles of a Lost Boy

People gather to see a stone cold face.
One by one they've come to pay their respects.
Rise, as the chorus sings Amazing Grace.
A day of tears no one ever expects…

"He was a good kid…" the preacher starts in.
Heads bow down in attempts to hush their cries.
Everyone remembers those times again…
His family wishing they saw the lies.

The kids, they beat him up at school all day.
A new bruise, a bloody nose, mom would ask…
He covered up, saying he was okay.
No one acknowledged what's behind the mask…

Now lay a boy, in his permanent bed,
Because of your ignorance he is dead.

Amanda Rivoire, Grade 11
North Point High School, MD

The Christmas Pup

My family's Christmas tree is now up!
We laughed and giggled all during the night
We cheered when we saw the lively small pup
His tiny little tail wagged in the light

The eyes of the dog were a bright maroon
Tiny paws ran around through the darkness
He always loved to chew on a small spoon
We went to bed and had to play less

Joseph Certesio, Grade 10
Delaware Military Academy, DE

Will You

You are the brightest star in the galaxy
You are my definition of love and beauty,
You stood by me through rough and tough
You made me believe in love,
I'm your knight and you're my armor
You have loved me through it all.

I don't want our love to set but rise
I need you as sweet music needs an ear,
I need you like air in my lungs.
You are the sunlight that makes our love grow,
I want us to grow old and gray together.

I ask myself how long I'll love you,
I'll not love you for days, months or years but forever.
Meeting you was not luck but fate
First time I saw you I feel in love with you
My love has taken a different turn.
Together we have and will outlast every storm,
I will be here from Genesis to Revelation.
Will you be my beginning and end
I want to know: will you marry me?

Sheku Janneh, Grade 12
Osbourn High School, VA

blacks and whites

in the beginning there were blacks and whites
then emerged from the dirt were the blacks and whites
sometimes I wonder if humans caused the blackness of night
why does black stand for wrong and white stands for right
why does black stand for dark and white stands for light
why does it seem that if you're white you're living the life
why does it seem that if you're black you're in jail doing life
is this reality or is this just a stereotype
why do blacks lie, and say they can't get a job when they don't apply
why do colleges have less blacks and more whites
why do blacks blame whites for self-inflicted problems
why when whites see a black do they want to hide their objects
life is in black and white don't be blinded
don't live life mentally unconscious
black and whites are both good
and some of both do evil
but at the end of it all we all are people

Deylin Lucas, Grade 12
Havre De Grace High School, MD

Greed

Greed is the destroyer of families and friends.
Greed is the destroyer of theme and prosperity.
Greed is the destroyer of peace and harmony.
Greed is the destroyer of singularity and growth.
Greed is the destroyer of the helpful and the charitable.
Greed is the destroyer of individuality and majority.
Greed is the destroyer of happiness and cheerfulness.

Lucus Mero, Grade 10
Woodbridge Sr High School, VA

Rainbows

Cold, dark, impersonal
like a jail cell or padded room.
What can I use as arsenal,
since I'm living in a tomb?
When no one can hear me scream,
wake me from this hellacious dream.
Now our painted faces have started to crack.
I could hear my world being torn,
as everyone was quiet as a mouse.
Losing my voice I couldn't warn,
you as you came into the house.
The fighting had already started,
when you stood up and quickly departed.
My madness is piling into a stack.
Running hopelessly down the street,
my vision impaired by salty tears.
Is this the last time that we'll meet,
which is the worst of all my fears?
No explanations to how I'm feeling,
just bottling it up and dealing.
But I know I'll never get you back.
Kari Louk, Grade 12
Bishop Walsh Middle High School, MD

Angel's Soul

once upon a stormy night
shadows creep with a fright
nothing seemed too convivial
though an angel tries flight

everything was dark and droll
creatures out to steal your soul
searching for that angel's light
don't go out for an evening stroll

once upon this creepy night
all the creatures come out to fight
fighting over the purest soul
and now there is no more in sight
Courtney Kessler, Grade 12
Madison County High School, VA

The Barnes and Nobleman

he sits in the bookstore every day,
drinking from his goblet of fiction
gorging on his feast of words
on his hard wooden throne
in his old black robe
and his pair of olden Levi's;
his subjects the books
his officials the bookworms
that weave in and out of his palace,

the dominion of Paperback.
Samantha Yangilmau, Grade 11
Eleanor Roosevelt High School, MD

Mistakes

When I look at you,
I see rage in my reflection, tight mouth, and bold fist,
How your lips speak such sneaky sections in seconds.

When I look at you,
I see pain through my friend's concerned affections, tired eyes,
Crystal clear that have had its last moments of protection.

When I look at you,
I see shameful arrays of life lessons.
I count my blessing, as righteous rich sweets that seep deep
Into the cracks of acceptation.

When I look at you,
I question how I could fall off cloud nine for a porch.
What I thought when my heart pounded like you were the flame to my torch.
Where was my brain when you said you wouldn't lie and
You cried since I was supposedly worth more.

Who was I when I considered you were good in your core?
Why did I trust you as my world falls to the floor.

When I look at you, I see a mistake.
A torn page corners bent running out of the ordinary.
Nothing bright left. No longer extraordinary.
Kallahda Hugee-Sillah, Grade 11
Forestville Military Academy, MD

Look

For the girls who can barely stand:
who are connected to the quivering strands of life
by the most fragile of skeletons' frames

I eat 200 calories a day to hear myself
devour the fruits of emaciation and satisfaction,
the sickeningly sweet juice sliding down my chin
and painting the floor with what's left of me —
all 87 pounds of it.

But it's still too much, zero zero — the number running
through my head, thundering through my thoughts —
but still, my dear listener: listen and learn, lest you
turn into someone like me and repeat
"nothing tastes better than skinny feels" to yourself every night instead of whispering
"and if I die before I wake I pray the lord my soul to take"

And as I was sitting in that hospital bed,
feeling my life slipping away, I realized too late that our fatal flaw is
that we realize too late who we should be

Instead of who society wants us to be.
Jesse Zhao, Grade 11
Maggie L. Walker Governor's School, VA

I Am

Love me or hate me for who I am;
an Atheist, Hispanic and vegetarian.
I am as quiet as a mouse,
with a personality as loud as two clashing cymbals.
My art is a colorful rainbow,
my writing is deeper than the sea.

I am timid yet fierce.
I am quiet yet loud.
I am loving and caring.
But most important of all,
I am the older sister of a precious child.

I can be your sunshine,
I can be your rain;
that's your choice to make.
Just remember that I am nothing but myself,
and that will never change.

Cassandra Hagan, Grade 10
Harford Technical High School, MD

Graduating

I'm graduating this year
As I graduate, there are going to be many tears.
They are tears for sadness and tears for cheers
I finally made it!!
Graduating, which was never my fear!!

I studied hard and did my best,
So I could achieve much success.
There were times where I struggled and cried,
But at the end I swallowed my pride.
Asked for help and did my best
So I could be prepared to ace that test!!
Graduating is a must for me.
And I can't wait to see what the future holds for me.

Toney Washington, Grade 12
Oxon Hill High School, MD

Those Great Outdoors

Those golden days in the great outdoors
Are better than those polished floors
To be outside with clouds so fluffy
Than be inside where the air is stuffy

The smell of fresh cut hay and grass
Cannot be compared to finger-stained glass
The sound of chain saws in the woods
Is better than discussing Mom's baked goods

Outside I can use all my energy
That being inside made me have, you see
So if you really want to hear the truth
The great outdoors is best for youth

Rachel Miller, Grade 10
Oak Grove Mennonite School, VA

Closed Eyes

As I sit there all the pain and sadness catches up to me,
I try and wish it all away, far away.
I close my eyes, wish, count to three,
Open but everything is still the same.
Everyone is crying over never again to see,
All over those eyes never to open.
My mother never again to be,
I miss you my mother, never to come back.
Oh God please help, to thee I bend on knee,
For once again to see those closed eyes open.
My locked heart never to unlock, you must find the key,
Though the one thing needed to unlock will never come.
No she will not come back as hard as I pray,
That's the truth that screams in my head.
They all apologize for the loss that's what they say,
Though no one really knows how it hurts, oh so bad it hurts.
I finally admit defeat, hoping the pain will stay at bay,
But it never does, and I eventually die with the pain.

Monika Spieker, Grade 10
Harford Technical High School, MD

Self-destruct

Things are fake
Things have no life
Things are what cause me strife
I have never seen someone with so many things
Things that are not necessary
Things you make others carry
But you don't seem to mind their pain
As long as from it all you gain
And yet you keep piling it on
Then one day you will drown in your own sorrowful song
No one is coming to your rescue
And you get what was due to you
So drown, drown, drown
Come back up I'll tear you back down

Godstime Ojinmah, Grade 10
Parkdale High School, MD

Patterns

There was a beach ball resting in the sand
until the tide went out, pulled it away.
I did not care to soak myself today
or salt my limbs with water from the ocean,
so there it went. Three miles out from land
my eyelids traced its journey through the spray.
No doubt it's on some beach in Uruguay
by now, where sun browned hands will pick it up
and perhaps (if the journey was not rough)
the thing will make a gift to someone's child,
or if no hand should take it home, then fall,
it may, for miles below the tropic surf;
and there in darkness deep it will be filed
beyond the reach of gentle wave's recall.

William Campbell, Grade 11
Grace Christian High School, VA

Something Gotta Change

Something gotta change
Me or myself
I can't stay in this rut
No more no longer
I need a change
I can't go on
Not like this
Something gotta change

Something gotta change
For better or worse
I can't be certain
In time things will turn around
Something gotta change

Something gotta change
Or all hope is lost
I can't go on anymore
If not even a mere thing will change
Or all else fails
Something gotta change
Katelyn "Katie" Lott, Grade 11
Woodbridge Sr High School, VA

Five Seven Five

Without formulas
Poems have no direction
A hard place to start

Writing a haiku
May seem like simplistic work
But it's really not

Free verse poetry
Is fluid and wonderful
Though it may seem strange

Maybe fitting thought
Into cement packages
Is the real puzzle
Maxwell Gollin, Grade 11
Eleanor Roosevelt High School, MD

Randan

darting through the grass
hiding in the shadows
I am camouflaged in the sand.
the ripples above me
wander out and cause me to drift.
a tiny randan slices through the surface.
I see faces peer down
looking for anything they can see.
but what they didn't know is
why I am hiding.
Kaiti Burger, Grade 10
Madison County High School, VA

Freedom Beyond the Cocoon

In and out of the towering blades of grass
Weaving through each one creating a design with her path
Flipping over and twirling about above the meadow
Grazing the premises of her homeland; wondering if she'll ever come back

Further her wings take her on the journey
As she lofts into the wind's gentle offering
It sped up her pace and helped her try to forget
Of the past she was leaving behind

Memories racked her fragile mind as she soared
But it was no use in swiveling her glance
She was gone away from her old life
In the midst of the new one lying ahead

As ideas of intriguing opportunities burst into her mind
She begins to accept fate for what it is
And flies with new colors in her eyes
Counting two joyous thoughts for every downbeat

Deep breaths fade with her self consciousness
As her heart races in anticipation for her new existence
Gabrielle Powell, Grade 10
Woodbridge Sr High School, VA

Life's a Trip

Life, sometimes good, sometimes bad,
ups and downs
good times, bad times
Blood, sweat and tears this life brings
Hate and pain, stupid old things

Make the best of it, you never know when your time ends
Every day's a struggle, so if you make it through happy, you're on another level
Life's no fair so get even, have fun in this cold, cold world
Don't let it bring you down, be bold and do your thing and make it shine
All the time

Life, hate it or love it, just know, it doesn't care about you
But use it to your advantage, only strong people make it through
Control your life, so it can be nice
Life is short, so have the time of our life
Dominic Akers, Grade 10
Forestville Military Academy, MD

Love Is

Love is

L asting when nothing stands.
O verriding when blemishes corrupt.
V erifying when friendships are down.
E xpressing when one is grateful.

Love is a warm connection that helps one show concern to another, when no one else cares.
Erycka Spears, Grade 11
Hampton Christian High School, VA

At a Glance

We'd see each other at a glance
Both of us too shy to engage in conversation
We'd Just stroll past one another
Not showing any emotion

The day comes to an end and you were still in my mind
We pass each other on our way to the buses
Our eyes met at a glance and yours lit up
A smile developed across your face and you waved

Weeks later we talked for the first time at lunch
As we talked I became lost in her voice so divine
Not once did we look away from each other
The bell rang and we reluctantly departed

A year passes and our relationship grew, but not for the better
Your voice that was once so divine became bitter
We exchange glances in the hallway and my heart sinks
With no emotion you strolled past

Now we are just two beings
Separated by conflicting emotions and actions
The harmless glances evolved into piercing glares
Rattling me to my core
Yet till this day I still find us meeting each other, at a glance.

James Roaix, Grade 11
Coventry High School, RI

Changed and Barred

Freedom rings throughout this so sacred place.
Never let them take it from your tight grasp.
Tell me why, why I cannot find your face.

Surrounded by the power of God's grace,
Sit in hallowed pew, watch rain on stained glass,
Freedom rings throughout this so sacred place.

Search the crowd, people and their daily race,
While millions of faces I must have seen pass,
Tell me why, why I cannot find your face.

I fall behind, can't keep up with this pace,
Drown in the crowd, lay down in earthy grass.
Freedom rings throughout this so sacred place.

If you are not within the calm, this place,
And I can't find you with the rest, the mass,
Tell me why, why I cannot find your face.

You left me alone in space, left no trace.
There you are in a cell, barred by brass.
Tell me why, why I cannot find your face.
Freedom rings throughout this so sacred place.

Ellen Berry, Grade 11
Madison County High School, VA

Life's Questioning Prance

What in life has taken its
Peak
So to speak
What in life has made through
The outer shell
But did not compel
Where in life has fate not been misguided?
So you could not have striped
Where in life did wisdom be at use?
So now you fuse

How can this change?
How will we manage?
So there will be another page

Open up life
And be wise use wisdom and strive on climb high and do not fall
Life is once it is not to pounce on,
But to go through it.

Hephza Varghese, Grade 11
Laurel High School, MD

Beauty

To look in the mirror
Only do you see the outside
A view no clearer
To know what's in the inside
Grace and looks of an angel
She is blessed with the most flawless of features
Deep piercing eyes dark as the pits of hell
Born of supremacy, the most delicate of creatures
Skin radiant as a ray of sunshine
A perfect view from every angle
For she is the epitome of something divine
To compete with her, no one is able
A fallen goddess, the earth happened to catch
Beauty so rare, personality to match

Tierra Lanier, Grade 12
Dinwiddie High School, VA

When the Wind Blows

When the wind blows, it tries to sway me different ways,
But it's my own road that I chose to pave.
It always blows me to the left, but never seems to blow me right
But I'm going to keep walking straight with all my might.
That wind, it tends, to scowl so mean
But I howl back at it with a determined scream.
How about this wind, rustling me down,
But these feet here, will continue to touch the ground.
When realizing defeat, The Wind! Proclaims to be my friend,
But it will be me, who has my own back at the end.
But I thank the wind for blowing me along,
Because it is the wind that continues to make me strong.

Bernita Randolph, Grade 12
Varina High School, VA

Living On

I wrote a story in class today.
In fact, it was about you — every page.
Every memory, and every kiss.
It consisted of everything I'll always miss.
It's hard to talk about losing a boyfriend.
Not because of a fight, but him speeding around a bend.
Today, I cannot help but to be mad, scream and curse.
I never imagined his last ride, being in a hearse.
There is one thing that puts my mind at ease today —
Joshua Michael lived his life, in every way.
I hold onto every day that he spent with me,
I just wish that June 6th, was never a bad memory.
But I keep his picture in my mind
right next to his liveliness, and the way he shined.
And rather than crying, I'll smile instead
to know my pictures, too, are forever in his head.
As I was writing a story in class today,
it no longer pained me to say:
Yes, I mourn my best friend who was my boyfriend too,
but he's not gone, his life continues on, through me and you.

Alexa Merring, Grade 12
Delaware Military Academy, DE

Talent

An action, a thought, an event, a sound
Does it come to me or have to be found
Is it blind? Trapped inside?
Too many questions
Too little time, for this one thing, ever searching.
And to this day, I hunt for my prey:
A talent, a future, an ending to this play
So as the sky closes its eyes,
And the night creeps to eat daylight away
Putting humanity to sleep
But I stay awake, to ponder upon
An endless debate,
The key to my history,
A rift to my mystery.
So I lay awake in this world of gray
Waking up to another foggy day.

Islam Abdelhamid, Grade 10
Parkdale High School, MD

I Love You

The grass is green, the sky is blue,
My eyes see no one, but you.
Happy times, angry times, sad times, and emotional times.
Our love is like committing a thousand crimes.
Nothing is like our love
Expect the heavens above!
They always say, "Love doesn't last forever"
Well let's make it last a life time through whatever
I never want to forget this,
Let's make it like it's our last kiss.

Nicole Ware, Grade 10
Forestville Military Academy, MD

Lost Love

Cast off in a faraway land
Empty heart and empty hand
Left deserted to live or die
Left alone to try to fly
Without wings, a heavy heart
From her life that's torn apart
Left alone to wait for her fate
In surroundings filled with hate
The rivers of death and misery
Only to break by images of he
Who stole her heart and ran
So far untouched by Cupid's hand
Left in the shadows while he's in the light
She fills with numbness, remnant of her plight
Inescapable as the day breaks
Her heart is torn apart and it aches
And she's left to live or die
Quietly crying her goodbyes
To life as it was, and fearing
How it shall be from now on

Katie Horn, Grade 10
Padua Academy, DE

Shadows

My name is Nightmare.
I am the darkness,
The shadow of the human mind.

My name is Death,
The shadow of destruction
that lingers inside.

My name is Defeat,
The enveloping failure
cast in hindsight.

In the end I will be weak.
I will be defeated.
I will die.
And when you wake, you will find me
only a dream.

Clint Johnson, Grade 12
Thomas Jefferson High School for Science and Technology, VA

Another School Day Completed

I get out my computer
About to check the time
After a regular day's finishing of homework
Hoping that it is not too
Late in the night
Knowing that it is probably
2 a.m.
Having to sleep again
Without ever waking up

Natalia Mikutina, Grade 12
Douglas Southall Freeman High School, VA

Oasis

I am parched.
Drained of life and hope,
No elixir to revive me.
This lone desert I wander,
My desert of desolate dreams.
I have not the strength to fight.
My steps falter,
I fall on the coarse sand.
How did I get here?
Sand envelopes me,
The vicious sun whips me,
The violent winds strip me,
My name is called out.
I look up and see the oasis
So close, so close.
Strength returns to my limbs,
There is no turning back now,
I must walk on, and on, and on.
Almost there, my breath comes out in gasps.
I inch closer, the oasis inches farther away
It is merely a mirage.

Pritika Tiwari, Grade 10
Westfield High School, VA

The Floods

Could I get some rain down here?
Just a drop,
a drizzle.
A downpour'd be nice.
It's been so long.
I forget the feeling.
And why not now?
See, now could be a great time,
to really make a change.
Now is the perfect time
to stop this drought.
My ground is cracked
and my air is dry.
I know you can help.
Will you?

Daniel Camunas, Grade 12
Madison County High School, VA

Fallen Angel

Fallen from heaven, Fallen from grace
Alone in the dark waiting to die
Once an angel, Nevermore
Slipping away into the darkness
No one to catch him as he falls
A fallen angel Who lingers in the shadows
Never to return to the light
As this world continues to fall
Fallen from heaven, Fallen from grace
Alone in the world Waiting to be save...

Madeline Kline, Grade 11
Harford Christian School, MD

Here Is Winter

One can always tell winter is here.
From the cold nights to the numb faces.
From the laughing children playing in the snow,
Laughing as they feel the sled sliding down a hill.

One can always tell winter is here.
From the 'thwack' of a snowball hitting its target.
Or a shriek of surprise when some poor soul touches the ice.
The shouts of revenge echoing into the distance.

One can always tell winter is here.
As you hear the 'crunch' of the snow while you walk on the sidewalk.
Or the 'thunk' of the snow falling off a tree branch when it weighs too much.
The rush of slow cars trying to finish their Christmas shopping.

One can always tell winter is here.
From the Christmas music blasting over the radio,
From the light humming outside as the Christmas lights hang on the houses.
The rustling of the wrapping paper getting around the present.

Erin Pelton, Grade 12
Coventry High School, RI

What We Do

Is writing not an art, or an extension?
Do we not just talk or do we speak?
If we hesitate we will rust, rust and we will die.
We always wish to say, surely it must be I,
I who will conquer the mountains, who calms the seas.
But what do we do when we lose our voice?
Lose our way to connect, to extend, to reach out?
What do we do when the one we love is out of our grasp?
We write to speak,
what we write is what we love, it's who we are, what we believe,
so why do we write in black and white?
Is the world so bleak? Void of understanding, potential left untapped?
What we do when we write?
To write a poem, to rhyme, to sing to chant?
Is it not human nature to inquire,
to want to know?

Anthony Yeldell Jr., Grade 10
Woodbridge Sr High School, VA

Becoming

Where to start? Where to begin?
I dip my brush into my memories
I dig deep, drawing up my most painful experiences
I search far to find my happiest days
I see through different eyes, through my eyes
I become a cavity in which the spirit of another can fill and take over
Metamorphically, I transform
My wings of another color spread
I take my place upon the soft, wooden stage
The lights come up
Scene.

Kelli Richardson, Grade 12
Dinwiddie High School, VA

Fred the Caterpillar

One day, a furry bug was crawling around.
He went this way and that remaining unfound.
His track was halted by a girl with a cup.
He tried to avoid it but had no such luck.

Caught by crystal clear cups, he foresaw his end.
He sought pity while he was being examined.
The girl admired his orange, threatening spurs,
Snow-white body, and small feet covered with furs.

She searched the web to classify the creature.
She discovered details about each feature.
He was a Sycamore Tussock Caterpillar.
A touch will cause discomfort, not much danger.

The girl rejoiced in her find, naming him Fred.
When expecting the worst, he got food instead.
He was as happy as a bee with honey.
Fred the caterpillar's days were all sunny.

Marlena Fernandez, Grade 11
Bishop Denis J O'Connell High School, VA

When the Relatives Visit

Oh honey you have grown so big
And they would laugh and snort just like a pig
Sweetheart do you play basketball
I ask because you've grown so tall
I remember when you were small
You would walk and talk and regularly fall
When she wants to hug me tight
She will never let me go
If I tell her how I want it and what is right
The right hand connecting to my face will show
At times I would hide in my room
And think many thoughts and watch the moon
Sooner or later the plan had failed
And back down to my family I had to go
We had, had some fun and made a show
One last hug and one last kiss
Then they are out the door without a hiss
The house is once again back to normal
But tomorrow might bring about another trouble

Priscila Omotoso, Grade 10
Parkdale High School, MD

Remembering

distant sound of train clicking along tracks
stabs your soul
forces you to remember
his eyes as they were in that train yard
Lighting. Electric.
eyes that haunt you
countless efforts to forget, all failures
like a nightmare you just can't shake

Jeannie Sutherland, Grade 12
Eleanor Roosevelt High School, MD

Reasons to Read

Books, books, books,
So much to learn, if only one looks,
Perhaps you'll read of King Arthur and his knights,
And learn of how they defeated evil in great fights,

Or maybe you'll dive into *In Search of Honor*,
And learn that revenge does not equal valor,
If you peruse the works of Aesop,
The morals you'll learn will not stop,

Sticking your nose into *Pollyanna*,
Reveals "being glad" gives you stamina,
Classics, adventures, comedies, and more
So many to choose from none are a bore,

Books, books, books,
So much to learn, if only one looks,
They benefit us in ways untold,
Open the pages to let the lessons unfold!

Jacqlyn Fletcher, Grade 10
Barrington Christian Academy, RI

The Clock Turns Backwards In My Mind

The clock turns backwards in my mind.
This thought I have tried to avoid.
By it I have become defined.
I am becoming paranoid.

This event took my soul, kidnapped.
The clock turns backwards in my mind.
Seeing this I wish I was blind.
By this guilt I have become trapped.

My pocket has the solution.
All I need is to consign, but
The clock turns backwards in my mind
Where I see my execution.

These memories flood my conscience,
Destroying sanity's balance.
I'm feeling doomed to decline, while
The clock turns backwards in my mind.

Steven Hartman, Grade 12
Red Lion Christian Academy, DE

Sleepy Eyes

Weary eyes I despise
As sleepy lids fall and rise
Paper, book, pencil before me
Tendrils of sleep to envelop me
Oh, resistance come to me!
How can I win
When all of me wishes to sleep within?

India Karianen, Grade 11
Hampton Christian High School, VA

Who I Seem to Be

I am a courageous young lady
I wonder if things will ever get better in life
I hear my tears slowly dropping from my eyes
I see darkness everywhere I go
I want to achieve my long term goals
I am a courageous young lady

I pretend that I am a beautiful young lady who loves, and lives life
I feel my dad is watching over me and protecting me from any harm
I touch the stars in the sky and make a wish
I worry when things turn out differently from the way I expect
I cry when I think about the bad days or sad days
I am a courageous young lady

I understand that everything happens for a reason, so life moves on
I say that if anything comes your way just take it as it comes
I dream of being a fairy and making all my tales come true
I hope I become the best I can be
I am a courageous young lady

Yvette Brown, Grade 12
Mount Pleasant High School, RI

Respect Responsibility Integrity

Respect is what you earn not command.
That is something some find hard to understand.
You earn respect if respect you do show,
From people in your life you've come to know.

Something I'm learning, something that I know is true,
The only person responsible for your actions is you.
What goes around comes around, as you may have heard,
you give and take, you receive what you deserve.

How many of us live with true integrity every day?
Do your work to the fullest, never cheat in any way.
Stay to the path you made up your mind to tread,
Falling away from truth never entering your head.

Juwan Cole, Grade 11
Forestville Military Academy, MD

Blue Regret

She is like water...
   I feel turquoise mist
   whenever her name crosses my mind
   and escapes my lips.
   Pools of aquariums in her eyes
   and I'm not sure if it reflects the sea
   or if it reflects the sky.
   Her posture, her ways
   are like the fiercest, softest rippling waves
   drowning me in another breathless daze.
   But now all I'm doing is sinking when I have tried to swim
   because what I thought what once was love
   was nothing but a horrible, blue, bleeding sin.

Koa (Casey) Beus, Grade 12
Woodbridge Sr High School, VA

Earth Day

Just a small trickle
of water
nestled between sandy banks

Hardly a river at all.

Upstream
the water gets deeper, dry shoes
are a lost hope.

Armed with gloves and plastic bags
we begin to clean
the mess that is not ours.

Dodging car bumpers, gathering empty beer bottles,
playing catch with bricks,
we sink further into the sediment with each step forward.

Mountains of plastic, invisible
beneath the rushing currents
trees scarred by totaled cars existing somewhere
upstream, half buried.

Bags full to the brim, clothes stained, aching bodies
we leave the river, leaving behind
what we can't change.

Alexandra O'Neill, Grade 12
Eleanor Roosevelt High School, MD

My Dream of Love

My heart burns for the sight
Of your beauty once more.
Your eyes are so radiant but yet mysterious.
It's as if you can look straight into my heart.

I wish I could give you the world.
For I am not worthy to be with a girl of such beauty.
You make me feel like a king and
You my queen, you are the most precious thing to me.

Though I don't say those three special words I would
Rather show you that I do care for you, and I
Appreciate everything you've done for me, I would
Rather shout out to the world that I love you.

My love for you can't be described; love is rich, love is
Pure, love is a thing no doctor can cure. When I look in
Your eyes all I see is you and I together with a
Wonderful life ahead of us.

True love can't be found with just the simplest interest.
Love can be found in the weirdest of places.
I love you with all my heart I hope to be able to live
My whole life with you.

Peter McPherson, Grade 10
Forestville Military Academy, MD

Teenage Love Story

Love is easy to give,
But not always easy to find.
It may be a hard
Difficult road for many.
Yet, I find myself
Loving you and wanting
You to think of me,
As I do you.
I want you to look
At me as I do you.
Oh, wait you do.
I see the way you
Look at me.
I hear what you
Say about me.
Yet you won't tell me.
Why do you do this to me?
Only time will tell me
The end of the teenage love story.
Missy Fox, Grade 12
Page County High School, VA

For Cold and Lovelorn Caterpillars

Deep within the freeze,
A pocket of warmth did shelter
A small cocoon alone,
Amid the howling winter.

The blooms of life will freeze,
Finding no hope of shelter.
Death all alone,
Amid the howling winter.

My blood will surely freeze,
Away from your arms' shelter.
Please leave me not alone,
Amid the howling winter
Neomi Rao, Grade 11
Eleanor Roosevelt High School, MD

Hurt

The sadness and sorrow
The grief and pain
With nothing to gain
Broken and all out
Shattered all about
Never fixed
Never right
All alone for endless nights
Revenge takes place
In this hallowed hole
Nothing's there
But pain and despair
This is my broken heart
Crystal Tippett, Grade 11
Great Mills High School, MD

School

We are the kids

Boulders on our backs
From the ring of one bell
To the next, the next
Hear the same speeches
But hate to listen

Sounds of lead and ink
Tear through ridges of processed trees
Touching multiple seats and sheets
And on returned paper,
An alphabet in red

Visible veins protrude
Teeth clench — grind together
Fatigued from lectures and work
Unsatisfied from a dull present
Future without hope.
Kalu Azu, Grade 12
Eleanor Roosevelt High School, MD

It's All the Same

Kick it, or throw it
Drive it, or putt it
Hit it, or pitch it
Jump in, or dive in
They're all the same

You practice daily
For what,
The glory, no
For the experience
For the pleasure

You work hard
You train hard
You work for one goal
Just that one thing
They're all the same
William Walsh, Grade 10
Delaware Military Academy, DE

Taste for Spasm*

Aroma so tempting,
Flavor so sweet;
Wrapped in fine cloth
Good enough to eat.
Dark chocolate hair,
Eyes just as deep.
Arms that could've rocked me to sleep.
Sarcastic humor;
You mean me no harm,
But you've caught me
With your outlandish charm.
My heart starts to spasm
Whenever you're close,
And when you leave
I become morose.
So hurry if you please,
Before you have to go,
Let me taste your lips.
And you had better not say no.
Jasmin Sparkman, Grade 10
Kecoughtan High School, VA
*Dedicated to someone special to me.

It's Death Again

It's death again and he's always there
Watching, waiting on the stair.
Every time I look behind
Or reach to pull the window blind,
I catch a glimpse of grubby hood
A little clue to where he stood;
The glint of light that caught the scythe.
Perhaps if I could pay a tithe
But oh, no use, he'll never go.
The adamant phantom; don't you know,
He will but wait until it's time
For me to hear his fateful chime
The toll that's only meant for me,
To say, "You're next, it has to be."
Patrick Clark, Grade 10
Forestville Military Academy, MD

That One Place

I feel the world lift my worries
away as I lay on a homemade hammock
placed right under a mango tree
When I want a snack, a fresh
mango will drop onto my lap and
satisfy my hunger and sweet tooth.
As I lay there rocking back and forth
watching the clouds go by
and the sun disappears
I hear the quietness of the night
come on as the freshness of the wind
passes by and rocks me to sleep.
Gabriela Blandin, Grade 12
Mount Pleasant High School, RI

The Weeping Tree

A tall willow stands alone
Its beautiful leaves folded and bent.

A little blue pond
Waves at the tree
But continues to stay within its home.

A wind comes by
Playful at first,
Then forcing the extensive limbs
To bend at its will.

The long delicate branches
Begin to sway to the
Sound of the lapping water.

It twirls alone
To its own tune
But at the same time it asks
"Will you dance with me?"

Jennifer Burker, Grade 11
Clear Spring High School, MD

Broken Glass

One day I'll run away
from this world of broken glass.
The shattered lives of many,
trying to overlook the past.
Teardrops fall like rain,
forever you will cry.
Won't the rain stop falling
from this godforsaken sky?
Broken hearts like fire,
burning in the heat.
Deep inside out hearts cry out
"I need to find relief!"
Death is like a demon
with little evil eyes.
Staring you down on the darkest night,
only coming to surprise.
I'll just keep on running.
Running far away.
One day I'll escape this world,
I don't think I can stay…

Erica Meusel, Grade 12
Annapolis Sr High School, MD

Love

Love is pure and natural
Natural is beauty and innocence
Beauty is found within
Within there is always a heart
Heart is always ready to hate and to love
Love is rare and infinite.

Christine Bangura, Grade 10
Woodbridge Sr High School, VA

Rag Doll

You'd play rough with me
during tea, my face colliding with our
plastic not-so-dreamy house or when you
swept my cheek across table tops and left
me dirty. You always turned the other Toys on the shelf
around, they only saw when you'd pet my hair gently
or pull my chair out like a chivalrous Ken doll.
You were more like Godzilla crushing my easily torn body
I was only a doll and you were my owner, you
were allowed to do what you pleased. When you were finished
with me I settled next to Barbies and Care Bears with my stringy hair disheveled
and my blue dress clinging in torn bits to my cloth skin cut open with
cotton oozing out from my wounds.
I'd lie to protect you, "I fell down some stairs." A Rag Doll has no brains
and you had fists like He-Man, it was obvious who would be the victor every time.
I understand now, a little too late, why boys were never allowed to
play with Dolls, he always played too rough.
Always pulled too hard, always defiled Dolls until
all my cotton was beaten from me, left a torn Rag.

Lisa Delao, Grade 11
Woodbridge Sr High School, VA

At the Coffee Shop

You can easily forget the time
when freshly brewed coffee flows rivers inside you.
I glance at the dust of school textbooks.
My fingertips remind me how skin feels as I wipe the exhaustion from my chin.
I have invested an entire evening into this stool; studying for tommorow's test.
I thought that this was a good idea;
I'm having second thoughts.
In this basin of idleness, I decode the enigma of boredom.

Wrapped around the taste of adrenaline injected scones and tongue torching coffee.
I just sit here.
Pouring ambition into this warm brew, adding sugar, desire, expectations... the future?
I drain away the night as I done countless times before
Hoping that one day,
I could go and watch a movie instead.

Jorrell Watkins, Grade 12
Open High School, VA

Insanity

These haunting memories can never leave my head
Striking the impure mind with blood, pain, and the dead
They curse and stain the tormented soul with sorrow
End the path of destiny, leaving nothing to follow
The howls of the lonely night crying out
Calling me to them no doubt
The darkness circulating my mind, injecting me with its twisted madness
As loved ones stand by, their eyes full of worry and sadness
Death watching, a dark evil smirk upon his wicked lips
Watching as if he were at a freak show while my sanity crumbles and rips
Thus being cast into the dark, empty depths of the forsaken abyss
The warmth leaving all around, only cold as I feel death's kiss upon my lips

Raymond Jones, Grade 11
Woodbridge Sr High School, VA

Now Over

Over the edge
and into the violent blue water
of his eyes,
I find myself irritatingly lost.
Over the truth
and viciously into the lies,
I fling myself.

I'm Over the past,
focused on the future.
Over him I will be,
and back into me.
I'm more important.
Over his needs and onto mine.
Moving over and past,
destroying all he laid before me.

Violence. Tearing the bonds
he held over me.
Over him now,
his villainous reign ended.

Crystal Fleshman, Grade 12
Dinwiddie High School, VA

Love

I love you with all my heart
Being together forever
Knowing we are never apart
Will I hurt you never
Whipping my tears
We fight our enemy
He looks away from what he fears
While we see our entity
Thinking of all the bad
We laugh and giggle
Wow what a time we had
As his eyes wiggle
Love is part of the mind
Something most can't find

Keshaunna Stith, Grade 11
Dinwiddie High School, VA

Myself or My Reflection?

Her body,
Is monstrous.
The skin that covers her
Is singed and burned.
The parts that make her whole,
Are lanky and awkward.
Where her curves should be lovely,
They're uneven and lumpy.
Singed,
Burned,
Flesh.

Kaitlyn Allen, Grade 11
Dinwiddie High School, VA

Sticky Little Kitten

All I wanted to do was pet my pretty little kitten
But she wanted to play
I tried to grab her before she fell in
But she got away
Now she's climbed out of the punch and her fur is wet
Her claws are bared
She's looking around for some unknown assailant
But no one is there
It can't possibly have been her doing
She's just a baby
It must have been demonic possession
Or maybe rabies
But in her right mind she would never do that
She isn't that careless
If she isn't careful she'll wind up dead
Or worse, hairless
Then she looked at me with her big, wet eyes
And realized the truth
Of how my sticky little kitten got herself in the bowl
She needed no proof
My little kitten who still loves me so, then told herself I pushed her into the bowl

Will Walsh, Grade 12
Bishop Walsh Middle High School, MD

The Girl

Take a look around you, what do you see?
Shelter? Clothes? The multicolored screen of your TV?
Alas, that's not the case for me; I have never had the opportunity to be free.
I am the girl, who walks the streets all day,
The girl society deems has nothing to say.
The girl who cannot read, nor write;
The girl forced to entertain men at night.
I am the girl, whose life is a dwindling fee,
The girl about to bear child number three.
The girl, who has no will or power,
The girl whose past has turned her sour.
I am the girl left bloody and bruised,
The girl constantly manipulated and used.
The girl whose tears could fill up the ocean,
The girl whose never seen positive devotion.
I am the girl whose life is filled with lies
The girl viewed as a blemish in societies eyes.
The girl whose days are ticking away
The girl who'll die with nothing to say.
Now, alas dear stranger, won't you help me?
Not now you say, my favorite program is on TV.

Denise Bonsu, Grade 11
McLean High School, VA

Never Back Down

When I think everything is right, something goes wrong right in plain sight.
I believe trouble has a way of finding me, knocking me down, never will I achieve.
Life has many ups, but downs constantly come, what to do at that point, I sometimes run.
But it chases me to a dead end, then that's when I face it and that's when I win.
If I continue to think like a loser, then losing I will do.
The right path to success is what I will choose.
Why do bad things happen to good people, something we will always ask,
but if I let it get the best of me, they get the last laugh.
No negativity should be beside me, I will eliminate every thing that reminds me,
Of the defeats I endured and tears I shed, my life is like a book, yet to be read.
No looking back, I am starting fresh, putting all the past times and rumors to rest.
So talk all you want, and call me all those names, this time it won't affect me it will not be the same.
Difference is I am fighting back now never to run away,
But to stand up for something and live to fight another day.
I might even go in alone with no one else around, but one
thing I tell myself is to never back down!

Maurice Williams, Grade 11
Forestville Military Academy, MD

The Undeniable Fact of Seasame Dobbins

A wall built of logs for as
long as the eye can
see.

Is it keeping you in? or are you keeping me out?
This barrier needs to come down life is not meant to be spent, in a cold
isolated world.

Is you life full of Happiness that I'll just never know? or is your facade everything you make it seem.
    I want it back
  to the way I had planned it
    I want it back
  to the way it was meant to be

I took your mind and your soul for granted
    now it's just selfishly me…

Rebecca Grubb, Grade 10
Tunstall High School, VA

My Rice Krispies

I opened the cabinet and took the bowl from the rack.
I obtain the milk from the giant fortress of cooled air.
Then, with a tilt of the carton, magic erupts!
Alas! Mesmerizing mouthfuls await!
My rice krispies are a symphony inside a crater of porcelain.
They snap, crackle, and pop at a mere wave of my silver spoon.
Better than Beethoven, they play with all their might and never miss a beat.
Float peacefully they do, in their calcium fortified mixture.
Their over joyous faces gleam with every beat like the bright sun beaming down on a summer day.
I chew and chew and chew yet, their roar is unfazed.
After I have finished preparing and enjoying and eating my rice krispies, I guzzle the bittersweet taste of success.
With a swipe from the back of my hand, my journey has finally come to a close.
Suddenly, I jolt up in bed! I look around only to see that it was merely but a dream.

Irina Boothe, Grade 12
James River High School, VA

Free to Fly

I am caged like the bird in the second window
Down
Wishing I could fly Fly Flying down
   Floating down

Wishing I could spread my wings and
Fly above the ground

If I listen to the left if I look to the right
I see the people staring cacophonous, not caring
Staring Staring Staring
Stupid stupid people

There are no cages on their window and no bars upon their door

Choosing not to fly Fly Fly down
   Float down
Just staring
Never caring
If they Fly above the ground

Choosing to remain like the bird in the second window
Down

Caged, like me in the second
Window
Down

JK Day, Grade 10
Woodbridge Sr High School, VA

Shooting Star

A fire burned in the eyes
Of two young lovers underneath
A sparkling blanket of stars
As they wondered at the mysteries of space
And sat in each other's arms
When the young girl saw a marvelous sight
A star shooting across the sky.

Not much time had passed
When again she saw
Yet another star fall.
In excitement she told the boy,
Who grinned at the sight of her joy
And told her a story
That he had heard.

Seeing one shooting star is rare
Seeing two on the same night is special
And one who does may make a wish.
The girl thought about what she would wish for
And immediately made a choice.
To be with him for forever
Was her heart's desire.

Kiersten Gausman, Grade 11
Madison County High School, VA

Lost

Lost is feeling alone in a room full of your peers.
Lost is forgetting your locker combination the first day of school.
Lost is a wren who has fallen from her nest.
Lost is a penguin in the Sahara.
Lost is being free like a leaf in the wind.
Lost is being confined like a bird in a cage.
Lost is a crying child stranded in the grocery store.
Lost is a box of old clothes and abandoned toys.
Lost is living at a house but longing for a home.
Lost is a TV show that makes very little sense.
Lost is an empty hole inside your soul.
Lost is a plethora of paths leading to the future.
Lost is a meandering road revealing the past.
Lost is a discarded cheerleader doll tossed under the couch.
Lost is a lone mauve button whose sweater was trashed long ago.
Lost is knowing you're missing something, but not knowing what.
Lost is drowning in a sea of emotions until you're finally
Found.

Jane Autumn Plummer, Grade 12
St. Elizabeth High School, DE

Not So Perpetual After All

Run! Don't pause, just get out of the way!
Don't hesitate, collapsing skies await!
Catastrophe of modern-day Pompeii
A true disaster imminent today!

Meltdown in Chernobyl's cousin-to-be
Domino skyscrapers line up perfectly
The Tower of Babel has nothing on these
Architectural dynamo-calamities!

World leaders, engineers, cry out in pain
Future dreams shattered — Goliath, slain!
Two thousand Tinkertoys and three model trains —
One careless jerk
and two days' work
goes down the stairs
and down the drain.

Linus Hamilton, Grade 11
Eleanor Roosevelt High School, MD

Until Then

Every day I wake up thinking something will change.
But I guess I was wrong, some things never change.
How many times does it take for you to understand,
Or do I have to realize the truth?
The truth is you will never change and I will never listen.
I will never listen to those who tell me otherwise.
Am I a fool and am I in denial? Maybe.
This is the thing about you that drives me crazy.
I will come to my senses one day or maybe that
Day will never come, but
Until then I will be waiting.

Nia Boone, Grade 11
Forestville Military Academy, MD

Quietly

Quietly sitting under this big oak tree
Wondering about life, writing a poem, watching the seasons go by
But this tree has stayed the same

Quietly kneeling by a beautiful lake
The sun smiled back at me as I glanced at my reflection
My feet dangling in the clear blue water
I sat with my notebook on my lap, sketching little stars
Quietly walking along the beach
Staring out into the vast ocean
Seeing a dolphin flap its tail, I waved to it
And imagined you here with me
Quietly watching the sun set
The orange and yellow rays gleamed upon my face
As my hair flows across my face with the breeze
You came into my mind
And before I could help it, your hand was on my shoulder

Quietly sitting under this big oak tree
Wondering about life, writing this poem, watching the seasons go by
But now you and this tree have grown

Miranda McLain, Grade 10
St Mary's Ryken High School, MD

Accomplishment

Nothing comes without pain
Without sweat, without blood
Glory is not achieved by working
Nevertheless it is achieved by hard work
Dedication
Determination
And discipline
Luck runs two ways
Good luck and bad luck
Luck cannot be achieved by prayer or by magic
Luck is earned by the player
The leader that stays after practice working on his faults
The group that is working in the off season for the upcoming season
The group that will never give up in any situation
Accomplishment is not appreciated without the taste of defeat
We all must taste defeat sometime in our lives
It is not about experiencing defeat
Rather than learning from the loss
Correcting mistakes
And getting that
Accomplishment

Brandon Kimble, Grade 12
Bishop Walsh Middle High School, MD

Just Because I'm Quiet

Just because I'm quiet
  Doesn't mean I don't know how to have fun.
Just because I'm quiet
  Doesn't mean I'm a loner.
Just because I'm quiet
  Doesn't mean I don't have a sense of humor.
Just because I'm quiet
  Doesn't mean I don't get along with people.
Just because I'm quiet
  Doesn't mean I never have my own opinion.
Just because I'm quiet
  Doesn't mean I'm not a good friend.
Just because I'm quiet
  Doesn't mean I have problems.
Just because I'm quiet
  Doesn't mean I don't care what people say about me.
Just because I'm quiet
  Doesn't mean I have no life.
Just because I'm quiet
  Doesn't mean I have no personality.
Just because I'm quiet.

Leigh Ann Lennon, Grade 10
Delaware Military Academy, DE

Morning's Night Watchman

some world between late night and early morning
last train to the last stop
we faced each other, ten, fifteen feet apart
an Asian man, eyebrows drawn, features frustrated, angry
older, long hair, frameless glasses, dressed in black and blue
eyes mistrustful, wary
wasn't angry, I realized, just tired
waiting for the end of the line, I struggled to stay awake
so did he, even as new passengers boarded
every now and again
he would close his eyes
sleeping on the job
each stranger attracted his gaze, look of caution
except me
innocent curiosity, wondering why, I was too tired to judge
half asleep dreams expected something unreal to happen
half awake musings thought he was stopping it
midnight morning
we reached the end
I went to the world of daylight and dawn
he walked the other way.

Emily Laughlin, Grade 12
Eleanor Roosevelt High School, MD

Youth Violence

We see it flashing big and loud on the evening news shootings, teens beating each other
We think yeah so that's hundreds of miles away or that's not one of my buddies who got busted up so what do I care
But stop and think that's teen vs teen
Lives changed forever one misstep
Someone's lying in a hospital bed the other sent away to rot in a cell
Both lived changed forever but let's not forgot the chain reaction the pebbles been dropped the ripples are moving
Can't call them back now
Boom the first wave hits a mom or dad a sister or brother lost now in despair and disbelief
Boom extended family get the shock
Boom now friends classmates teachers those passing on the street can't believe the news or the scene they saw
Then those feelings got nowhere to go so another act of violence drops another pebble
Then it repeats
And repeats
And repeats
Someone's got to yell STOP! Break the cycle why not you and why not now?

Sam Ruff, Grade 10
Indian Creek Upper School, MD

Senior Year

Senior Year…
We have made it this far, but this far is not enough, there is nothing less that we would wish for. Our time together have grown short, as we grown taller and more mature. As the final days of our great four years come to an end, we'll shed many tears that'll show the true feelings we hid behind dimming smiles. We'll say, "Hey! It'll be okay, we'll keep in touch and than when we meet again, it won't be hello, it'll be where have you been!?" As we smile and laugh and take our last big breaths as our names are called, we pant, sneeze, twitch and sweat. As we shed more tears that we won't regret, we'll look upon the crowd as we cheer each other on. A smile that'll jump on our faces, and the tears will flow harder, but the only thing we can all say is…
We accomplished it!

DeAndre Weaver, Grade 12
Dinwiddie High School, VA

Just Because I'm Smart

Just because I'm smart, doesn't mean that I don't have a life or friends just because I study all day.
Just because I'm smart, doesn't mean that I'm a video game junkie.
Just because I'm smart, doesn't mean that I'm not social, or that don't like to be talked to.
Just because I'm smart, doesn't mean that I'm in all the available school clubs.
Just because I'm smart, doesn't mean that I'm a loner and push away relationships.
Just because I'm smart, doesn't mean that I dress weird.
Just because I'm smart, doesn't mean that I don't have a sense of humor.
Just because I'm smart, doesn't mean that I am a nobody.

Garrett McCarthy, Grade 10
Delaware Military Academy, DE

The Difficulty of Life

when I walk home from school I'm always hearing get your homework done dad's always calling me I get so mad it just makes me crazy I tell him that I'm in high school now but that don't mean anything to him all I have to say is wow when I'm done I want to relax hang out with my friends and bros pretty late but since it's a school night I'm not allowed to I just feel hate I have to wake up early to catch the bus at a whole other neighborhood and stand in the cold and I don't even have a hood to protect me from the rain it just brings me a lot of pain so you see what I go through every day makes you feel that you're lucky that you don't have to see my ways

Joshua Kerr, Grade 10
Delaware Military Academy, DE

Not a Game

If life is just a game, why do we feel the pain?
There are no pauses, resumes, or start-overs.
Our life isn't counted by hearts, stars, or clovers.
We've only got one chance, but for how long
Before we screw up,
Or something goes wrong?
Our allies change sides, everyone tells lies,
Sometimes you get lucky,
But not everyone gets out alive.
There are no special codes, cheats, or walkthroughs.
There are just many roads,
And the paths you must choose.
There are no heroes and villains, drawn from black and white lines,
But there are all kinds of people,
With different personalities and minds.
We don't always win, we sometimes face strife,
But this isn't a game,
It's a thing called life.

Brittany Bartley, Grade 11
Fort Defiance High School, VA

Success

The little girl weeps, tightly hugging her knee.
Her friend calls, beckoning, from up in a tree.
Her running tears sparkle in the clear autumn light;
He swings from branch to branch with all his might.
The wind picks up, and dancing leaves fly.
The friend doesn't notice as the little girl cries.
She sits on the ground in the dying green grass
While he reaches for heaven, just like every boy has.
And from up in the branches, he let out a cry:
He had reached the top, therefore touching the sky.
The hurt little girl, stuck firmly on ground,
Craned her neck just to see what he'd found.
But the boy paid no notice to her questioning eyes
For she was on Earth, and he in the sky.

Halle Burns, Grade 11
Cab Calloway School of the Arts, DE

Don't Walk Crooked

You move with a slouch and a deviant face
Your joints crackle and pop with utter disgrace
The manner of your clothes infers something wicked
And your lascivious grin makes my skin turn frigid

Worst of all, your strides are lopsided
The sickening movements with revulsion provided
A dance, a jig, a crooked shuffle
A waltz of contortion as you gently chuckle

Don't walk crooked, you look stiff and brittle
Your wood-carved face is littered with spittle
A man such as you isn't easy on the eyes
Kind gentle ways have a horrid disguise.

Johnny Griffith, Grade 11
Madison County High School, VA

My Personal Philosophy

My personal philosophy
is to reside within my apathy, to
just close my eyes and count to three
and let the time sail by me. And as I start to sleep,
deep within my slumber things start to
appear that make me wonder if the world is
all a-plunder or asunder —
could it be we're falling under?
To change my mind and disagree,
I open my eyes and count to three, and
wait for thought to enlighten me as
I start to wake up from this dream of
danger, mistrust, and grief that
I feel so far beneath the worn surface
of this decrepit rusty sheath that I do call
my own skin. Such disbelief! to feel so queer
in one's own skin; so I'll close my eyes and count to three
to reside within my apathy,
as that is my philosophy.

Katie Hall, Grade 12
Tucker High School, VA

I Want to Hold You Close

I want to hold you close
And take you far away
I offer you my love and pray
To the God up above
That he can make us last and keep us together
Because we are perfect for each other
You walked into my world with a smile
So let's just pray you will stay for a while
And never leave
Because you're starting to mean the world to me
I never thought
I would find someone like you
Someone so funny, someone so smart
And someone who knows the real me
Before I tell you

Britni Adams, Grade 10
Parkdale High School, MD

Poison

A heavy feel, the poison of sleep.
Soaking through her veins, pushing in deep.
The burning invades her flesh, forcing her to cry.
Her screams seem silent, and she can't find why.
Breathing in deeply, her stomach in a knot.
She tries to relax, but can't shake the thought.
That she may never awake from this nightmare.
She will forever haunt the middle of nowhere.
THUMP! goes her chest, as she sees no one is around.
Then. She's flying off a cliff, and wakes on the ground.
Her chest eases as she comes to see.
There was no poison, just wild dreams.

Cherry Shutler, Grade 10
Stone Bridge High School, VA

Paranoia vs Paraphernalia

Social vagaries,
Tis impossible to even fathom the possibility of embracing them.
Those who try are often left gallivanting aimlessly,
Or in worse cases driven to the brink of obsessive insanity.
Yet why don't we label them as the ones with the problems, defects, dilemmas, and so forth?
Instead we decide to investigate and instigate.
To excavate for research and preservation,
Then to emulate ignorantly without moral discussion.
Such profligate trends are short lived and soon berated,
Yet through it all we have cleverly manipulated...
By the evasive government who all the while prospers.

You see once one's integrity comes into question all attention diverts,
Even I have fallen prey to these situations. I thought that I had deciphered the scheme at one point,
Sadly it 'twas but an illusion — a figment of my imagination.
So after my spark of insanity I became a wanderer, petrified of the eyes the world gazed upon me with.
The ever growing fear of not fitting in pilfered my breath,
Until my lungs themselves were virtually gone with the wind.
That's when I had a revelation and noticed that being a consumer only led to self doubt and ignorance.
Only in a society obsessed with public affinity,
Will we be left to their own devices with every other problem, thus we are left
Assuming ourselves to death.

Brandon Artis, Grade 11
Benjamin Banneker Academic High School, DC

Hysteria

Panic. I'm terrified.
I go to sleep at night wondering if I will wake up in the morning.
I walk through the streets paranoid, turning at every sound I hear.
I pull my sweater tighter around me. A dog barks, I jump. A stranger bumps into me, apologizing, and I shiver.
I'm not crazy.
There's a buzzing in my ear that won't go away. I don't close my eyes, when I do, I see scenes unfold like a horror movie being
played on a screen.
I'm not crazy.
My body is numb with fear and yet I feel my whole world crashing down around me. I see flashes, things that aren't there. I hear
my name, my heart beats faster and my throat closes because I'm scared.
I ask why me every day, but no one responds.
I'm not crazy, that's what I tell myself.
I'm not crazy.

Sophie Perrotti, Grade 10
The Prout School, RI

Pawn

I look through you. Translucent you are, fading in and out as if your past has been altered. A simple pawn in your plan, used
I was, as a queen...you would win, but I would not lose hope. I see your feelings unfold and I realize that you strategized and
thought out your moves. A crystal piece, solid in every step, moving closer and closer to the other side. Confused and enraged by the
manipulative words you spoke, I tried to break you, maneuvering around your pieces of anger, guilt, and frustration. I tore down
all of your "puppets," yet you stood strong as if YOU had already won the battle. You mustered up all the strength that remained
within you, and released it in one move. As I fell in defeat, I new that it was over, I had been conquered. The crystal shards of
memories, yours and mine alike, were all that remained of our intense quarrel. As I began to dwindle away to nothing, all my
energy consumed, I used the last bit I had left to form the dust that I would become into a "parting gift." It would read...
"check-mate"

Ian Harris, Grade 10
Parkdale High School, MD

Dreams

I've been told countless times that they're only meant for when we sleep
A form of escapism that only lasts until we open our eyes again
But if dreams are so superficial then why do so many dreams come true?
Martin Luther King had a dream I could have the same privileges no matter what color or creed
This would have never happened had it not been for one man who had a dream
You see dreams are just the seeds of what can become reality with perseverance and faith
Dreams are what the world is made out of.
They're meant for anytime of the day.
They inspire us to do the impossible
Dreams are the pennies thrown in a wishing well only they don't sink to the bottom.
Without them, the world would be hell on earth.
A place full of empty souls just existing instead of living
So let's come together and dream big
Not for fortune or for fame
But for those people starving in Africa
The victims of the earthquake that rocked a nation
And those people who have lost all hope
That they too will knock the dust off their knees
And join us as we dream

Gabrielle Wynn, Grade 11
Elizabeth Seton High School, MD

Dear Josiah

I just wanted to say I love you
Also, I miss you a lot,
I wish that I could see you,
You are amazing,
We all love you very much,
I no longer mourn
I celebrate everything about you
From your precious hands and feet to your beautiful, adorable, unforgettable face
I wanted to thank you for opening closed eyes
The day that I get to see you, I will cry, but you shouldn't worry, they are tears of joy, I promise
You will have to tell me everything
About the funniest, best, saddest, happiest parts of our lives you have been able to watch
I just wanted to tell you
I Love you

Love,
Courtney

Courtney Yarbrough, Grade 10
Tunstall High School, VA

The Edge

My whole life I have lived in the quiet serenity of my father's home. But now that I'm older it's time for me to take hold of my life and my future. In order to achieve this freedom I must, as my ancestors before me, leave the quiet serenity of my family and jump off the edge. But there is one problem, I'm scared. I am afraid of going off the edge, but I shall be strong. As I go towards the edge my legs go rubbery. I start to sweat uncontrollably. I tremble with each wobbly step. As I reach the edge I look back to see my friends and family urging me on. You can do it, they say. Jump, they chant. I wanna run back where I will be safe. But no I must jump. I step forward. I bend down on knobby knees. I reach my arms as high as I possibly can. The chanting ceases. All is still. All is quiet. My heart takes on a rhythm unfamiliar to me. Now, I tell myself. Jump now, I say. My legs stretch out under me. I did it. I jumped off the edge.

Megan Lawrence, Grade 11
Allegany High School, MD

Run Forever

Gasping
Dying
Trying
for just one more breath
Pushing
Dying
Trying
for just one more step
never knew it was this hard
to move my legs
Why
do I keep doing this
Can't
wait for this to be
Over
but then it is over
and every time
I
Go
and do it
all over again

Adam Rossi, Grade 12
Bishop Walsh Middle High School, MD

Nighttime

The moon sings to the stars
The owl hoots along
The coyote howls with the owl
It is a beautiful song

It is calm and peaceful
All is at rest
All are relaxing
This is the time I like best

Soon the sun rises
Soon the stars go
Soon we are awakened
By the rooster's crow

A.J. Brady, Grade 10
Delaware Military Academy, DE

Around the Rabbit Hole

Around the rabbit hole,
children jump and play,
Inching closer around,
daring to take a peek.
All around stories are traded
of leaping cards and a Hatter.
But, one girl gets too close.
So, the others lay around the rabbit hole
and watch her fall down to Wonderland.

Alice Shanfelter, Grade 12
Dinwiddie High School, VA

I'm Sorry

I never knew what I really had until you almost walked away.
I never knew what could have been up until this very day.
You've been there all my life and I've never taken notice,
Never even acknowledged you until this moonlit solstice.
I'm sorry that I took so long to finally hear my heart.
I'm sorry that I took so long to finally play my part.
I never knew how funny you could be, how it could be so contagious.
Yet under that jester's mask lies a heart, truly courageous.
I sat upon my throne all day, basking in all my glory,
That I never knew how you really felt, and for that I am dearly sorry.
You saved my life that rainy night, and have made it easier,
And even when I couldn't listen, you took your time, at leisure
To tell me how you truly felt, to tell me that you loved me.
You've loved me all our lives and yet I never managed to see…
Because of this, I nearly lost you; if I did I wouldn't know what to do.
I'm sorry that I took so long to say that I love you.

Luke Coleman, Grade 10
Heritage High School, VA

Saying Goodbye

Saying goodbye was *not* the easiest thing to do
Especially when I knew I'd be spending the rest of my life without you
When reminiscing I'd just want to lay down and cry
Ya know thinking about all the reasons "why"
Why I won't be able to see your beautiful face ever again
Why you won't be here to play with me, tea parties, princess, pretend
I still think about you, yeah, every single day
You might not be present
But in my heart you will stay
Saying goodbye was *not* the easiest thing to do
Especially when I knew I'd be spending the rest of my life without you

India Dandridge, Grade 10
Forestville Military Academy, MD

Tears in My Eyes

Sleeping with tears in my eyes
Going through my life without a purpose
Needing you to help guide me in the right direction
Walking with a glassy tint in my eyes. Do you notice? Probably not.

Tears flow down my face like the Mississippi River never going to stop
I look at you
You look at me
We reach our hands out and intertwine our fingers
I look at you again and weakly smile with the joy in heart slowly dying
But when I blink…you're gone.

Erika Hardy, Grade 11
Bethel High School, VA

Death on the Blind Side

Death does not always
seem as a kind friend
some see brutality
others practicality
But no matter the case
we all meet our end
at some point of time

It is seen as a monster
under our bed
the boogieman in our closet
or maybe just maybe
the nightmares within our dreams

I stare beyond
the cold dark shadows
of the atmosphere
only to be blinded
by the path on the road
when my journey
comes to an end

Caroline Boles, Grade 12
Tunstall High School, VA

Colors

A rainbow of colors
flying through the air,
only to come
back down to the earth
to be caught in empty hands.
There was purple,
followed by vibrant
streaks of blue and green.
All flying around in circles
left and right
up and down
then suddenly…
nothing
no movement
no sounds

Carrie Birkett, Grade 12
Madison County High School, VA

Stars and Stripes

A fluttering flag,
The flying eagle,
Little kids playing,
We do what we want,
We say what we want,
We're the brave and the free,
We stand for what we believe,
Our life is our own,
We are America.

Michael Soong, Grade 12
Homeschool Plus, VA

The Afterthoughts of a Breakup

You weren't a regret, you weren't a waste of time
I loved you so much it should've been a crime
And I'm not going to lie; it was hard for me to say goodbye

No, please don't feel ashamed; you were not to blame
This was just the price paid to play the game
Yes, there will be others in line
But getting over this will take me some time

You told me your love was true, for this I didn't need a clue
I loved you so dearly, hopefully you saw this clearly
But it's not you, it's me; not being the boy you wanted me to be

This was the hardest thing I've ever had to do
No longer could I be doing this to you

I'm sorry I didn't hold up my end of the deal
Your wounds aren't the only ones that will never heal
You gave me your life; you gave me you soul
Sorry for breaking the promises I said I'd hold

Sorry I have to take away my hand
Someday you'll hopefully understand
Sorry it had to succumb to your number one fear; but it was something that you had to hear
And you have no clue how much it made me to pay
But it was something that I just had to say

Ian Bruce, Grade 10
Delaware Military Academy, DE

A Better Future

I sit here, trying to analyze what's going on in the world
There's war, there's hate, humans killing other humans
We're killing off our own race like animals
Like animals, we'll be extinct one day
Yet, I can't help but wait for peace to come to the world
To the souls who truly need it

They say time heals wounds
I question whether what they say is true
Whether time heals our wounds, or whether the faith we have in time heals them
Faith that time, will bring a better future for ourselves
Maybe that's what really heals wounds
Having faith that one day, we will have a better future for ourselves
A better future in exchange for our tragic past
But now is the time, to begin planning for the future
We can't sit around, waiting for something to be done
When we ourselves are the ones who must take action
Against the war, against the hate
We are the makers of the better future that awaits us
We WILL change the world
As I sit here, I realize that this world will be changed
Everyone has a role to play and it all starts today

Cindy Navarro, Grade 10
Parkdale High School, MD

I Waste Away in the Company of Diamonds...

If you crushed my body
It would precipitate
Diamonds
They would fall
With breathtaking urgency
On hard concrete
Hail from pale white bones
Destruction from glitter
It's so easy to conquer children
Using stones
They fall with me
Jewels dusted with dying laughter
We fall into the melting pot
Of Society
And evaporate as chalk dust
Sprinkled black from your ashes
We are strewn with the Pixie Promise
Of Freedom
We are dead
They corrupted us

Amitie Hylton, Grade 11
Tunstall High School, VA

Road to Normality

I think to myself...
What lies ahead?
Future?
Family?
Thoughts of impurity?
Confused, I am indeed.
But compelled by those thoughts.
I realize I'm enjoying my disorientedness.
So intrigued...
Never thought I could have those thoughts.
Never thought I could have an imperfect life.
Feels good to be NORMAL.
I sit,
I ponder...
I think to myself...
Imperfectness is the normality.

Jasmine Reid, Grade 12
Tunstall High School, VA

Ballin'

Basketball is the sport
Dribbling the ball up and down the court
This is a fast pace game
You should have no shame
Try to score
Buckets are the core
Two points, three points, shoot from the line
Jordan and LeBron the best of all time
You must master all
This is the game of basketball

Cody Dotson, Grade 10
Delaware Military Academy, DE

Time

Time is a bead of water slipping off a stone
With each drop of water comes a new beginning and end
Every new bend in the rushing river has something to behold
A power that rivals the sea

Time pursues our lives
Nipping at our heels
A blizzard in the night
A cold chill

What makes it so different
It's subtle beyond comprehension
The sage of our existence
Creating the past
Living in the present
Molding the future
Shifting the earth

But no matter how long you want to hold onto a moment
You can't stop time from moving on

Tim Torre and Russell Rusko, Grade 10
Harford Technical High School, MD

The Noctivagant Swain

A waxing swain,
My waxing swain,
He comes apart on his noctivagant ways,
Ambling forth to an awaiting horse; they trod the nights away.
Here comes he, here comes he, wide-awake and barely asleep,
I on the bassinet of lethargy, he comes to me, he comes to me.
As I rouse, I hear the hounds, I stumble to my casement.
Up he comes, he has me spun, I resemble shock, displacement.
He unfastens the hinge, I permit him in, exulted we both are.
But we must be silent, for things may become violent,
Our relations are exceedingly thin.
We dash away, we dash away,
Desires to become unchained
Scatter throughout our brains.
A waxing swain,
My waxing swain,
He has been shot; he has been maimed.

Bethany Perez, Grade 10
North Smithfield High School, RI

The Soul Within Me

Within my heart my soul dwells;
listening and waiting for the day
it may burst from its cage and be inspired.
Inspiration being its key to take on a new beginning;
the new beginning being its savior.

My soul longs for its savior in a suicidal manner.
It burns quietly while my heart is at the controls.
If only the inspiration can be found...

Katelynn Wilson, Grade 10
Woodbridge Sr High School, VA

Blank Canvas

I was born a blank canvas free of irrationalities and any mental poisons
I grew to learn and memorize guidelines, regulations and barriers society noises in all of our ears
Over the years I took it upon myself to take what was once a deteriorating mental state
And revert back to my purity, of which I was initially given,
And with that, I found something that tied me back to the world of which
I once grew to hate; the world of which we live in
Through images I paint, metaphorically and literally,
I found a new way to deviate pain, love life, and strive to eliminate the strain

I was born a blank canvas, now it's my destiny I choose to create
A right which I think somehow in my mind began to fade,
It's now alive and well enticing me to be and create something of great virtue
My environment is the mural which my peers revert to create and somehow destroy at the same time too
Now that the pen is in my hand, my job is to add a piece that is here to stay
A piece that is too great to ever write over, draw over or mark in any way
My life has become something through art I learned to appreciate

I was born a blank canvas,
Over time I've collected dust and markings that have been difficult to take away completely
There remains a faint residue of imperfection,
A worn surface that has been misplaced and shoved repeatedly

I was born a blank canvas, now I'm a classic mural on the wall
Telling a story of timelessness, and dare I say beauty, that I hope captures you all.

Maria Miller, Grade 12
Forest Park High School, VA

Focusing

An infinite number of dimensions…
Unseen, unheard, unnoticed…except for
The first three barely perceived,
The fourth's concept barely conceived.

An infinite number of universes…
Existing side by side behind invisible layers;
As far away as the space between the nucleus and its electron,
Every chance and choice occurring everywhere, but only one here.

A finite number of galaxies, though the number is unknown…
A finite number of possibilities, but of what type is unheard of.
What started with the Big Bang could end up with the Big Crunch or expand into the Big Freeze or beyond.
Andromeda, the Sombrero, the Large and the Small Magellanic Clouds, and last but not least, the Milky Way.

A finite number of solar systems, possibly several billion…
Containing several odds and oddities.
Generally, a sun or several in the center,
Surrounded by a smorgasbord of far smaller celestial bodies.

A finite number of planets; what used to be nine, now eight…
Both big and small, hot and cold, gaseous and solid,
The Earth is home and at the perfect place,
Location, location, location, even in space.

Amndeep Singh Mann, Grade 10
Thomas Jefferson High School for Science and Technology, VA

Almost a King

The day has come,
He walks to the throne.
People are watching,
as he walks to the throne.
The cobblestones quiver,
as he walks to the throne.
The dogs start to pant,
as he walks to the throne.
All is silent,
as he walks to the throne.
POW!
All is chaos,
as he falls to the ground.
The dogs start to bark,
as he falls to the ground.
The cobblestones turn,
as he falls to the ground.
People are screaming,
as he falls to the ground.
The day is done
as he falls to the ground.

Nick Paxton, Grade 11
Madison County High School, VA

Shadows

I feel you watching me,
Though in the shadows you hide.
I know that you are stalking me,
Though proof I can't provide.
You are there, I know you are,
No matter what they say,
My instincts guide me better
Than any rational prey.
I can't fight what I can't see or hear,
So I guess that makes me weak,
But I would fight with all I have,
If ever we should meet.
One day you won't move quick enough,
And a glimpse of you, I'll catch,
The darkness in the shadows,
The sunlight in a match.

Alexa Marshall, Grade 10
Home School, MD

Rise

Even in darkness,
Light will follow.
I lay on my marshmallow mattress
as forgotten souls haunt me.
Every sleepless night
wanting only but destruction
in my mind.
But in my mind,
I will rise as trees had never been cut down.

Abass Kanu, Grade 10
Eleanor Roosevelt High School, MD

25 to Life

I cut back to relax on the fact that I don't need you anymore
How you can expect me to pour out my life to you
When I've been in deep battles and still carry the scares
I know you saw a veteran when you first laid eyes on me
No wonder I was shy around you
I couldn't be myself around you
You was right I was walking on eggshells
Only because your expectations and requirements were hard to climb
Even after I climbed Everest there was still thousands of miles to go
I almost couldn't breathe in your presence
Now that I want to ignore you and move on you want to talk
Call my number more than ever
And what did that produce???? Just a few words
If you want to talk come harder smarter and stronger than that
I KNOW for a fact that you can do better
Your endless voicemail hurt me
But I can get through it I'm a new man now
I won't settle for seconds anymore
I know that God wants me to have the best in my life
So he gave me the keys
And said that my life sentence is over

Austin Caver, Grade 12
Benjamin Banneker Academic High School, DC

Definition

I wish I could
open you like a book,
read your life
chapter-by-chapter,
scroll through an
index of your thoughts,
study the glossary
of your slang;
practice the pronunciation
of your expressions,
analyze the etymology
of your smile.
I would examine you
cover-to-cover,
and armed with
my careful study
have not a word
more of vocabulary
to explain the conundrum of my heart.
love (lu v), n., v., the sum of all the words in the dictionary at once;
the act of having this feeling. [Origin: unknown, possibly the beginning of time.]

Tarika Sankar, Grade 11
Richard Montgomery High School, MD

Inspired by Shakespeare

My mind dies when my eyes close.
My hated past life is simply faded.
The weakness in my vision,
Is not a cheerful collision.
All built up in my mind,
Like temples and Towers left behind.
My mind is disturbed,
With dreams that are dissolved.
With beams of light that aren't that bright.
When my eyes are closed,
The spirits behind my eye lids
All are still filled with hatred.

Taylor Sessums, Grade 11
Dinwiddie High School, VA

The Chinese Waltz

Can it be right? Is it just;
for Americans to be sitting at
home driving cars that have rust?
When we go to a store we scarcely
find products made in the USA
Americans are out of work the economy
is so bad people have bills that they
cannot pay how did our country the
greatest in the world sell its working
people out not giving them a chance
Welcome to the new age
Welcome to the Chinese Dance

Danielle Griffin, Grade 11
Tunstall High School, VA

Grades 7-8-9
Top Ten Winners

List of Top Ten Winners for Grades 7-9; listed alphabetically

Kate Brady, Grade 8
Wren Middle School, SC

Eileen Collie, Grade 7
Providence Academy, TN

Stephanie Jill Davis, Grade 8
Swampscott Middle School, MA

Natalie Drury, Grade 7
Lebanon Jr High School, Grade OH

Lynzee Linnarz, Grade 7
Heritage Middle School, ID

Joanna Liu, Grade 8
Bret Harte Middle School, CA

Kianna Matthews, Grade 7
Eagle Point Middle School, OR

Hannah Ritchie, Grade 7
Sailorway Middle School, OH

Austin Siegel, Grade 9
Saint Stephen's Episcopal School, FL

Celeste Watson-Martin, Grade 7
Landisville Middle School, PA

All Top Ten Poems can be read at www.poeticpower.com

Note: The Top Ten poems were finalized through an online voting system. Creative Communication's judges first picked out the top poems. These poems were then posted online. The final step involved thousands of students and teachers who registered as the online judges and voted for the Top Ten poems. We hope you enjoy these selections.

So Much Depends Upon

So much depends upon
your loving caring
mom
loves you unconditionally
forever
works hard for
you.

Sure you'll mess up
sometimes
sure you'll make her
mad
sometimes maybe, she'll even
cry
mother isn't perfect no
being is
but she is still the perfect mother
for me.

Keala Fletcher, Grade 8
Highlands School, MD

Music

Music
Has been around for ages
That was founded
Thousands of years ago
When you feel that beat
And you move
Your feet that
Groove that gets
Into you you don't
Have to prove you can dance it's just
That music is
A way of life that
Helps you feel good
Through the good
And bad times
Music is a great part
Part of life that
You can use to express your life

Thomas Gregg, Grade 8
Sacred Heart School, MD

When I Grow Up

When I grow up,
I want to be a doctor.
I want to follow in my mom's footsteps.
She works in the medical field.
I have always
Found it interesting.
I love watching
People get blood drawn.
I go to my mom's job all the time.
I love it!!!

Caitlin Documet, Grade 7
Tasker Middle School, MD

Beautiful Angel

My love, the one missing in my stone cold heart,
You fill my thoughts all the time and pierce my mind like one of Cupid's darts
The clarity of her figure will always be plastered to my memory
Eyes that are the heavenly blue skies bringing me serenity
Your long luxurious golden blonde hair shines warmth into my rejuvenated soul
Intoxicating aromas of a meadow of flowers wraps around her celestial body
The universe cannot separate me from embracing your fiery figure
Suddenly our embrace transitions to a passionate kiss engulfing my full mind
Awakening, my reverie of my one desire ends and my heart reverts to cold coal
Sadness overwhelms my heart and tears flow down my ice cold face for you
I will always remember the dream of my beautiful angel.

Alexander Fish, Grade 8
St Catherine of Siena School, DE

Ode to a Reese's Cup

Oh dear Reese's cup your eyes plead to me from the store shelf;
Asking me to pick you up and buy you.
You are a bandage on my wounded heart.
If I had a choice I would eat infinity of you, but unfortunately I don't.
You are as beautiful as a butterfly on the grave.
You are mine, all mine, I will treasure you forever and for always.

Andrea Smith, Grade 8
Paul L Dunbar Middle School for Innovation, VA

Memories

So many memories
So little proof
Not even snapshots
That hold the truth
Living and laughing
Dreaming and crying
No picture can show
No letter can prove
How we really are
Everything so fleeting
What looks like forever
Gone in a flash
How do you describe it?
When you thought they had your back
Ripped away with memories that remain
Scars across your heart
How do you capture the essence
Of who we are

Caitlin Woodson, Grade 8
Bishop Walsh Middle High School, MD

Summer

Cool, refreshing breeze comforts my body,
Hot, grainy sand between my toes,
Clear, blue skies with warm sunshine,
Happiness bringing families together,
These are brilliant sensations of Summer,
Coming slowly,
Leaving quickly.

Julia Pezzullo, Grade 8
St Rocco School, RI

Black and Gold

A cold, crisp fall day starts the season
Teams compete
The championship is the top prize

Hard hits, penalty flags
Screaming, cheering crowds
Cool catches, from every angle
Touch downs scored

Games won, games lost
Who is going to make the playoffs?
Teams fight hard
For survival

Players fighting, talking smack
Championship on the line
Black and Gold has 6 in the win column
Steelers all the way

Eric Shipley, Grade 8
Sacred Heart School, MD

Football

Football
Athletic, healthy
Passing, running, catching
Energetic, surprising, tiring, passionate
Sports

Javell Middleton, Grade 8
Lafayette Winona Middle School, VA

Defense

Defending the end zone,
Tackling the running back,
Sacking the quarterback —
It's all about the defense.
We keep the other team from scoring.

Don't let them score.
Hurt them more.
Stick them. Stick them.
Tackle even more. Hit them harder.
It's all about the defense.
We keep the other team from scoring.

Defense is my heart.
It's where I always love to start!

Zach Jacobs, Grade 8
Chickahominy Middle School, VA

The Ultimate Sin

Just like the apple,
So very much enticing.
Its flesh smooth and silky,
In a variety of colors:
Dark, bitter, and dangerous,
Milky, velvety, and lustrous,
White, sweet, and crisp.
The seductive aroma,
Playing snakelike through your nose.
So hard to resist,
So easy to succumb.
It is greed,
It is gluttony,
It is the ultimate sin:
Chocolate.

Alison Lindsay, Grade 9
St Anne's Belfield School, VA

A Marriage of Seasons

Vivid trees,
Sway in the breeze,
Screaming winter is near.

The frigid wind roars,
Creating a spinning leaf galore,
Piercing my face like a spear.

The day is dull,
The night prolonging,
I drink apple cider mulled.

It's boreal and damp,
Not inviting to a tramp,
Surely winter is here.

Imran Alam, Grade 8
Midlothian Middle School, VA

The Sunrise

As I look at the morning sunrise
I see so many colors
Purple, blue, and orange
Shining bright on the Earth

As I look at the morning sunrise
I imagine greater places
Laughing, smiling, and relaxing
Running with friends through the tall grass

As I look at the morning sunrise
I remember the memories
Family, friends, and pets
Playing games, winning and losing

As I look at the morning sunrise
I lay down to enjoy life
Taking every second as a miracle
Living every day as if it was my last
Enjoying my life as it is
As I look at the morning sunrise.

Caroline Phillips, Grade 8
Sacred Heart School, MD

Why Can't It Be?

Yes sir you really must know
that I do truly love you
and I do not want us to part
I once read a story book when I was little,
one about a prince and a princess.
Everyone says that the ending is happy,
well, I never got that far
but to me, you're my prince
and I'm your princess
you're appearing to me as my destiny
but unfortunately we're stuck in the middle
of this story
the middle where the fights start,
the tears fall,
and the heart begins to crack
no matter how many times I tell you
that the ending is happy,
it never clicks in your mind…
Why can't it be
the happy ending already?

Sheridan Chattin, Grade 9
Independence Secondary School, VA

Sammy's First Fish

Sammy finally fulfilled her wish,
To for once in her life catch a fish.
The fish flipped and flopped,
And it never stopped,
Until her first fish landed on her dish.

Nicole Rogers, Grade 7
St Joseph School-Fullerton, MD

When I Was Young

When I was young
I had a brother
And he was my mother's son
He never did drugs
He never robbed a store
He wanted to be perfect
And he wanted to do more
He loved me very much
He always showed it
He loved me we always know it
He never held a gun
He is the one
For every girl in the world
This is my brother
He is so cool
This is my brother he's not a fool
This is his life this is the end
This is his life I hope he starts it again!!

Alexis Gordon, Grade 7
Tasker Middle School, MD

So Much Depends

So much depends
upon
a giant redwood
tree.
It is very
shady
and generously
provides
shelter.
For the scurrying little
ones
and the owls that
hoot
and the woodpeckers that
peck
and the humans that
breathe.

Price Dawson Reeder, Grade 7
The Highlands School, MD

Introduction to Poetry

Read poetry as if
There are no ifs

Read it like you are building a sand castle
Start with the ground

Don't look for answers in a poem
Look for questions

Read it like riding a bike down a hill
Read down the paper, to the bottom

Casey Emerson, Grade 7
St Jane De Chantal School, MD

The Moon

The moon…

Is so beautiful
   It makes everyone smile,
It's like a home to those who fly high
   A dream to those who sleep at night,

Soothing to infants
   But romantic to adults,
Small to us on the ground
   Huge to those who are in the air,

Love and happiness is what you see
   Free as a bird is what you feel,
Dance in its light when your heart is full
   Scream and shout, and it will feel your pain,

The moon…

Nicole Bader, Grade 8
Brandywine Springs School, DE

At the End of the Rainbow

At the end of the rainbow it is not a pot of gold I see
But the essence of life
The pureness of love and happiness
The beauty of why we live
Why it is we have life in this world
At the end of this rainbow
I see not the bad in the world
But the good
At the end of this rainbow I see not an end,
But a beginning
And now looking into this rainbow
As I get lost in its wisdom
I realize that you should live life to the fullest
That we should go for our dream in life
That we should take chances
And as this rainbow goes away
I know that I will never forget
What I learned at the end of the rainbow

Isabel Muir, Grade 7
Grace Episcopal Day School, MD

Family and Dreams

Family and dreams
You think they go together
They do in many ways
Your family helps you make a dream reality
Don't you agree?
Family isn't just blood line
It's also people you care for
Those that help you along the way
These people are important because life is always just a path
A path to your dreams

Isaiah Coles, Grade 7
Benjamin Tasker Middle School, MD

Wind

It whooshes it swooshes it spins all around
to the peaks of mountains, to the lowest of grounds
it swirls and twirls all over the air
up in the sky and all through your hair
it takes the papers right out of your fingers
in the coldest weather it makes the snow linger
it flies with the birds, it sails with the seas
it's all over the flowers with the hovering bees
it helps the planes fly way up high
it's with the clouds floating in the sky
all through the day and all through the night
its force of nature is an amazing sight
it sways the grass it shapes the land
it leads your way, it grabs your hand
its always there where ever you go
it goes very fast, then goes very slow
it quietly whispers with the slightest breeze
it blows the pollen that makes you sneeze
although you might not notice or care
the wind is the one thing that will always be there

Annette Yospe, Grade 8
Sacred Heart Glyndon School, MD

I Am a Poem

I am a poem.
I am happy; I'm sad.
Jolly and mad.
Flowers and unicorns are written above my lines,
And words like graceful,
Prance, and sing,
All dance afloat,
In the paper-maché skies.
Black and gray is what I can make you feel.
I can make you think your head is spinning on wheels.
Jealousy and sinister are scribbled on my forehead,
Along with modest and beauty printed in sharpie red.
I will tell you a secret. A surprise, you may see.
But I am unwritten.
There is still too much to be.

Jordan Rodgers, Grade 7
Kilmer Middle School, VA

I Love Baseball

Baseball is my favorite sport.
I love playing it.
It's the best sport I have ever played.
I would never stop playing ball.
I play a lot of positions.

I have played baseball most of my life,
Baseball was my dad's sport too.
I would watch baseball forever.
I would teach anyone who needs help with it.
I can't stop thinking about baseball.

Ben Wright, Grade 8
Chickahominy Middle School, VA

School

School isn't very fun,
But you have to get it done.
Teachers always giving too much work,
It will do anything but make you smirk.

Everything is so hard,
Don't even tell me about my report card.
There's way too much to get done,
And it's never any fun.

Homework is like a volcano waiting to erupt,
There's so much you could say it's corrupt.
It fills up your whole room,
And your heart with a sinking feeling of doom.

Overall school is so boring,
Sometimes it will have you snoring.
Even in your favorite class,
Sometimes you won't pass.

Blake Schmidt, Grade 8
Brandywine Springs School, DE

Basketball

Basketball is a sport most people play.
Basketball is used with an orange round ball.
Basketball is a sport that people have to run a lot.
Basketball is a beast sport.
Basketball can make a person famous.
Basketball is used with two goals.
Basketball has a rectangular court being played on.
Basketball is also a contact sport.
Basketball takes practice to play and learn.
Basketball has teams.
Basketball takes points.
Basketball has a rule who ever with the most points win.
Basketball is another sport I love.

Richard Daniel, Grade 8
Paul L Dunbar Middle School for Innovation, VA

The Balloon

I float effortlessly as if I command the skies
My yellow hue more powerful than the Sun's own rays
I look down at all of the people below me
If only they knew I was up here
Maybe they would bring me down
Or just watch me fly away
I float effortlessly as if I command the skies
Up up up
Until I'm out of Earth's atmosphere
And "pop"
I'm gone
Gone forever
I wish you would have brought me down

Patrick Yeboah, Grade 8
St Rocco School, RI

In the Moment

SMACK! As the ball and the bat meet.
One second to react.
The ball flies over my head and into the outfield.
But wait.
Does she catch it?
The batter runs like a puma around the bases.
Coaches yell, "RUN!"
Caught in the moment of hit and run.
The world falls on me
as the ball flies.
Centerfield strong and brave; dives.
The crowd grows quiet.
"Did she catch it?" says a voice.
But the ball plunged to the ground.
A home run.
The other team cheers.
We move on.
Although we lost the game,
others will come.

Leah Coles, Grade 7
Blue Ridge Middle School, VA

Poetry

Poetry —
either it flows like the waves of the sea
effortlessly
or every syllable pains your soul and your hand
and when you go back to read it
it is terrible

But once in a while
the pain and frustration is all worthwhile
and when you read it
you smile
because you know
it is true poetry.

Elizabeth Larson, Grade 7
Parkside Middle School, VA

Women's Right to Vote!

Susan B. Anthony
Fought for women's rights
You see with a right
To take a vote
And to take a stand
We all count in this
Great land she was
One of the most honored
Before now everyone treated
Her like she's poor
My poem is over now
Talk to you again sometime
And turn your frown upside down!

Rasheen Haythe, Grade 8
Paul L Dunbar Middle School for Innovation, VA

Strike 3

I am a pitcher
I wonder if I will get this strike out
I hear the crowd, a dull background noise
I see only the catcher's glove; the batter is of no consequence.
I am very nervous

I pretend to be composed
I believe I can get the out
I touch the ball

I feel sweat dripping down my face
I worry my fielders will let me down
I cry tears of joy to be in a position to help my team
I am checking the signs

I understand the catcher's signs
I say to myself, "Throw the curve"
I dream I will strike him out and win the game
I hope for a good pitch
I am ready

Johnny Spadaro, Grade 8
Sanford School, DE

Anger I Live Each Day

It was just like a dream.
Never as it seems.
They're always on teams. I just want to SCREAM!
Go Away!
Leave me alone!
I walk down the hall in a daze,
Never able to get through the misty haze.
People day in and day out,
Plan ways to make me go insane
It racks through my brain
Each day my brain cells snap.
SNAP! SNAP! SNAP!
They laugh like I have no comeback
They should never think that
As quick as a slap
I make a comeback
Then it turns into a nightmare.
What a scare, I fed into their talk,
When I should have just walked.
Then I realize I was just all along angry.

Ashleigh Sutton, Grade 8
Tasker Middle School, MD

Friends Should Be

Friends should be kind
Friends should be honest
Friends should be trustworthy
Friends should be able to express their feelings with each other
Friends should be comfortable sharing their ideas freely

Ryan Sneddon, Grade 8
Ballenger Creek Middle School, MD

Cowboys or Cowgirls?

The Eagles had an important game
The fans were very eager
And even though their coach was dumb
The other team was extremely meager.

They were against their rivals from Dallas
An injured and struggling crew
And when the Eagles saw Tony Romo playing quarterback
The whole team cried, "PHEW!"

It was a very good game for the Eagles
Like a bear versus a trout
When the final second ticked on the clock
Jerry Jones, like a school girl, began to pout.

Cowboys fans wish that this story was false
But all that they feel is pain
For their team is off to a terrible start this year
A 2-7 campaign.

Dominic Cicconi, Grade 8
Brandywine Springs School, DE

She's a Brave Robin

She's a brave robin
braver than ever
She's independent
but not like others,
She shows real emotions
And true with every step
She never gives up
no matter how hard life gets
She's a strong robin
She never lets go
She's a brave robin
Until the day she goes
onto the Heaven above.

Mia Davis, Grade 8
Paul L Dunbar Middle School for Innovation, VA

A Dream Fulfilled

What happens to a dream fulfilled?
Does it shine
Like the stars on a clear night?
Or flow like an upbeat song —
And make you dance with all your might?
Does it dance like a thought through your mind?
Or soothe your throat?
Like tea of some kind?

Maybe it soars majestically
Like an eagle in the sky.

Or does it just flutter by?

Haley Adams, Grade 7
Marshall Middle School, VA

The Greatest Game

When you are playing soccer it's so much fun,
Especially because you get to run.
Before you play you get pumped up for the game,
And all of your teammates are doing the same.

My position is defense in the game we call soccer,
I stand in front of the keeper which would make me his blocker.
I'm as fast as a plane racing in the sky,
When I pass the other team they just stand there and cry.

In the game of soccer you must always be smart,
If not the other team will score making you feel like an old fart.
My goalie is a mountain in the way of the other team,
But he can't block everything that would just be a dream.

What we Americans call soccer has many different names,
But no matter what country you're from it's all still the same.
I love the sport where you put the ball in the back of the net,
I hope to keep playing soccer and not stop yet.

Colin Lussier, Grade 8
Brandywine Springs School, DE

The Love of Siblings

Although we may be apart
You'll always be in my heart
Our bond will never be broken
I have promised like I have spoken
Whenever I felt lonely
You were always there for me
Like a GPS, you guided me when I was lost
Now, when you are stressed, saddened, or in trouble
I'll be there on the double
I'm always a phone call away
Like the sun, I'll frequently make your day
The first time you left
I pretty much died internally
But I know our special relationship
As brother and sister...
Will never change
Proud — is what I am — to be called your
"Little Big Brother"

William Villamayor, Grade 8
St Joseph School-Fullerton, MD

Footprint

The sand feels cold beneath my feet,
As I walk along the banks of the shore
My traces of footprints are erased by the ocean,
Hiding all of its secrets.
My feet sink deeper into the sand imprinting summer's memories
Summer's ending...
The sun sets behind the water,
Hoping to wash all of its secrets away too.
Waiting for next year to come again.

Gabby Elia, Grade 8
Ursuline Academy, DE

Hope, Believe, Dream

I hope that there will be joy to everyone,
I believe that there will be freedom to everyone,
I dream that all pain will turn to peace for everyone.

I dream that there will be no more wars.
I dream that love will reign forever.
I dream that all pain will turn to peace for everyone.

I believe that joy will come back,
I believe that happiness is just around the corner.
I believe that love will reign forever.
I believe that life is a gift of beauty.
I believe that there will be freedom to everyone.

I hope for the wars to end.
I hope that love will reign forever.
I hope for the goodness in everyone.
I hope that there will be joy to everyone.

I hope for joy to everyone,
I believe for the freedom for everyone,
And I dream for all pain to turn to peace for everyone.

Keira Zirkle, Grade 7
Hampton Christian High School, VA

A Message Amidst the Snow

The dance of a snowflake is unique indeed,
Thousands of dancers in a relaxed stampede?
It seems so messy...so many at a time,
From the heights they fall, truly sublime...
From the clouds to the ground their performance is short,
But lengthened by the gusts that they consort.
The pure white snow stands out from the gray,
While to the wind's howling music trees sway...
Focus on one, their dancing is chaotic,
But see them all and it is hypnotic.
In this way snowflakes are like mankind,
Separate and solitary our achievements are confined?
They say all snowflakes are matchless...so are people.
Though some are christened the same name under a steeple,
Once there is an effort from each and every one,
There is truly no limit to what can be done.

Eric Zhao, Grade 7
MacArthur Middle School, MD

Untitled

Love is something special, and very hard to find
Peace is what we want, and what the world needs
Pain is what I bring —
Smile and frowns are what surround me
Karma is who I am...
You can love me or hate me.
You can be my friend or my enemy
Because it's not going to phase me.

Breanah Cole, Grade 9
Independence Secondary School, VA

Baseball

Baseball is fun,
to play every day.
I play for a team
on most Saturdays.
My team is the Yankees
who wear blue and white.
Although orange and black
are the colors I like.
I play as a catcher
with a mask on my face
but my favorite is pitcher
making the batter try to chase.
I catch fly balls
while in the outfield
but my favorite place to stand
is in the infield.
While I am at bat
I hit really hard
I send that ball flying
right out of the yard!

Phillip McGregor, Grade 7
Sacred Heart School, MD

World Cup

There is a buzz in the air
and a breeze in my hair

I have the ball at my feet
and I have a good beat

It's the fans cheering
there's so much I am hearing

I dribble the ball
the crowd is in awe

I shoot the ball
it goes in the hall

The Hall of Fame
I won the game

The World Cup is ours
I feel so much power

Andrew Reter, Grade 8
Sacred Heart School, MD

Winter

W e gather as a family for Christmas
I nside because of the icy winds
N ot enough of sun
T oo cold
E veryone plays in the snow
R ide in sleighs on a fun snow-filled day

Geena Brown, Grade 8
Lafayette Winona Middle School, VA

Championship Game

Hours of practice, hundreds of laps,
We've come here for one thing,
To hear the spectators sing,
"Brandywine Springs you are the champions!"
The bus ride to A.I. was filled with screams and shouts,
"Brandywine Springs is coming you better watch out!"
We got off the bus, H.B. is warming up.
Let's get started if we want to win that gold cup.
The whistle is blown, it's game time ladies!
Sticks down, eyes up, be on your toes, we all know how this goes.
The game is going by fast,
H.B. players are whizzing by,
Fast as a cheetah; give it your best try.
H.B. scores once, twice, three times
"That's the end," the referee chimes.
We held up a good fight, as tough as an ox!
Even though it's my last year, I try not to shed a tear.
"I am going to miss this team," I said,
My coach says next year, "We'll knock them dead!"
"Expect to see me at your games next year," I told her.
My field hockey girls will always have a place in my heart, even though we will be apart.

Taylor Hazewski, Grade 8
Brandywine Springs School, DE

My Plan In Life

Get good grades in school!
Don't act like a fool.
Grades get you far in life as you get older.
Keep things organized in your folder.
Study for a test or quiz.
You'll be a whiz.
If you don't study for tests, quizzes, and don't do your homework just know you're wrong.
Now life will be hard and long.
My motto in life is to never give up on your dreams.
Life is not always as it seems.
If you try your best and never give up,
You can walk by people proudly and say what's up.
As you can see grades are important but you should never give up on your dreams.
If you try your best and never give up, I guarantee you will succeed!
Now you're ahead and in the lead.

Alyssa Swift, Grade 7
St Augustine School, RI

On Your Plate

You need this to live,
You need this to spice things up,
You need this on your plate,
You need this in your cup.
Carrots, broccoli, corn, green beans, eat these to stay healthy, by all means.
Brownies, cake, candy, ice cream, these junk foods make your eyes beam.
Cereal, pancakes, donuts, toasted bread, these sound great when you get out of bed.
Taco, spaghetti, burgers, fries, we're already eating supper, time flies.
Soda, juice, water, milk, quench that thirst with some silk.
Food.

Brianna Tomchick, Grade 8
Benjamin Tasker Middle School, MD

Sick of You

I'm so sick of you,
so sick of all your little lies.
so sick of you,
with everyone by your side.
but what you don't know,
is how great it feels,
to let you go.
I'm happier alone,
I don't care who was wrong or right,
I'm done with all the lies
and I'm moving on to the next guy.

Kelly Noon, Grade 8
Chickahominy Middle School, VA

Lockdown

Trapped.
Nowhere to go.
Nowhere to hide.
So quiet I can hear my heart beat.
Going to die in a white sealed room.
I know I deserve it.
Body fills with madness.
About to go into rage.
I can't hold back.
I must get out.
Of lockdown.

Matthew Gaertner, Grade 7
Blue Ridge Middle School, VA

The Penguin

I'm cold and I'm wet!
Life here's a breeze,
Swimming all day,
Sleeping long nights,
With all of us huddled
together,
We keep warm.
Thank you, God, for making
me that day,
I'm special and loved —
In a slippery way!

McKenzie Richerson, Grade 8
Homeschool Plus, VA

We…

We live…
We die…
We find love…
We go through changes…
We succeed…
We can be happy…
We live…
We die…
That's all…maybe.

Adrianna Stallworth, Grade 7
Tasker Middle School, MD

Waves

Waves are swift waters drifting upon the surface.
With one glance, I see their texture of a bright outline.
I hear the soft whisper that forms upon gracefully hitting the surface.
The waves get larger and larger,
As I take each step towards the wave,
I feel the coolness of the water being thrown against your foot.
It eases up to your ankles giving you a shiver,
And you feel you are in the midst of the sea.
The waves crawl to the shore rising upon the wet sand.
I plunge into a wave,
Whenever I catch the eye of a large wave,
I duck right under and feel the gust of water thrown in my direction.
As the sun is setting,
I glance towards the sea full of waves,
Which makes a beautiful texture,
And a smile casts upon my face.
I begin to draw the feel of the wave,
And with every swish of the brush,
A new wave spreads upon the beach.

Margaret Dent, Grade 7
Grace Episcopal Day School, MD

Feelings

Look before you fall.
"Don't fall for someone if they are not going to catch you."
Girls, don't give everything you have to a boy.
Boys, life is not all about girls.
Forget your pride.
"Live, Laugh, Love."
You life does NOT revolve around one person!
Take your medicine if you have any.
Listen to your parents, they might know what they are talking about.
If your friends bring you down, they are not friends.
If you make a promise, keep it.
Don't let anyone take advantage of you.
"Never regret anything because at one time it was exactly what
You wanted."
Rich or poor isn't a big deal.
Don't let yourself come second to anyone.
Love animals, they are defenseless.
People HAVE feelings.
"Love gives someone the power to break you."

Autumn Price, Grade 9
Tunstall High School, VA

School Life

Get up, Yeah! My first day of middle school.
At the bus stop, I'm excited. No more lines, no more teachers to walk me around the school.
On the bus, it's noisy as a whole school at recess.
In the school, the bell rings for the first time. Am I late on my first day?
At my locker Crash! Things fall out.
And I don't have the right materials for class.
Teacher yells like a gorilla.
This day did not go as it had in my head…

Bryan Huffman, Grade 7
Blue Ridge Middle School, VA

A's

I am nervous
I wonder how to write this poem
I hear people furiously typing away
I want to get an A
I am nervous

I pretend I know what I'm doing
I believe I can write this poem
I touch the smooth keys that hold the future to my grade

I feel the pressure to get an A
I worry mine will not be an Amazing poem
I cry out that I am frustrated
I am nervous

I understand that I can do it
I say I can do it
I dream of my poem being the best
I hope it is an A
I am nervous

Lisa Rocca, Grade 8
Sanford School, DE

Problem

If two trains are heading toward each other
In opposite directions at the same speed
And collide at one point,
How many cars were there and
How many people were killed?
And if the smaller number is the greater negative, then
What was the name of the brakeman in the window?
If the total murders made is an irrational number
The sum will go on forever.
And when you multiply the number of deaths
By the age of the child
Who was playing on the platform of the station
And the tickets gathered by the agent earlier that morning,
Sooner or later it becomes irrational
And when numbers become irrational
They go on forever
And when numbers go on forever
Sooner or later
They have to
Repeat.

Jennifer Coleman, Grade 9
Atholton Adventist Academy, MD

Beautiful Wolves

One of the most magnificent
Creatures in the world to me
Would have to be the wolf,
You can find the majestic wolf
Roaming around almost anywhere in the world
They hunt,
They love,
They fight,
They cry,
Are they not like us?
Why do we harm them?
Of all the many types,
I cannot pick a favorite,
For they are all…
Beautiful Wolves

Sydney Price, Grade 7
Benjamin Tasker Middle School, MD

New Shoes

When I bring in new Nike's to school.
Everybody looks at them for a while and says they're cool.
They are clean as a whistle and sharp as a razor.
I have several shoes that are new and they are called Nike Blazer.
Mostly all of my shoes are Nike and two are not.
My brothers spilled juice on them so now they have red spots.
Most I use for sports and others I use just for looks.
People think I steal shoes because they haven't come out yet.
If I had more money, I would make a bet.
My aunt gives me new pair once a month.
But she doesn't care.
She wants to make sure I have everything I need.
Because she cares about me, yes indeed.
I have at least ten pairs of shoes.
I've got so many shoes it should be in the news.

Channon Young, Grade 8
Sacred Heart School, MD

July 3, 1863

The Battle of Gettysburg ended on July third,
And there were many cries to be heard.
For men had died.
Their bodies lied.
Waiting to be buried.

The battle had a cost.
The Confederate suffered a loss.
But the Union still couldn't bear.
For they should have ended it there.
So the war went on for two more years.

Matthew Linz, Grade 8
St Joseph School-Fullerton, MD

What Am I Doing Here?

I came here to start a new life.
I came here to start a new dream.
It didn't turn out as expected
It didn't turn out as wanted.
I couldn't see the shining gleam.

I need to keep looking for the ray.
I need to keep my smile.
Life is never as expected.
Life is never as wanted.
I will continue this journey until I've done the mile.

Matthew Szczuka, Grade 9
Delaware Military Academy, DE

Paris

Ah, the city of lights!
It is such a delight,
To see the Eiffel Tower,
In my only free hour.

The clothes are never out of date,
Shopping till you drop with your mate.
There are a variety of dresses,
From Louis Vuitton to adorable Guess.

Go out and eat crème brûlée,
And watch Cirque du Soleil.
I promise you, you won't be dismayed,
Once you watch Scene de Ballet.

There are so many things in France,
So book a ticket in advance.
Trust me, you'll be very appalled,
By the most admired city of all!

Fiona Do, Grade 7
Longfellow Middle School, VA

I Know

I fell in love with a boy I don't know
I fell in love with the thought
Of us as a couple, dancing slow,
Although I knew him not

I fell in love with those brilliant eyes,
That brilliant shade of blue
I fell in love with my own lies,
The boy I thought I knew

He up and left, that brilliant boy,
With a girl he loved and knew
The change I saw, that rush of joy —
He'd found his true love, true

I learned my lesson at a cost;
For first I had to fall
But 'tis better to have loved and lost
Than never loved at all.

Kay Whitman, Grade 9
Coventry High School, RI

Love

Dear love,
Why do you make me hurt?
You bring tears to my shirt.
Why do you make me smile?
I can spot you from a thousand miles!
Love is needy, but don't be greedy.
You never know what love will bring.

ShaDonna Walker, Grade 7
Chickahominy Middle School, VA

A Flash and Then Snickers

If my camera could talk, he'd do nothing but snicker.
I could not have made him a cynic any quicker.
He feels he's been doomed to a monotonous existence
so I think he'd be surprised that I'd give this admittance.
When he accompanies me he scoffs at the appearance
of the "wonders" surrounding him because he knows from experience
that my pictures, though numerous, will capture only a small part.
They'll show just a little lovely that doesn't even start
to show the places or moments that I actually toured.
Anything that doesn't draw a crowd will be ignored.
If you asked him about me he'd rant with a nasty smirk,
"She ignores the graffiti, any sour faces, anything she feels would not be a perk
in her 'perfect' little album of this 'perfect' little place."
So maybe he is justified; it's a lot to face.
But let's hope he's paid well for his challenging occupation
because I don't think I regret it, despite his vexation.
Some might call it ignorance, others good attitude,
but I'm not sure how I think my habit should be viewed.

Rose Baker, Grade 8
Paul L Dunbar Middle School for Innovation, VA

The Terrible Tale of the Twisted Tree

The twisted tree was magnificent. A truly beautiful sight,
With branches like mahogany, and leaves so small and slight.
The branches swayed in the wind, the boughs thrived in the light,
And so the twisted tree survived no matter; come day or night.
So summer changed to winter, then back and back again.
And the tree was still alone like it always had been.
The tree had no one to eat its fruit or to play on its boughs,
It had no one to nest in its branches, or to use its wood for a house.

The tree was very lonely and very sad as well…

Many years had passed many a day had gone,
Summer came and left, the tree was still alone.
I do recall now when that twisted tree gave in.
So I look back, on a very cold winter,
What I heard that day was a very quiet crack, an almost silent splinter.
The tree was old and full of rings so those things in spite,
The magnificent twisted trees' life was done, on that silent night…

Emma Houser, Grade 8
Brandywine Springs School, DE

Red

What does red represent? Is it just another color in art?
Or the color of beauty? Or maybe the color of our hearts.
What it really is, is the color of love,
Red is what you feel when you're falling in love.
It is something you can never resist,
After having your first kiss.
Red is the sweetness you feel inside,
When you know everything is going all right.
Red is the feeling you get when you and your special someone have finally met.

Mariam Sargsyan, Grade 7
Kilmer Middle School, VA

The Way People Are

The way that I m treated,
Like I don't even matter.
I get shoved and defeated,
Oh my heart it has shattered.

The way people are
The way that they act
They should know when they've gone too far,
For that is a fact.

A fact I have known,
I have experienced first hand.
My opinions are shown,
Like they're written on sand.

I may not care what people think,
For that's what I should do.
When life flashes by in a blink,
How would you feel if it was done to you?

Chelsea Keyton, Grade 8
Chickahominy Middle School, VA

Three Wishes

In a place long ago
lived a nice king called Diaria.
King Diaria owned a small village
with nice people.

Everyone was nice
except for this one
little witch.

One day the king took a stroll
the witch crossed his path.

She gave him three wishes
and he took them.
He decided not to use the wishes

He was content with his life.
You could learn a lesson from King Diaria.

Darrick Crews, Grade 8
Paul L Dunbar Middle School for Innovation, VA

My Life

My life I dream about being something one day.
My life I want grow old and happy.
My life I want to do something extraordinary.
My life I want to be known worldwide.
My life I want to have no excuses for lying.
My life I want the Giants to win three more Super Bowls before I die
My life I hope we end hatred and come to world peace.
My life I hope I never make enemies.
My life I want to be successful.

Kelvin Whitaker, Grade 8
Paul L Dunbar Middle School for Innovation, VA

Mom

Mom,
I love you so much,
more than you may know,
you care for me,
and help me grow.

Sometimes I think,
I know more than you,
but you always say,
I've been there,
I've been through.

We had long talks,
that I thought meant nothing,
but at the end of the day,
they meant a great something.

You tell me to do right,
when I do wrong,
you believe in me so much,
and I thank you for it all!

MaHogany Matthews, Grade 8
Paul L Dunbar Middle School for Innovation, VA

Hope

In the worst of times it's there to bring up your spirits
It cannot be seen
Nor can it be heard
It is the thought of hope

It doesn't always help those who are wealthy
But in time of need it will be there
To guide your heart
And soothe your soul
It is the thought of hope

Although we cannot see it we all have it inside
To make us feel all right
And to help our pain disappear
It is the thought of hope

Dillon Loose, Grade 9
Delaware Military Academy, DE

Endless War

The screams of men went on for miles,
As evil grins turned into eager smiles,
The sky lights up like fireworks,
But the deaths of many only hurt,
Laughs like hyenas float over the field,
Creeping and crawling into other's ears,
The sounds of this battle will always go on,
Until another one just as bloody comes along,
And even then when that war does come,
No man will be forgotten; not ten, not one.

Michael Villanueva, Grade 8
St Rocco School, RI

The Ring*
There came a black horse
Upon him there rode
A deadly king in search of his foe.

A ring he must find that is
One of a kind.
This ring rules them all
And if found we will fall.

A hobbit carries the fate
Of Middle-earth from Rohan to the Black Gate
He must leave the Shire and the comfort of his room
To search for Mordor and the fires of Mount Doom.

The eye of Sauron is ever watchful
So Frodo and his friends must be very careful.
Will Frodo finish his journey into the land of fire
Or will he succumb to his own desire?
Mark Padilla, Grade 8
St Joseph School-Fullerton, MD
*Inspired by "The Lord of the Rings" by J.R.R. Tolkein

Sunset
The day is almost over as the sun sets,
bountiful colors flowing behind it.

It seems to smile at you as it shares
its last bit of warmth and beauty
in this everlasting hour.

A bird flies into the sunset as if bidding
it goodbye until it returns again.

The bears and deer cuddle up in their homes
preparing for the cold of the night
savoring these last few moments.

An owl hoots waking up from its tiring nap
staring as the sun slowly fades into the darkness.

I wave goodbye longing for its return,
as I slowly trudge home.
Cassie Smith, Grade 8
Paul L Dunbar Middle School for Innovation, VA

Family
Family will always be there no matter what
Through thick and thin
Through lightning and thundering
Family will always have your side
You might have ups and downs
Sorrow and disbelief
But no matter what family will always be there.
Denekqua Glover, Grade 8
Paul L Dunbar Middle School for Innovation, VA

Me
Mom's voice — she never cleans her room
And never uses a broom
She's always watching TV
But never really listens to me.

Dad's voice — when it comes to sports she likes them a lot
Also she's a fan of polka dots
She loves to play volleyball
Even though she's not that tall.

Brother's voice — we'll always be partners in crime
Even thought we fight sometimes
She yells at me most of the day
But that's ok I'll always love her anyway.

Friend's voice — she likes it when there are sunny days
And likes most things to go her way
Not everything works out like that
But no matter what, we'll have her back.
Lauren Canard, Grade 7
Marshall Middle School, VA

About Me!
My mom says I'm crazy
Outgoing and fun
Also kind of lazy
And she loves me so much.

My brother says I'm annoying
As weak as can be
He also says I'm boring
But I know he loves me.

My dad has called me "Cricket" since I was two
He says I've been beautiful
Since I was brand new
And I will be his little girl until the end of time.

I think I'm kind of funny
Totally insane
Always acting sunny
Don't like being plain.
Ivy Olinger, Grade 7
Marshall Middle School, VA

Friendship by the Heart
A friendship is like a roller coaster. Emotions rise and fall.
Your friend is always by your side I can count on you through it all.

You're supportive, admired, nice, respectful, and amusing.
Just in case you didn't know, you're the one I'm choosing.
Friendships begin in many ways and ours will never part.
You always know what to say, for that you're in my heart.
Briana Wilkerson, Grade 8
Chickahominy Middle School, VA

Smells of Nature

Ah, the sweet smell of honeysuckle
The gentle rain's fresh scent
These smell good to me

Sticky sap flowing free
Yummy for me
Citrus oranges acidic smell
Sharp and tangy never waning
These smell good to me

The ocean air salty and wet
The desert air gritty and dry
The tundra atmosphere sharp and pointy
These smells are good to me

I could live without my ears and eyes
But leave my nose for me
To smell the autumn leaves
These smells of nature are good to me
Emily Sutphin, Grade 8
Auburn Middle School, VA

Options

Everyone has options.
You have to choose.
No one else can
Pick to win or lose.

Options are everywhere.
You have to be able
To choose by yourself,
Just play the cards on the table.

What should you do?
Family or friends,
Whatever you choose.
There will be consequences in the end.

Everyone has options.
You have to choose.
No one else can
Pick to win or lose.
Karrah Bauserman, Grade 8
Chickahominy Middle School, VA

I'm Hungry

I'm hungry,
Whose idea was it to make lunch at 12?
Not everyone has time for breakfast,
And school food is just,
Nasty,
So why can't kids who bring lunch,
Eat in class?
It's our food.
Jebrail Dempsey, Grade 8
Benjamin Tasker Middle School, MD

Home Run Dream

I am a baseball star.
I wonder if I am going to get a home run.
I hear the crowd go wild.
I want that home run.
I am physically powerful.

I pretend to see myself running around the bases, getting the winning run.
I believe I can obtain that game-winning hit.
I touch the baseball bat, with my gloves on my hands.

I feel the pressure on me with 2 outs, in the bottom of the 9th inning.
I worry that I will let my team down.
I cry for the pitcher to throw a fastball right down the middle.
I am focused.

I understand my teammates are watching me, and hoping I get a home run.
I say I will try my best.
I dream for that winning home run.
I hope that my teammates will not be angry at me if I don't succeed.
I am a baseball star.
Chester Burnett, Grade 8
Sanford School, DE

Little Brothers

Little brothers wiggle.
Little brothers shout.
Little brothers cry.
And little brothers pout.

They sneeze.
They cough.
Sometimes I wish I could turn them off but I can't.

But what can you do they're family they're practically attached to you.
I love them on days. Well most of the days. It must be a phase of the little brothers.
Well I gotta go it's the end of the show I gotta go watch my brothers now.

I love you even if we get in fights.
I love you through all the days and nights.
To me you'll always be little and small.
I see you grow up so, so fast.
I just wish time could last.
Me and you will always be close.
You guys will always be the ones I love the most.
Alexis Brock, Grade 7
Tasker Middle School, MD

Life

Life is hard do not forget
You have to give something to get
Nothing is free you pay the price and only then you get your prize
Sometimes we all forget what precious things we gave to get
Those little things we never saw they disappear and now they're gone
So pay attention don't forget for if you do you will regret.
Valerie Vozhol, Grade 8
Bishop Walsh Middle High School, MD

Contender

I am a contender.
I wonder how this game is going to be.
I hear the crowd preparing.
I see the warm ups starting.
I want to win.
I am a competitor.

I pretend I am going to the win the game.
I believe the chances are not good.
I touch the grooves of the ball.

I feel anxious.
I worry more with every step I take closer to the hoop.
I cry inside when I make a wrong move.
I am a challenger.

I understand I have to do this.
I say to myself, "Everything is all right."
I dream of getting to the top.
I hope this ball goes in…
I am a basketball player.

Hadiya Tucker, Grade 8
Sanford School, DE

Change

Please never change the way the trees turn colors in the fall,
Or the way my friends stick up for me,
Because they're true friends, all in all.
Never change the way squirrels run around trees,
The way the snow falls,
The way my life is full of ease.
Never change the forest,
Or the stars, the moon, the sky.
Never change the birds,
And never change how high they fly.
Never change the amount of happiness
That we all some time in our lives,
And never change the plants and the flowers,
Because the beauty helps the world survive.
Never change the smell of flowers,
Never change the beautiful sun,
Never change humanity, except to make up all as one.

Alexandria Dannhardt, Grade 7
Kilmer Middle School, VA

Bright Comes Natural

Bright comes natural
As if I'm a bright star in the dark sky filled with darkness,
Brightening the souls of the females
Because of the bright star that I am,
The shine I have gives me an advantage over other stars,
Meaning that I can't be outdone.
The dark sky is a place where not many lights glow but
The one that stands out the most represents me.

De'Xuan Smith, Grade 8
Lafayette Winona Middle School, VA

Winter

Ring Ring Ring!!
That is my alarm clock
It is screaming at me
To wake up. I open my eyes but some thing
Is pushing them down
I sit up in my bed and look out my window
My once green grassy backyard is now a white blanket of snow
My once bare apple tree is covered
With a fluffy white substance
Outside is a snowy wonderland filled with joy
I run out pushing against the heavy snow
I drop in the snow and look
Up at the sky the sun stares at me
As it hides behind the clouds
Snow flurries fall on my nose as I close my eyes
My mom shouts that school has been canceled and I should come in
She tells me that she has just made
Some warm hot chocolate with cream
I push myself out of the snow and run towards the warmed house
I look back and shout that winter has come
To the unknown world beyond me

Ashley Wells, Grade 7
Blue Ridge Middle School, VA

Fear

My heart pumps.
Boom boom
I pay for my ticket.
I start walking.
The sky holds a full moon.
The smell of hay turns my stomach.
The scary spooky maze.
I keep a steady pace
despite the screams that make me nervous.
A zombie chases me with a chain saw.
I tell myself this is not real,
but it feels like it.
I tell myself
I have to get out.
My head throbs with fear.
My heart jumps out of my chest.
My face burns red as I see everyone laughing at me.

Francheska Molina, Grade 7
Blue Ridge Middle School, VA

The Chicken

There is a chicken in my house.
He is lazy all the time
Oh how I hate that chicken
He drives me crazy

He can't cook, he can't clean he is just there
He is the cause of all my problems
He is procrastination

Jimmy Cummins, Grade 7
Tasker Middle School, MD

Desserts

I ordered some food at the county fair
The menu came at the speed of a hare
The words were as big as bears
And what I saw gave me quite a scare.

There were cookies and cakes and crumbles
Enough chocolate to feed a city
Oh how it made my stomach rumble
I got up and danced and sang a ditty.

I shouted for the waitress
To come and take my order
But if she were any slower
I would've had to run over.

But when the speakers came on
I stopped and went inert
Because the dreadful message said
"We're out of all our desserts."

Richie Kimball, Grade 8
Brandywine Springs School, DE

Snakes

They are sacks of venom and muscle
They are always on the move
You can find the smallest one
In the tiniest little grooves

All though they're said to be mean
They're really not that bad
Even if you get bitten
It's not all glum and sad

Snakes are smooth and sleek
The way they slip and slide
If they had wings
I bet they'd even glide

Snakes are like sharks
They come in different sizes
It'd be funny if you hit a piñata
And snakes were all the prizes

Jeffrey Leggio, Grade 8
Brandywine Springs School, DE

The Moon

The moon
secret and dark
mystery, emotions
rip tides, currents.
Gravity engulfs the mind.
We're all connected
but are we?
The sun comes up.

Peter Pagliarini, Grade 8
St. Rocco School, RI

Baseball

Sweat gleamed on his forehead as he walked to the plate,
He was so nervous he could hardly stand up straight.
It was the last chance they had to bring home the win.
As he stood and readied for the pitch he knew, it was all up to him.
With a glance to the runner on first, the pitcher threw the ball.
The runner took off, running so fast he looked as though he might fall.
Strike! He missed the ball by a hair.
"It's all up to me" he thought, "that's not fair!"
He knew if he struck out his coach would be very mad!
The second pitch came in, and swung with all the strength he had.
Strike two! The crowd erupted in a torrent of unhappy shouts.
"It's the bottom of the ninth with two outs.
The home team is down by one and it looks like this may be it."
It zoomed in like a rocket and he prayed for a hit.
He swung at the ball with all his might.
And at that instant he knew that he hit the ball just right.
It was sent sailing out of the park for a home run.
Winning the Championship was a lot of fun!

Daniel Schmidt, Grade 8
Brandywine Springs School, DE

Someone Special

Every morning when I wake up and get ready for my day ahead,
    I will always think of you.
When I am with my friends at school,
    I know my day will be special because I know I have you.
When I get home from school,
    I know I will have a good night of sleep because I know I have you.
If I am lonely,
    I know that I have you to cheer me up.
I have someone who will love me no matter what happens.
    While I am at home,
I know that I will always have that one special place in your heart just for me.
Even if I had every thing I could ever dream of in life,
    I would still love you the most.
Every day and night of the week as time goes by,
    I know that you are always going to love me.
So this poem is specifically for you, great-grandmother. I love you.

Chris Elston, Grade 8
Chickahominy Middle School, VA

Snow Day

Tiny snowflakes, slowly building up,
Scalding hot chocolate, twirling in my cup
Frosty windows blur my view
My little sister peeks out to something entirely new,
She screams, "SNOW! SNOW! SNOW! Isn't this great?"
I looked a little puzzled, trying not to take the bait.
But when I look outside the window, my eyes saw such a sight,
Everything in my neighborhood was blanketed in fluffy white.
Like a little kid on Christmas morning, my heart was filled with joy,
Because the sight of snow to me is like a brand new toy.
I skedaddled upstairs, put on layers of clothes and a warm hat on my head
Tied up my boots, put on my mittens, and now it's time to sled!

Samantha Behnke, Grade 8
Brandywine Springs School, DE

A Dream Fulfilled

What happens to a dream fulfilled?
Does it shine
Like a colorful rainbow?
Or flow like a crystal river —
And clear stream?
Does it dance like a frog on a lily pad?
Or soothe your feelings —
Like ice cream after having surgery?

Maybe it soars in the sky
Like a bluebird

Or does it sparkle like an eagle's eye?
Bianca Dodson, Grade 7
Marshall Middle School, VA

Living

Flowers, frogs, humans
What are they?

Living beings on Earth
What does it mean to live?

To be alive

It's really that simple
Nothing more

Nothing less
Live life to the fullest
Sara Yaseen, Grade 9
Oakton High School, VA

He Doesn't Care

Whenever I say hi
It's like he says bye
Whenever I say what's up
He says shut up
I always try to be nice
But he is as mean as ice
I try to give him a hug
But he just gives me a shove

There's only so much I can say and do
But it's up to him to like me
I try so hard but nothing.
Because when I say hi he says bye
Menaal Saeed, Grade 7
Kilmer Middle School, VA

Fall Is Soon to Be

Leaves fall to the ground.
Pretty colors fall slowly.
Fall is soon to be.
Abigail Guite, Grade 7
Marshall Middle School, VA

Worst Day Ever

It was the best day of all
Sun is out; I'm smiling with an open mouth
I don't usually have good days; but today I won't pay
I went to school with 100% pride; by the end of my first mod I cried
Who knew Mr. L would give me an "E;" I didn't because it was the best day to me
The day is not over I still have time
All I have to do is keep my pride
Second and third mod was ok; not what I was going for on my best day
But don't give up so quick it's still a good day
Time for P.E.; it's time to be free
It was time for basketball and I have moves; by the first shot I lost the groove
BREAK! BREAK! BREAK… All my shots missed
But the good part is nobody watched me play
P.E. wasn't the best, but two more mods can save the day
Then one more mod and it's Math; Ha it's Friday I'm going to pass
But NO we have a quiz; Hmmm — should be a piece of cake
By the time I put a pencil on that paper; I didn't have a piece of faith
Of course I got a "D;" and by the time I got home I took a long sleep
Then I remembered P.E.; I'm home with flip flops, not the shoes my mom just bought me
I'm not getting my shoes back because it was the last day of school
Now I can officially say it was the worstttttttttttt day in the entire world!
Justin Davis, Grade 7
Benjamin Tasker Middle School, MD

Getting the Solo

I am a singer
I wonder if I will succeed
I hear the other students trying out for the solo
I see the nervous faces of the other students
I want to succeed
I am a singer

I pretend to be an accomplished singer
I believe that one day I will get a chance to sing a solo
I touch the notes on the page

I feel my hands shaking
I worry my voice will shake
I cry tears of joy inside of me because I know I did well
I am a confident singer

I understand I did my best and whether I receive the solo or not is out of my hands
I say to myself "Be confident"
I dream of singing the solo and seeing my parents smiling at me
I hope I will get the solo
I am a very confident singer
Breanna Mendell, Grade 8
Sanford School, DE

Summer

Summer is like a nice cup of tea. It is my best friend.
Summer gives me a pat on my back every time I see him.
The temperature it gives off for free is a million times hotter than any other season.
Summer is a wonderful time to be with family and friends.
Caleb Denton, Grade 8
Paul L Dunbar Middle School for Innovation, VA

Love Is a Precious Thing

Love is something precious to me.
I can't let just anyone take my heart
And let them tell me they Love me.
That they will never hurt me
Or that never want to lose me.

They think that it is okay to have my emotions toyed with.
They think my heart is made of stone,
Like I don't even care if my heart is shattered.
It seems like they don't even care about me,
Yet we are considered friends.

To even think that I actually cared for them.
To tell them I would do anything in the world to save them.
I admitted that I love them with all my heart and soul.
But I've come to realize I don't

That's why love is a precious thing.
Love is a complicated thing.
In my world, love is the most puzzling thing,
But it's the most
Precious.

Allison Sevidal, Grade 8
St Joseph School-Fullerton, MD

The Steelers

#7 Big Ben,
I will always know Hines Ward will catch it when he throws.

I love the saying "Run like El,"
he's a good one to have, I can tell.

Polamalu is one of the best,
you can tell when he's put to the test.

Jeff Reed kicks it high,
and the ball goes soaring by.

Thanks to the rest of the team too,
because boy these games are really flying through.

So bow down to the black and gold,
they are surely a sight to behold!

Aurash Aidun, Grade 7
Carson Middle School, VA

Blue Beauty

Blue is a pair of jeans,
Reliable and comfortable
For many, many years.
Blue is sadness,
The deepest despair,
When everything is against,
Like a tidal wave against you, engulfing you.

Ariana Wheeler-Lafuente, Grade 7
Kilmer Middle School, VA

Strokes of Light

The color strokes sweep across the canvas
The color and light
Lighting up the darkness
With each consecutive stroke
More emotions rise

I am almost done
Just a few more swipes
I look at the painting, it is complete
I am finished
I feel like I have accomplished something internal
I am ready

I step back
To look at my work
Its beauty takes me aback
The strokes stay put
It is luminous in the dark
And the strokes will glow for eternity

The strokes of light

Danielle Foley, Grade 8
Chickahominy Middle School, VA

Sailor

I am a sailor
I wonder what lies beyond the horizon
I hear the way the waves roll about
I see the glory of the ocean
I want to see everything of the sea
I am a dreamer

I pretend that I am always out there, though
I believe that I will not be alone
I touch the ends of the earth in the dreams I often have

I feel the boat slicing through the waves
I worry for nothing in the tranquil capes, and
I cry only when this paradise may end
I am at peace

I understand the waters of the world
I say that I'm going to sail them all
I dream that I am the first to do so
I hope that my dreams fulfill themselves through my actions
I am a sailor

Trevor Long, Grade 8
Sanford School, DE

The Les Paul Standard

The red Les Paul standard is very big and shiny too.
It includes many cool features that are made just for you.
The Les Paul comes in many colors that look really nice.
If you save some cash, you can buy it, since it has a huge price.

Thomas Visalli, Grade 7
St Joseph School-Fullerton, MD

McNabb

The Redskins are the best,
They put the others to rest.

No one can sack McNabb,
He doesn't even have one scab.

He used to play in PA,
Loved to play during the day.

Now he is a skin,
He wears a pad on his chin.

He throws very well,
If he messes up he doesn't dwell.

He throws many touchdowns,
The other team just frowns.

Indeed he is staying,
For the skins he is playing.
Donte Divincenzo, Grade 8
Brandywine Springs School, DE

Trains

Carrying passengers alike,
Just for a hike.

The comfortable seats,
In the high class suites.

The people relax to see a landscape,
Amazed as if it's on a tape.

People from all around,
Come just for the sound.

The clatter of the tracks,
Gets people so relaxed.

The train starts to slow down,
Getting closer to the town.

The ride is finally done,
Everyone knows they had a lot of fun.
William Johansen, Grade 8
Brandywine Springs School, DE

Dedication

This poem is dedicated to me
Because I am me and I love me like always.
I am fabulous, and gorgeous.
I'm intelligent and I'm a princess,
No matter what anyone says
I love me.
Andrea Clinkscales, Grade 8
Lafayette Winona Middle School, VA

Christmas Spirit

A man who didn't believe in Christmas, happiness, or joy,
would change to cherish all people and children, just because of a little boy.

This man never put up any Christmas lights, or even said, "Happy Holidays!"
He was actually like a regular Scrooge in many, many ways.

But one night he was sleeping, resting his little head,
and he heard someone creeping beside his antique bed.

He sat up and turned on the lights,
and what was there gave him a fright.

It was a little boy, with rosy cheeks and pointed ears,
and a smile that was full of cheer.

He took the man out of his bed, and they vanished from the room,
landed in a joyful place, contradicting the gloom.

It was happy and bright, and made the man's heart warm,
this place was not gloomy in any way, shape, or form.

There were elves like this one wrapping gifts with bows,
some were tall, but some stood on their toes.

Then a man with a red suit came out;
He was cheerful, rosy, and stout.

He looked at the man, and the crotchety man knew
what the pudgy man wanted him to do.
And he was never mean again.
Matthew McDonald, Grade 8
St Joseph School-Fullerton, MD

Christmas

Snow falls silently outside your window as you rest your head on your pillow
You hear a noise! Munch, munch, could it be? Munch, munch
Santa Claus eating the cookies! You spring out of bed and run in a fright
To find your dad eating the cookies in the moonlight
You go back to rest your head, but only for a short while
Because its Christmas morning, and you're excited like a child

A few hours later

"Wake up, Wake up," you hear, as your sister screams in your ear
"It's Christmas morning! Wake up!"
You get up to look outside to see the world looking like a sea of white
"It snowed, too," she said, while jumping up and down in the light
You both run into the kitchen, to find a cooking chicken, when you get to the den
You see a stack of presents with your name and stack with Grace's name
Rip, rip, crumple, crumple, open faster!
Yeah! It is just what you wanted an action figure of the Evil Disaster
For the rest of the day you play in the snow, and drink hot cocoa
At dinner when your parents ask how your day went
You say "This has been the best Christmas ever, and it couldn't be better!"
Mattie Mason, Grade 8
Brandywine Springs School, DE

Thanksgiving

T hanksgiving is
H appiness
A ll the family and
N eighbors
K indness
S erving
G iving, and
I nviting
V arious people
I nto our family
N ever ending
G atherings

Jude Makhmreh, Grade 7
St Joseph School-Fullerton, MD

Turtles of the Sea

Silently in the water
the sun slinks
Through the liquid silk
and reflects
Off to the scarred shells
Like an eagle
Each sweep of the flippers
is graceful and smooth
Churning mini tornados
with every stroke
This is the beauty at its best
the turtles of the sea

Tanushree Singh, Grade 7
Rachael Carson Middle School, VA

A Dream Fulfilled

What happens to a dream fulfilled?
Does it shine like silver?
Or flow like shining rain in the sun.
And gentle water?
Does it dance like leaves in the wind?
Or soothe gently like a calming song?

Maybe it soars wildly.
Like a bird in the wind.

Or does it just happen?

Chase Bowdoin, Grade 7
Marshall Middle School, VA

My Dog Sam

My dog's name is Sam
My dog Sam likes to have fun
My dog Sam is great!

Robert Weidle, Grade 7
St Joseph School-Fullerton, MD

Skateboarding

Skateboarding is a way to express yourself,
From the way you dress to the way you do tricks.
It doesn't really matter as long as you love it.
So many setups to choose from, a wide board to a skinny board,
high trucks to low trucks, bearings to wheels.
Oh, how I never get bored.
Skateboarding is like a drug, Never to quit and hung over from bruises.
Sometimes you just love it 'till death. From getting kicked out,
To having long sessions,
It's really just fun to go out.
Skateparks, backyard pools, and home built ramps,
All the kids love to skate,
Even if it means skipping their date.
From five in the morn'
To eight in the evening,
From dusk 'till dawn.
Aspirations of becoming a pro,
It's baby steps from flow to pro, doesn't matter if you're pro or not
The love for this sport
Is stronger than the love of a loving parent
Just remember who brought you into this planet.

Arturo Zarate, Grade 8
Brandywine Springs School, DE

Evanescence

Have you ever felt like you weren't good enough,
That the weight of the world was just too much?
The stress and pressure is taking over you
And you think you are the only one.

Well let me give you some advice before you lose control,
So you don't end up farther and farther away, until you breathe no more.

Now you search for a field of innocence; a way onto cloud nine.
But contrary to popular belief, it is very hard to find.
You must discover the balance between succumbing and going under,
And living in an imaginary world that will lead you to a blunder.

When you feel your life is haunted by your constant sweet sacrifice,
Hope and prayer is the tourniquet that will bring you back to life.
So when life is bad, don't say you're broken, because then you are everybody's fool.
God has a plan for all of us, and it is not to make life cruel.

Have a bit more faith. Don't fear this is your last breath.
Do not say goodbye; Say hello…and conquer your Evanescence.

Margaret Dolan, Grade 8
Brandywine Springs School, DE

Pizza

You scream at me from the pizza box yelling "eat me, eat me."
I open the box as your scent lifts me up like I was tied to a rocket ship.
I take one of the slices and eat it like I have a million more to go.
Your smell is like a cologne I wish I had.
You are a spaceship touring me around space.

George Branham, Grade 8
Paul L Dunbar Middle School for Innovation, VA

The Wild Wind

The wind flows,
Like it is the sea.
It is so wild,
So free,
Able to do as it wishes.
The clouds are its fishes.
The storms are its sharks.
It is sometimes rolling, sometimes calm.
The wind is so brave.
He and his friend the Sun,
Together are so daring.
Earth to the Wild Wind
Is its play thing.
The Wild Wind watches us,
It loves us,
The Wild Wind.

Taylor Lane, Grade 7
Kilmer Middle School, VA

2012

Society has just fallen apart,
    No more culture or beautiful art.
The world that was once so great,
    Has ended on this very date,
    Like it was destined by fate.
The people tried to save this earth,
    They tried and tried,
    But could not give it new worth.

The forests that were once so green,
    May never again be seen.
The water as blue as the sky in the oceans,
    No longer in fluid motion.
The once beautiful place,
    Now gone, erased,
    The people searching for a new space.

William Barndt, Grade 8
Brandywine Springs School, DE

Music

Music flows through the air,
Weaving its way through the clouds
Like a stream twists past the rocks.
Mortals say music has a certain form.
Restrictions.
But this surely cannot be so.
Music can be free.
Limitless.
It can reach new heights.
Skyward.
I think this as I strum at my lute,
Weaving through the apple orchard
Like music through the clouds
Or a stream past the rocks.

Alaina Keller, Grade 8
Monsignor Slade Catholic School, MD

Fire

The heat is high;
Yet I feel it escaping my fingertips.
My toes,
The air has a different smell.
Sweet, yet bitter somehow.
The fire is only in my heart right now.
I can hear you speaking,
But I can't seem to answer.
Then something changes.
The fire is gone.
But my heart is iced over.
I sense something coming.
Everything is still, calm.
The air smells of different.
And I know something new has begun.

Emily Garzon, Grade 8
Norfolk Christian Middle School, VA

Summer's End

Clovers dance.
They happily spring and prance
in the whistling wind,
while I wonder
what it would be like
to whisk and whirl, a ballerina,
in the slight summer breeze.

Trees swirl,
their branches eloquently twist
in the flowing wind.
While I walk by,
the breeze blows gently,
the world at its best.
Summer's End.

Molly Magoffin, Grade 7
Blue Ridge Middle School, VA

The Travels of a Hockey Puck

Back and forth
Back and forth
Up and down the ice
The puck moves with blinding speed
Like a shooting star
In the night sky
As it dances around the rink.
All the players
On the ice
Try to get to it first,
But once someone hits it
Good luck finding it now,
For anyone could have it
But there is no telling
Who will.

Allyson Westfall, Grade 8
St Joseph School-Fullerton, MD

Live Love Hate

L iberating
I magination
V aluable
E xhilarating

L aughter
O ptimistic
V ibrant
E nchanting

H orrendous
A crimonious
T reacherous
E xecrate

Josh Mundy, Grade 9
Delaware Military Academy, DE

Pretty Red Dress

One drop descends
From the millions that fall
Into the hands
Of one little child in awe

She jumps with joy
At the incredible feel
Unaware it was just destroyed
For now it lies on her hand in the heel

But that one little drop
Gave its life up in happiness
By giving that girl a little hop
To bounce her pretty red dress

Samantha Warner, Grade 7
Parkside Middle School, VA

Angels

Angels, angels
up in the sky
Their hair falls around me
enveloping me
comforting me
protecting me
erasing my doubts
giving me strength
Just when I thought I would fall
fall
fall
falling
but I don't
because they catch me

Crystal Goldman, Grade 9
Mount Pleasant High School, DE

Basketball

Basketball is my favorite sport
I like it when they dribble up and down the court,
Jump shots, fade aways, and finger rolls
Scoring the most is part of many goals,
Lebron James, Kobe Bryant, and Dwayne Wade,
When they drive down the lane
Watch the step back and fade,
When they make the shot
The crowd begins to hop,
Blocking shots and getting steals
It makes the players
Start to play for real,
When you win the championship
You get the ring
Then you can show off your fancy bling,
Players can range from different sizes
Starting from John Wall to Pau Gasol,
There's only one thing that's bad about basketball
It's when the referee makes a terrible call!

Julian Issa, Grade 8
Sacred Heart School, MD

Shattered Heart

Shattered heart
I'm falling apart
Broken inside empty and shattered
Is how my heart resides
I won't ever let
Go of you in my life because then all I'll feel
Is broken inside
Take my heart
And do what you wish
Just don't tear it without 1 last kiss
Your memory remains
In these hollow eyes
Because now that you left me
I'm broken inside

Andre Bucham, Grade 8
Paul L Dunbar Middle School for Innovation, VA

The Terps

The Terps are up by 5.
Our Coach is giving the players high five's.
Florida State runs a pass,
But we sacked him right into the grass.

Florida State has the ball.
Our fans are banging against the wall.
Florida State attempts the kick,
But our player flicks it.

We win the game,
But this win doesn't feel the same.
We are going to play in the ACC championship!

Nick Billings, Grade 7
Tasker Middle School, MD

The Last Goodbye

This is it,
Our last goodbye,
Now it is finally here,
How time went by,
We are all gathered here,
See how we all have grown,
From the time we were young,
I cannot believe after all these years,
All the hardships,
The laughs and cries,
We have been through so much together,
Our strong family will never come to be again,
The friends we made here will never leave our hearts,
We will never forget each other and the great times we had,
For that is certain,
As well as we hoped so much for this day to come,
We never know the best things in life until they are gone,
So now we hold hands together one last time,
We look into our future,
Never will it be forgotten,
Our last goodbye.

Nicole Bowman, Grade 8
St Rocco School, RI

The Man

There is a man who always cries.
We try to help him.
He said he's tired of lies.
He said his name was Jim.

He doesn't like to fight.
To stop trouble he has to be funny.
He's always wanted to learn to write,
But instead he steals money.

He is followed by a stray pet;
He said he couldn't keep it.
He sits in the drizzling rain getting wet.
He wears a jacket that doesn't fit.

So we helped Jim.
I think it changed us more than it changed him.

Trevis Claxton, Grade 7
Paul L Dunbar Middle School for Innovation, VA

Fire Wall

All I'm doing is digging fire.
I think I am burning softly
I feel myself crying but I'm scared to admit it.
I have a soul that keeps me going.
I call out for help!
But nobody hears me.
I finally died with a remembrance.
Of a person that dream so deep.

Machiah Hamlett, Grade 7
Paul L Dunbar Middle School for Innovation, VA

Earth's Mirror

Reflections in the water,
Show ourselves how we are made,
How we have grown as a person,
How our old selves start to fade.

Qualities that were once there,
Turned into something new,
You might not recognize yourself,
But your new self has found you.

Searching for your inner self,
Not just the outer core,
You might find you're a stronger person,
Than what you sensed before.

All reflections have a purpose,
Which we find out on our own,
Earth's true mirror,
Is a natural given loan.

Erin Swierczewski, Grade 8
Chickahominy Middle School, VA

Disguised Love

I wake up every morning,
to the sound of her feet stomping the floor,
opening and slamming doors,
Mom tells her she's late.
I wish she would go away,
but she can't.

When I go downstairs,
the Chaos never stops.
She runs around like a chicken
with its head cut off.
I wish she was at school,
but she's not.

As soon as she walks out the door,
into the cold, dark world,
I realize her annoying presence,
makes me myself,
and that I love her so.

Morgan Widdifield, Grade 7
Blue Ridge Middle School, VA

The Sound

"Whoosh" did you hear that
It might have been a bird
But did you hear that
Maybe it was the wind
Or maybe it was a car
That just passed by
But let's go check it out
And maybe crash by.

Sumant Bhupathiraju, Grade 7
Carson Middle School, VA

Fatal Patience

Even in the face of death, she embraces life,
Covering every inch of reality with struggle, love, and strife.
Eternally and classically it's a story of love and hate,
Where she lay she anticipates, but alas, her prince is late.
Let her sleep, restlessly at peace, for the price of forever's love,
Swaying gently, falling like a lone, forgotten dove.
Despair so quiet, distress so clear, losing hope with the passing years,
Insanity tangibly closing near, all because her prince was here.
All comes down to will and dreams of bliss and happy endings,
Most are found too late and all too close to breaking, bending.
She's lying on the floor awake behind the binding door,
Waiting, wishing, wanting, but always wanting more.
Simply addictive obsession comes close to how the damsel felt,
She fell pleadingly with surrender's demise, and on the floor, she knelt.
Anger and sorrow finally turned to a twisted, sickening glee,
She lost her vengeance of questioned malice and died with a final plea.

Michael Greene, Grade 8
St Augustine School, RI

The Box

Every day I walk through the seemingly endless halls.
I ask myself, "Where am I?"
Everywhere I go it's always the same thing.
I see familiar faces but the surroundings are very strange.
I feel as if I'm crazy maybe even deranged.
No one is talking, only staring and walking.
I start screaming, screaming with terror.
I yell, "What is wrong with me? Help me get out of this terrible place!"
Yet it's like no one is there to hear my heart race.
Not anyone to stop and save me from this awful space.
I feel boxed in.
I push on the walls of this box trying to make my escape from this terror.
The walls just keep coming closer.
It seems as though no matter what I do I'm always trapped.
One day I will make it out.
And so will you.

Kaitlyn Bradley, Grade 8
Sandusky Middle School, VA

Micaela

Micaela Dominguez
Who is creative, smart, fun, a cousin to Marissa and Marques and Alexis
Who is a sister of Tammera Arnold
Who loves my dog, my mom, my poppi
Who feels happy, confident, and excited
Who needs love, care, and fun
Who gives ideas, love, and fun
Who fears snakes, bears, and wolves
Who would like to see bats, dragons, and bobcats
Who shares a room with my dog
Who is awesome

Micaela Dominguez, Grade 8
Paul L Dunbar Middle School for Innovation, VA

Life

Our life begins when we are born, and first open our eyes.
And then it goes on from right there, life's just like a surprise.
We walk, we talk.
We eat, we sleep.
We grow, we learn
We work, we earn.
We give, we take,
And cook and bake.
We tell the truth and then some lies,
So that people don't recognize,
Some things we wish we hadn't done
But don't feel bad, it's just begun.
We laugh, we cry,
As time goes by
We'll say hellos, and then good-byes,
To all the world that passes by.
But sure enough, and who knows why
We get to live and then we die
It's time to tell the world good-bye,
And float like a balloon
Up into the sky.

Emelyn Frazier, Grade 8
Brandywine Springs School, DE

Painting a Picture

Painting a picture so pretty and bright,
My artwork brings people a gift of light.
People ask why I paint so well,
I laugh and I say,
"Because I think its swell."
I paint their portraits for free,
While the model sips on her tea.
I go out to the park,
To give my brain a spark.
I see a child running with her kite,
The wind is pulling at it with all its might.
When I see a sight like this,
It brings me bliss.
This is why painting to me is swell,
Because of the stories my paintings get to tell.

Miyah Boyd, Grade 7
Paul L Dunbar Middle School for Innovation, VA

Waiting

I wait for peace.
I wait for love.
I wait for unity.
I wait for no tears.
I wait for no sickness.
I wait for no divorce.
I wait for no race.
I wait for no gang.
I wait for true freedom.
And still I wait…

Joshua Doyle, Grade 8
Paul L Dunbar Middle School for Innovation, VA

Goodbyes and Goodnight

A temporary goodbye
Is all I hope it will be.
Because when we separate
You keep a piece of me.
I never feel complete
Without you here with me.
If we were to separate
For a permanent ending,
I could only hope
That you end up happy.
I may cry
And fall to my knees
But you being happy
Is all that matters to me.
Each night I dream,
Dream of you and me.
Sometimes I wake up
Hoping to see you next to me.

Christian Wilkes, Grade 8
Paul L Dunbar Middle School for Innovation, VA

Taken Away*

1. My eyes betrayed me
2. My ears left my face
1. I see black, but I hear the color
2. I see the color but I hear black
1. The world I hear is not right, not complete
2. The world I see is not right, not complete
1. What do they do?
2. What do they say?
1. Do they mimic me?
2. Do they speak smack about me
1. Do I care?
2. Do I care?
1. No
2. No
1. I give my eyes more sound than they need
2. I give my ears more sight than they need
Both: A piece of life was taken, but I was given more.

Vasanthi Rathnakaram, Grade 8
Carson Middle School, VA
**A poem for two voices.*

Happiness

It makes me feel all cozy inside,
and forgives, forgets, and loves.
It eases our pain and hunts down the bad,
it fits just right like a glove.
It abolishes the sad, the painful, the mad,
it's a gift that comes from above.
I call it happiness.
It encompasses me every day.
It's the best feeling that nothing can beat,
no how, not possible, NO WAY.

Gisele Iafrate, Grade 8
St Rocco School, RI

My Cat Memories

I heard a sound, a sound of tears
That was coming in my ears.
When my cat died,
My step mom cried and cried.

I cried and cried,
I was very sad.
Then my dad came in and saw she was dead.

Oh when will I get over,
That my cat Mrs. Kittie had died.
Oh, Oh, I was very sad,
But all I could say is that my best friend was dead.

I got new kittens
So I wouldn't be sad,
But nothing could replace what I already had.
I will love and miss you, and never forget you.

Garrett Grady, Grade 8
Chickahominy Middle School, VA

Real Happiness

I've once heard that no one dies until they know
what real happiness is like.
They say a dog's life
is one seventh of humans.
Do they die so much earlier
because they know real happiness?
All a dog does is
take your couch space
eat your food
and make you clean up their poop.
A dog know everything about you
He knows when you get up
what you eat
and knows what hurts you.
All it takes to make them happy is love.
By patting them, petting them, or giving them a belly rub.
That is real happiness for a dog.
For a human, well, I'm still here so I can't tell you that yet.

Erin Morgan, Grade 9
Leonardtown High School, MD

I Am

I am a mountain,
With many layers of feelings,
Nipped at, beaten harmlessly, by the wind of emotions,
Dwarfed by the surrounding mountains of siblings.
I am a tiger,
Attacking the deer of challenges,
Swimming into unknown frontiers,
Hunted by the daunting devils of memories.
I am a paper,
Mercilessly cut by the scissors of life.

Nikhil Sakhamuri, Grade 7
Kilmer Middle School, VA

Belief

I am a believer
I wonder if every human being has felt loved and safe
I hear families worrying about finances
I see people who have lost jobs on the streets
I want everyone to be secure and happy
I am a believer

I pretend that there is no war; everyone loves one another
I touch the newspaper and read about the horrors in the world
I believe that it will come to a happy ending

I feel hopeful for the future generations
I worry if I am the only one that believes
I cry for the people that are suffering

I understand that this is "normal" for our generation
I say that no hardship should be considered normal
I dream that everyone and everything is loved
I hope the world will find eternal peace
I am a believer

Rachel Farmer, Grade 8
Sanford School, DE

Shoes

Shoes might be the thing on your feet
But shoes can make the
Sound of a beat

Shoes can be a little kid's dream
Or a dog toy
Made up of strings and seams

Some people use shoes as a decorative fashion
With bright colors and brands
As a necessary passion

Either way you look at it they are protective for your feet
Until you get tired
Then you need to take a seat.

Colby Roloff, Grade 8
Sacred Heart School, MD

You Are Special

Life is basically a big book,
Full of billions of pages…
And we are the pages.
Each holding precious information,
That makes the whole story a story.
Each and every one of us, like the pages of a book,
are very important and special in our own specific way.
What is a book without its pages?
What is a story without its characters?
We're all here for a reason
YOU are special!

Sydney Leonard, Grade 7
Warwick River Christian School, VA

Sensationally Willing
Stepping over, crossing the line
That's been drawn
Stepping over into a newer dimension
Slowly losing air
Going under, sensationally willing
To feel the urge to give up
Maybe I could…
Maybe it would make it all better
If I just dropped off the face of the Earth
Feeling easing in my body, feeling numb
No control, no remorse
To come back, caring for no one
Not even myself
Feeling like dirt being stepped on
Hurting so badly, feeling so invaded
With my heart feeling heavy, my head held down
Dizziness bringing me low
As my head hits the floor I break out into coolness
Shaky, jittering, and helpless
I have never felt as much pain as I do now
Closing my eyes, I fall into the distance.
Pamela Gray, Grade 8
Thomas Walker High School, VA

Love's Blazing Fire
Love is a fire burning inside you
It warms you up
The sparks it gives off sends chills up your spine

Fire destroys
And love leaves heartache
But through that heartache we are stronger
As we build better on fire's victims

Love is terrifying, beautiful, and powerful
The same for fire
Love petrifies you; it makes you vulnerable
Love is beauteous like the colors of a fire raging
Love is powerful; it alters your life permanently
Love and fire go hand in hand
They are one and the same
Love, is a blazing fire
Kaitie Eileene Leach, Grade 9
Covenant Life School, MD

Dancing
There's Hip-hop, lyrical, and ballet too
There's nothing you can't do.
Letting everything out; going wild
In the heart I am just a great big child!
Moving, shaking, grooving to the beat,
After all it makes you want to get up off your feet.
Letting everything out with a care,
And yes, people are going to stop and stare.
Monica Stemski, Grade 8
St Joseph School-Fullerton, MD

Society
Less tax dollars
for white collars.
Is this the reason we should be scholars?

If the government would be fair,
More and more people would definitely care.
Then would everyone pay their share?

Why are there cheaters who play pro sports?
It seems like all of them end up in court.
Shouldn't these players' careers be cut short?

We have our soldiers in Iraq,
Fighting to get others' freedom back,
A quality that many others lack.

Many people lose their sobriety,
Almost all have forgotten the virtue of piety,
Just another thing wrong with society.
Harrison Zambarano, Grade 8
St Rocco School, RI

Basketball
Basketball is a fast paced game
Nobody wants to take the blame
Everyone needs to pass the ball
But no one does it as well as John Wall
Lots of people like to take the shot
Your shoes need to be tied in a tight knot
Also there needs to be time on the clock
Just make sure you don't get blocked
In basketball you will sweat
Also, people like to make bets
If shots will not fall
Then you really need to just pass the ball
In the NBA they give you a ball called spalding
Also it's funny that some players are balding
If a player makes a hard foul
You'll definitely hear the other player howl
There are six fouls and you are out
So to have some respect don't shout
Jack Coffren, Grade 8
Sacred Heart School, MD

As Time Goes By
It's amazing how time goes by
Every day gets harder and harder I wonder why I even try
Some days I feel like I'ma roll over and die
Every day gets harder and harder as time goes by
Now I understand why people commit suicide
But I'm still here and I'm alive
I'm a walk the face of the Earth until the day I finally close my eyes
Don't worry though as of now I'ma live my life
As time goes by…
Brianna Hawkins, Grade 8
Paul L Dunbar Middle School for Innovation, VA

Soaring

Wind rushes under wings
Pushing you higher in the sky.
A powerful force, with a desperate dream
To raise you up this time.

Yet often, because we're humans,
You and I will fall.
For though wind is powerful,
You are the stronger one, after all.

People, other people,
Can help you achieve your dreams.
But in reality, it's up to you.
No matter what it seems.

Life is simply a trial.
And a hard one, it's true.
But you are the conquering hero.
So put on your armor
And be you.

Battle your enemy.
The force of gravity won't conquer you.
So fight your hardest, and you will make
Your own dreams come true.
Katelyn Dalton, Grade 8
Chickahominy Middle School, VA

Dance of Life

We are born,
    And the floor opens
We are taken by the hand.
    And through our ups and falling downs,
We learn how to dance.

We are children,
    And we grow.
We're done with dance lessons,
    And we fly on our own wings,
We now dance alone.

We live, we learn,
    And the dance goes on.
We with emotion swirl around.
    And a few take us by the hand,
We help each other dance.

We tire and grow weak,
    And time's left for but one song.
We join with the final partner.
    And start a slow, soft waltz,
We finally dance with death.
Brittany Maynard, Grade 9
Hampton Christian High School, VA

Smile

Don't let that smile fool you,
    inside I feel like crying.

I put on an act for the people around me,
    a whole different, happier side of me.

It gets better every day,
    and soon I'll be almost whole.

But there's always going to be that hole,
    right where you're supposed to be.

My smiles get more real,
    My laughs a little fuller,

You help me,
    even after you're no longer
        with me.

My smile glows bright,
    because someone like you
        put it on my face.
Amanda Reid, Grade 8
St Rocco School, RI

Nightmare's Ceased

The screaming stops, only for a moment
The pain is killing me now
Sunshine makes me sick inside
I want the torment to stop
Do you know what I need?
No, of course you don't
Paper stars wrinkle in the night
Don't forget to tie back the dogs
Chains make the birds suffer
Keyboards shatter on the floor
Things never really seemed okay
Splits show up in their faces
Blood pools up at their feet
We never know what's going on
It's time to run away
Sometimes it's hard to tell the truth
Sometimes nothing is better than it all
Memorize your summary
Throw the sheet down the drain
That's what they taught us to do
Peel away your mask of lies
Jordan Hudgins, Grade 9
Tunstall High School, VA

The Ocean

Hearing the waves crash,
I use my ears immensely,
Hear world around me.
Jake Smith, Grade 7
Linkhorne Middle School, VA

The Chase

They feel something
On their tail,
I must find
Out what it is,
They say.
So they start
Going round and round
Getting the tip of
Their tails every time.
They wonder
If they will ever
Catch it!
So they must
Keep going,
It's a fair chase,
They think,
But the tail
Always wins!
Jamie Teramani, Grade 8
St Joseph School-Fullerton, MD

Ideas

They're floating around.
In our minds,
And in our hearts.
They're the tic toc of the clock.
The clicking of our pens.
It's in our words,
Our laughs,
Our thoughts,
Our actions,
Our smile,
Our sorrow,
And our adventures.
We can't let them float away.
Like a cloud in the sky.
But if they do...
They'll come back...
Oh, One day
Oh, Someday.
Nicole Price, Grade 7
St Joseph School-Fullerton, MD

Show Them What You're Worth

Don't let people put you down
Don't believe what they say!
They don't know what you got
Come on! Let them know you're worth
Your original and cannot be replaced
They don't know what the future holdsfor you
So...show them what your worth!
Jennifer Gonzales, Grade 7
Tasker Middle School, MD

Snake

Whisper in an ear
A sweet voice of deception
I listen to lies
Sifting through sand
Searching for truth
Lost in mistruth
True treason
The fall of an angel
Are you the snake?
Look at yourself
Do you put on the pretty face,
The innocent eyes
Are you
The whisperer,
The deceiver,
The liar,
Or,
The Snake.

Cullen O'Hara, Grade 7
Blue Ridge Middle School, VA

Who Am I

Am I the
Light or the dark
The sweet or the bitter
The liar or the truth
The lion or the lamb
The mountain or the hill
The puddle or the ocean
Am I the
Sky or the land
The bird or the ant
The monster or the hero
The smile or the frown
The happy or the sad
Am I
The giant or the dwarf
The pillow or the cloud
The rain or the lullaby
The girl or the poem

Cassie Gwinn, Grade 8
Chickahominy Middle School, VA

Field Goal

The	Snap
Is	Good
The	Hold
Is	Good
The	Kick

Is
Up
And
It's
GOOD

Kevin Lazo, Grade 7
Benjamin Tasker Middle School, MD

When Life Gives You Lemons

Lemons, like the bright yellow shining sun,
Sour juice escapes from the inner core.
Yellow as can be, lemons bring the fun. Lemons, a brother to limes, never bore.
Its rough skin sliced into halves and quarters,
Seeds spring out, breaking free from the peel guards
Lining up in the fridge, they make borders.
Lemons, sitting in a bath of water,
So sweet and sour like Sour Patch Kids.
Cold Lemonade made from freshly squeezed juice,
Citrusy and bright, enough to get bids.
Lemons on trees swaying, hang very loose.
Great on hot days they live in your tummy,
Lemons, always refreshing and yummy.

Rachel Leibowitz, Grade 7
Kilmer Middle School, VA

Cherish

Cherish the memories of you and I.
Cherish the dreams of reaching for the sky.
Cherish the good and all it's worth.
Cherish the world's God-given birth.
Cherish the beauty that lays on this earth.
Cherish the things that are great.
Cherish the moments before it's too late.
Cherish the dreams to open the gate.
Cherish letting go of all your hate.
Cherish the day that you where born, for life treasures they are sworn.
Cherish all that's dear, for when you need them they are here.
Cherish what holds you near, for you'll need them and the years.
So cherish with your heart and never let it part.

Tinee Henry, Grade 8
H B Dupont Middle School, DE

Basketball

Basketball is my favorite sport of all times.
Some people say I play like Dwight Howard.
Usually when I pick up a basketball it tells me what to do and where to go.
The only people I admire in the NBA are Dwight Howard and Shaquille O'Neal.
Sometimes I keep thinking that I'm playing for a million years.
I was run fast like a cheetah on the court.
I always be dominated in the paint every time.
Playing basketball is being in heaven.
Basketball will always be in my life no matter what.

Ty Tracy, Grade 8
Paul L Dunbar Middle School for Innovation, VA

My Favorite Season

My favorite season is spring.
I like spring because the air feels like a cool air conditioner.
When its spring time, the beautiful weather calls my name over again to come outside.
Spring is the best season ever I wish it was spring every day.
Spring is a warm cover when you outside.
That's why spring is my favorite season.

Courtney Walton, Grade 8
Paul L Dunbar Middle School for Innovation, VA

The Keeper of the Stars

It was September when I first met you. I remember coming out into the world and seeing all those bright stars. Oh, I do.

Isn't it amazing how we can all see the stars? I think of just how beautiful they are.

Black sky above going on forever. Forever. Along with nice early fall weather.

Others say the stars are too far away to be. I say, no. They are right here with you and me.

The stars, too many to count. Bright dots of light. So far away in distance and height,

or so you still think. As they are gone if only in a blink.

All of my favorite memories are those of the stars above.

The stars are those who are watching over us all. They see when we can take it and when we have to crawl.

Of all the things in this world, the stars they stay the same. Maybe that's why I take comfort in them. That I'm not the one to blame.

When you think of me, no matter where you are. I hope you wish upon a star.

And so I thank the keeper of the stars for crossing our paths and joining our hearts.

Kathryn Beddoo, Grade 8
Montross Middle School, VA

Closed Door

The sky becomes dark like a closed door.

I stare out the window and wait.

As the door closes, so does my mind for I am nervous and shaking in place.

I have no idea what will happen beyond that door, as my imagination becomes overwhelmed by fear.

As the noises draw nearer, my heart races and I find my mind is unclear.

I start to hum a relaxing tune, but nothing will work for me now!

I shiver as I open the door, and out jumps my big, gray, cat saying, *Meow*!

Shannon Czapla, Grade 7
St Joseph School-Fullerton, MD

My Favorite Candy

My favorite candy is Reese's.

Its peanut-buttery taste calls my name when I'm standing in front of a vending machine.

While I feed my money into the vending machine, my mouth starts to become a waterfall falling down into happiness.

I could eat a million and one of you if I had enough money.

You fall down quickly and smoothly, leading to a big thump.

Tabitha Lindsay, Grade 8
Paul L Dunbar Middle School for Innovation, VA

Snap Crackle and Pop

When I hear Snap, Crackle, and Pop, it's like a musical beat trying to whisper something to me.

When I put it closer to my ear, they appear to be yelling and shouting.

Sometimes while eating, I can feel the snap, crackle, and pop in my stomach.

After a while in there, the music stops.

Christian Denmark, Grade 8
Chickahominy Middle School, VA

Friends

Friends are people who can make you smile when you're sad. When someone pushes you down, friends help you back up. They encourage you to do whatever you set your mind to. Everyone needs a friend. They are gifts you give to yourself. Friends are the people that you can act crazy around and they will still love you. Friends are people that you can create wonderful memories with. And friends are people who will be there for you, forever and always!

Kara Hibler, Grade 7
Berwyn Christian School, MD

To Whom It May Concern

Dear Socialist federal government leaders,
We can do without you.
We care not whether you're red or blue.
We are tired, and with the people's backing.
We can send you packing.
We want our country back,
We want to fix this crack;
We can grow together,
We can stand in all kinds of weather
We won't succeed if we are divided,
We citizens together must stand united.

The American people
Susannah Martin, Grade 9
Homeschool Plus, VA

Residents of the South Pole

Portly Penguins
Waddling on the ice,
Gliding on your belly,
Huddling for warmth,
Slipping and sliding into icy water.
Your black back and white belly,
The orange on your ears,
All make up your custom tuxedo.
Your sharp, slick beak,
Slender and swift,
Help you hunt for your favorite food,
Fish.

Virginia Pan, Grade 7
Kilmer Middle School, VA

Golf

Sitting and waiting in a bag all day
Waiting for my chance to get out and play
Finally when I see the light
I know it is time to take my flight
Sitting on a slim wooden stick
I hope I do not sail like a brick
Suddenly I am sent up high
Hoping to land in a place that is dry
Rolling close to the edge I stop
Awaiting for the next smooth chop
As I land I make my final spin
Knowing I am in the pin

Daniel Montgomery, Grade 8
Covenant Life School, MD

The Jaguar's Words

"I am the Jaguar;
I creep about in the dark of night.
Run away now,
If you fear my bite."

Christina Martin, Grade 7
Homeschool Plus, VA

Training

I am an athlete in training.
I wonder when I will take the field.
I hear my teammates calling for the ball.
I see the other girls working and pushing to be the best.
I want to be among the top players.
I am an athlete in training.

I pretend that I will be the star.
I believe that someday I will be playing with the most skilled girls in the world.
I touch the pinny as it is thrown to me.

I feel training hard will get me where I want to be.
I worry about my future as a player.
I cry through the pain as I train harder and harder each night.
I am an athlete in training.

I understand that I cannot always be the best.
I say that I will have a future as a starter on the field.
I dream of being on the field as the whistle is blown.
I hope training and working hard can get me where I want to be.
I am an athlete in training.

McKenzie Frederick, Grade 8
Sanford School, DE

Flight

I am like a migrating bird
I wonder if they will like me
I hear them whispering about me
I see it getting harder with every year I move yet;
I want the best for my parents.
I am like a migrating bird.

I pretend that I am the luckiest girl in the world.
I believe the moving will all stop and I will have a place I call my home.
I touch the new air that I am in.

I feel the plane taking off into the sky.
I worry that my friends will forget about me.
I cry when it's winter.
I am like a migrating bird.

I understand that it's life and you have to sacrifice…
I say it's no big deal.
I dream of having just one school.
I hope they understand,
I am like a migrating bird.

Jane Motion, Grade 8
Sanford School, DE

Slavery

Slavery, a slithering snake that slips between the cracks
And breaks somethings true and all things just
Lacking sensibility and sanity bringing shame constantly back.
Come God's people for their sake, so shun this lust for them we must.

Brooke Ford, Grade 9
Hampton Christian High School, VA

Friendship

Friendship is a boat rocking back and forth steadily
Faith and trust surrounding the boat, a wall

A bold barrier from you and the water
It is a soft pillow to safely savor your head down on

The strong boats last forever without a crack in sight
But the weak ones sink deep below the bright blue

Clank clank — but sometimes the boat hits hard
The boat runs into steep rocks in states of anger

And you wonder if there was a reason your rode the boat
But then you realize how safe, strong, and secure the bond is

The boat is your old photo book — it lasts forever
Sailing on and on with precious pleasure and pride

Swish Swish — The roaring river ride of friendship never ends —
Keeping you safe and happy through the whole ride

And whenever you need it the most — it is there
Friendship is a boat rocking back and forth with pride and power

Friendship is there for you
At terrifying torturous times when you need it the most

The nature of the ride makes you proud, tweet tweet
And by the end you realize how pure friendship really is
Asmita Shah, Grade 8
Carson Middle School, VA

Looking Back

I'm looking out a dirty old window,
Looking out at who I used to be,
Running down those paths we call memories,
Unwanted tears slip down my cheeks,
They always did get the best of me,
Now, looking back on them, all the things I've ever done,
And all the battles I fought…I never did win a single one,
I'm still looking out that dirty old window,
Still looking out at who I used to be,
Running past those paths we call memories,
They've never done any good for me,
Through all the battles I've fought and never won,
I've always lived to see the next one,
Now I'm gone from that dirty old window,
Not bothering with who I used to be,
Running down that path we call life,
Into the coming dawn, on to now,
I'm done with the past,
Because through all those battles,
I never stopped looking back,
And now I'm done.
Sandra Webb, Grade 8
Poe Middle School, VA

Laugh!!

While living life be sure to laugh,
It's the best medicine you can take.

For laughing only brings joy to people
And is better than eating chocolate cake.

Never forget this important tip if you do
It will only be bad, for heaven's sake
Laugh! Laugh when you're happy, laugh when you're sad,
Laugh when you're angry and laugh when you're mad.
Doing this will only make you a better person,
And it will also make life more fun.
For laughing all the time
Makes you shine as bright as the sun.
People will want to be around you
And no one you make laugh will want to run.

Being happy starts with laughter and from there it doesn't end bad,
Stay positive and cheerful, because then everyone will be glad!
Jen Hayes, Grade 8
Brandywine Springs School, DE

October 31st

As the full moon soars in the dark night sky,
through the children's costumes they tell a lie,
cautiously wandering along the streets,
going from door to door collecting all sorts of treats,
in the distance a scream is heard,
when animals and crows become absurd,
throughout the children's body is sent a chill,
it's only the beginning of a suspenseful thrill,
up ahead is a dark eerie home,
in the windows gleaming eyes are shown,
stories of terror cause unearthly moans,
creeping up the steps what is found are bones,
it can be such a scary scene,
on a witchy Halloween!

Amanda Mellendick, Grade 8
Sacred Heart School, MD

My Friends

When we get together, we talk it up.
We hang and chill out 'till 3 am!
We dance around and sing at the top of our lungs to the radio
We throw on cool hats, neon tees, and all kinds of colorful jeans.
We play really awesome games.
My friends and I are one wacky scene!

My…
Pals
Friends
Comrades
Companions
Together Forever — My BFF's and Me!
Sara Tolentino, Grade 7
St Joseph School-Fullerton, MD

Winter

The white flakes fall from the sky
They melt as they touch my skin
As quickly as it fell
it's gone
the sky is completely white
as if a huge blanket was keeping the warm out
Frost bites me
as if a cat was nipping
at my fingers
But, deep down, in the bottom of my heart
I like the below freezing temperatures
they bring back memories of the past
the silence winter brings amazes me
Listen…
Nothing is here to distract me
not even a nipping cat
So I watch the flakes fall
until it melts on my skin

Tyra Smith, Grade 8
Sacred Heart School, MD

The Little Black Dog

There is a little black dog
That rules from the front lawn.
When neighbors and dogs set out for their jog,
She fusses and carries on until they've gone.
She prances with pride
And holds herself high.
Always thrilled to go for a ride
In the driver's lap is where she lies.
Her favorite toy consists of a Ping-Pong ball
That we can hear bounce throughout the house,
And up and down the hall.
She is quick and agile like a mouse.
Her black coat is soft and shiny
And she has white slippers on her feet.
Her body is very tiny
About the size of a soccer cleat.
This black dog may be small in size
But has more character than any other.

Luc Mortemousque, Grade 7
Linkhorne Middle School, VA

Soccer Star

Everything is perfect as he strides onto the field.
He has practiced all year to get to this point.
He is the star.
He is the best.
He is finally in his correct jersey.
The number that gives him power.
He is #8.
In his ruggedness he is irresistible.
At kickoff he stands tall and proud, ready to win.
At final whistle he rejoices.

Caroline Stiger, Grade 7
Mary of Nazareth Catholic School, MD

Ode to Dance

I thank you for giving me life
Without you I would have nothing
I would be clumsy and awkward
You gave me life

The way I have the freedom to do anything
I have no boundaries
I can spin, twirl, and jump
I feel weightless

When I see other people dancing
It makes me want to laugh and dance, too
I keep twirling around you over and over again
I will spin around you 36 times
 Until I fall to the ground

But I will still have life
Thank You, DANCE

Merissa Collins, Grade 8
Grace Episcopal Day School, MD

Sister

Sister

Jesus brought us together in this world
So we can be the best of buddies forever
I will catch you when you fall
We have pain sometimes
It's wonderful to have a sister like you
For whom I love the most
We share a lot of things together
We laugh at every argument we have
We act normal to the world
Loving you as my darling, sweet sister
Means a lot to me
I wouldn't trade a dime for you
I won't leave your side if you ask me too
I will always be in your heart

Forever your Sister!!!!!

Alysia Watts, Grade 8
Paul L Dunbar Middle School for Innovation, VA

The Dance

You dance with all your heart
Spinning in circles and circles around the stage,
Sweat beading off your face
Nervously doing glissades, Padas has, and degas hays
Your feet gently touch the ground
As you land your jump,
You move to the next step,
Gracefully spinning
Not having one flaw, and your dance finally ends
As you hear the applause.

Breana Uhl, Grade 8
Bishop Walsh Middle High School, MD

A Snowy Christmas

I awake in the morning to the smell of cocoa.
My eyes open for the first glance
only to see the snow.
I run down the stairs
only to slip on clothes.
I scream to my mom here it goes.
I wake up my sister.
She yells and groans.
I tell her it's Christmas!
She says here it goes.
I wait impatiently at the top of the stairs,
Screaming and yelling,
waiting for the rest of my family to come.
What's under the tree? No telling!
I find the perfect present — a colorful box.
What could it be?
Is it a pair of socks?
Now, Christmas is over.
Where has all the fun gone?
It ran away until next year.

David Beard, Grade 8
Chickahominy Middle School, VA

The Unlucky Jar of Jelly

Once there was a jar of jelly,
He was as smelly as the grocery deli.

The jelly man was sitting there very relaxed,
Then out of the blue he was being attacked.

There was a small kid trying to open his lid,
But maybe that kid should not have done what he did.

The jelly man was bumped, and knocked to the ground,
But now there is jelly all around.

The jelly man was hurt and yelled a scream,
It felt like being hit by a football team.

The jelly man lived a horrible life,
He was always being stabbed, and poked with a knife.

The jelly man probably wanted to die soon,
His expiration date was from last June.

Benjamin Harrison, Grade 8
Brandywine Springs School, DE

Be Safe

My room is my safety zone
I feel safe there
It's not safe on the street
It's better at school
But my room is best
It's good to be safe

Malik McDaniel, Grade 8
Paul L Dunbar Middle School for Innovation, VA

The Winter Day

The winter days come,
With much to bring,
The love and cold,
That will take over the air.
Families will huddle together,
And share the bond of love and fright,
And go through a trial of newfound problems they might.
But the winter days will bring in peace,
That will ride on the wind,
And over the seas.
And the oh so freezing ice,
Will sweep over the land,
Like a blanket on a child.
Light will get dimmer,
But snowflakes will shine bright enough,
For one to see,
Through the foggy path,
That one will walk.
And bring the winter day will careless cold,
That will zoom through the crowds that get together,
Cause the winter day that has come will bring many joys to one...

Ravdeep Mathone, Grade 8
Sandusky Middle School, VA

The Magic Candy Store

I didn't notice it before.
The Candy Store.
At the end of the block it was settled,
tucked into the corner of the street.
I couldn't believe my luck; a place to get some treats!
I ran over to this store,
as fast as my legs could.
The window candy was so enticing...I wondered if I really should.
I looked at the clock,
it was only four past nine.
Mother shouldn't be expecting me, so I'm fine.
I walked into the store, but no one else was in the room.
I stared at the candy, and wondered with all my might,
would it be a crime if I just took one bite?
My stomach started growling, so I grabbed the closest dessert.
And soon I grabbed another, oh, what a pleasure they were to eat!
After some time, my stomach was satisfied with treats.
Knowing well mother's rules,
I checked the clock and could not believe the time.
It was only four past nine.

Sarah Phillips, Grade 7
Linkhorne Middle School, VA

Candy Bar

You are the candy bar, I'm the vending machine.
I can eat you a million times a day.
You are smooth like my skin.
You winked at me today.
I love you so much I would buy you every day.

Tyler Childress, Grade 8
Paul L Dunbar Middle School for Innovation, VA

While Mom Sleeps

It's ten o'clock and time for bed.
I go upstairs and lay down my head.
My light is off and my TV volume is low.
I'm pretending not to watch my favorite show.
   By ten fifteen, my mom is asleep.
   And that my friend is when I creep.
   I go downstairs with Mudge my dog.
   While mom and sis sleep like logs.
The flat screen goes on and my Xbox lights up.
I open the Raspberry Ice Tea and fill up my cup.
I put on my headphones and insert my game.
I hope the free-for-alls tonight are not lame!
   For hours on-line with my friends I play.
   Who cares about tomorrow, I am happy today.
   Just before dawn I fall asleep.
   Tired and exhausted I don't say a peep.
Morning comes and it is time for school.
Mom wakes me up and that's not cool.
Into the shower and into my clothes
Off to school and nobody ever knows.

Jordan Navarro, Grade 9
Delaware Military Academy, DE

Nature's Boundary

The river whispers past the cold, hard rocks
Bending towards the sapphire waterfall.
Snakelike and slithering, the river talks
Carrying boats along at a slow crawl.
Slug, beaver, and dragonfly hug its bank,
Safe from the intimidating brown bear
Feeding on small fish with eyes staring blank
Under the fresh water's icy cold glare.
The wise, old river, swimming in beauty,
Tumbling over fast-moving, rapids fierce.
The swirling water can be quite moody,
Going from flowers to sharp pointed spears.
   The river is a puzzling mystery,
   Nature's most reliable boundary.

Kat Hanna, Grade 7
Kilmer Middle School, VA

A Dream Fulfilled

What happens to a dream fulfilled?
Does it shine lightly
Like the reflection of glass?
Or flow like the shiny river and the dirty brass?
Does it dance like the rain falling from the sky?
Or soothe softly
Like a butterfly fluttering by?

Maybe it soars near the mountain
Like the snow in the wind?

Or does it just move in circles?

Karen Poston, Grade 7
Marshall Middle School, VA

Coldness' Embrace

As I walk outside I feel coldness' embrace,
I feel it on my very face.
My gloves I put on one at a time,
So focused I didn't even care to rhyme.
When I turn my back and a cold ball hits the ground,
And in curiosity, I turn around.
Then I realize that it was my brother,
After all, there is no other.
I threw one back and he threw one again,
Then I knew a snowball fight was about to begin.
Few minutes later, I missed my show,
And at that moment I had to go.

I sit down with my nice hot chocolate,
I figured out that I was not too late.
Soon, my dad turned the heater on,
And in relaxation, I started to yawn.
I no longer feel the coldness' embrace,
The feeling or sensation had left my face.
I could now feel nothing but warmth on my face,
So I guess my next poem is "Warmth and its Embrace."

James Moore, Grade 8
Tasker Middle School, MD

The Chains of Love

I don't understand this feeling in my mind.
How can I have a crush on someone so unkind?
You say that you hate me for no reason at all,
You say that you won't date me because I have many flaws.
You walk around like you don't have a care in the world.
You don't know you are hurting this girl.
ME! You know the one you hate?
The one you won't date because it would be a mistake.
Well I've got news for you bud,
I don't want to live this way.
I don't want to have my heart broken every single day.
I'm done with you.
I am starting new.
I'm going to be happy with the far from perfect me.
I am finally free!

Jade Grubbs, Grade 8
Oklahoma Road Middle School, MD

Never Thought

I never thought I'd be the one to get hurt this bad,
I never thought I could actually feel my heart break in half,
I never thought all of this pain could come from you,
I didn't know you never meant it when you said you love me too,
Can you hold my hand and tell me why you chose to hurt me?
Can you put your hand on my chest and notice there's no heartbeat?
Can you look me in the eyes and feel the same pain I do?
Can you feel my anger and sadness amongst you?
I guess sometimes people just aren't meant to stay,
Cause I never would have thought your love would slip away.

Briyana Nelson, Grade 8
Tasker Middle School, MD

One Day After Another

There once was a time
Full of death and despair
Full of such utter sorrow
The damage beyond repair

Jews and gypsies were stolen
Like a thief in the night
They were gone
To the place of pain and death
Where joy was out of sight

Every day was a struggle for life
Often, they would be burned to ashes
Not unlike their dreams, hopes and wishes
Putting one day after another
Adding them up to get a number
Seeing how many days they could live
That was the Devil's Arithmetic

Elizabeth Bose, Grade 8
Norfolk Christian Middle School, VA

The Love of Basketball

I love basketball because,
It seems like I'm one away from
A phone call, I play basketball
Because I'm real tall,
I look up to a player
And his name is John Wall,
In basketball you get a,
A chance to make people fall,
And when I'm in the NBA
I'm going to live at the mall,
It's different from most sports
Because it's a Spalding ball,
I chase my dreams,
Despite how many are
On the team, every time I
Step on the court I feel clean,
Off the court we can be friends,
On the court I'm real mean.

Zuri Smith, Grade 8
Sacred Heart School, MD

Cream of Glory

The soothing power of ice cream.
All my thoughts
are swallowed up by the creamy taste.
Hot days become swirling blizzards.
Stress is released from its prison,
as I float gracefully on a cloud of freedom.
Another bite,
another gulp of happiness.
My worries are gone,
and so is my pain.

Jared Schoeny, Grade 7
Blue Ridge Middle School, VA

Chance Encounter

It is quite possible, in the grand scheme of things,
To be forgotten.
To lose yourself in the business of the world,
In the noise that we forget to hear and the whirl of colors we don't see.
Quite possible to forget yourself in the competition.

This is the world now, save for a few select places.
To me the woods are a healing place.
Far removed from the whispers of hurry up, and be the best
That I hear all day long.

Mother Nature forgets no one; she opens her arms to me,
Sweeps away my storms and clouds with a gentle breeze.
To her, everything is important,
Everything is needed.

I don't know how long I stay there,
Joining my inconsequential melody to the everlasting song.
She appears, a flash of brown amid
The swirl of reds and oranges and yellows
She and her fawns gaze at me, all of us frozen in time,
Scared, frozen, and yet peaceful.
We stay there forever for us, but moments in the scheme of things.
Until the world catches up and we both need to go.

Sarah Nakasone, Grade 8
Monsignor Slade Catholic School, MD

Final Moments

Midnight.
She sits up with a start, chest heaving.
He jerks awake, in the chair beside the bed.
Lights softly blinked, machines hummed.
She remembered where she was, and it hurt.

One a.m.
She slept once more, the strained breathing cutting through the dark.
He relived the past.
Easy living, difficult times, moments, years.
She had stayed strong, he, felt weak.
His mind drifted to more recent memories, the night she collapsed.

Two a.m.
Her breathing became more labored.
His eyelids drooped, his head sank.
Yet he must stay awake,
For it would not be long now, soon he would need to be strong.

Three a.m.
She was awake, and fading fast.
Hands reached for each other, found final security.
As she took her last breath, he cried his first tear.
Together. Alone.

Sarah Larson, Grade 8
Chickahominy Middle School, VA

The Performance

She brings up her left arm with the volleyball in hand,
like a lieutenant leading her troops into battle.
She steadies the ball, then tosses it up with a quick flick of her wrist.

"Awww," the crowd sighs.
The toss isn't high enough.
Never losing her cool, she catches it lightly in her palm,
then quickly flashes a confident smile at the crowd.

She determinedly looks at the ball,
and one more time, tosses it up in the air.

As she tosses, her right arm comes up above her head.
It seems, for a brief second,
that her arm wonders where to go.

Then it straightens up,
and smashes into the volleyball with a firm "smack!"

The crowd is on the edge of their seats,
they're holding their breath, and then, "WHAM!"
The ball slams into the ground on the other side of the court.

The crowd goes wild.
With a casual wave, she exits the court.
She is a performer,
giving her curtain call to the music of the audience's cheers.

Alison Luckett, Grade 7
Kilmer Middle School, VA

Life

Some people say life sucks
Others say that life is the best
Well I say life is a question, now I just ask:
Why is it hard to find the good qualities in yourself?
Why is it easy to find the bad qualities in yourself?

Why is it easy to find good qualities in other people?
Why is it easy to find the bad qualities in each other?
Why do we insult one another?
Why can't we just live with it, when we get hurt?
Why is it hard to forgive and forget?

Why do we love?
Why do we say no?
Should love be a question too?
Why is love so hard to understand?
What is the real meaning of hate?

Why is it hard to find the reasons why we are here?
Why are people good?
Why are people bad?
Now I have only one more question for you
Life?

Khadijah Wilson, Grade 7
Benjamin Tasker Middle School, MD

The Olympics

Every four years, people wait anxiously for
these special games,
Where countries compete to earn medals like
gold, silver, and bronze
Australia, Canada, Korea, Japan, Mexico, Jamaica,
China, US, and many more wait for their turns
to win.
Where will these special games be held next?
From winter to summer, so many sports,
Winter's short track, luge, ice-skating,
to snowboarding and skiing.
Then summer's track and field, volleyball, marathon,
to gymnastics and swimming.
Many athletes practicing and waiting to shine,
When it's their turn to perform,
Waiting for the torch to be lit,
Waiting for the flag to go up,
Waiting to see that special symbol of these games,
Waiting for their country to cheer them on,
And especially waiting to take their part in the
Olympics.

Bhakti Panchal, Grade 7
St Joseph School-Fullerton, MD

My Broken Heart

It wasn't that long ago that I was shattered
My heart deciding it had been broken too many times
I got tired of the hurt and pain
Tired of seeing your face each day
Every day I want to cry
Until the blood runs from my eyes
Until I disappear into the darkness
It wasn't that long ago that I loved you
Used to love everything about you
The way you looked, your appearance, everything
Now I can't stand the sight of you
Rage and hurt build up inside of me
Nightmares still plague me at night
I still have the unwanted memories
It wasn't that long ago that I left you

Mersadez Sewell, Grade 7
Grace E Metz Middle School, VA

Lost Memories

I stood and watched my home go into flames
My tears suddenly begin to fall
My memories started to fade
No home to come to at night
No place to stay
Nobody cared so I began to pray
Falling to my knees helped ease the pain
Asking God "Why me?" didn't change a thing
I still had no home
"Why me?" I continued to say

Mikkia Jefferson, Grade 8
Paul L Dunbar Middle School for Innovation, VA

Macin

I am a concerned sister.
I wonder what his future will hold.
I hear my brother's laughter.
I see him getting older.
I want the best for him.
I am excited for the future.

I pretend that I don't care, but I do.
I believe he is a strong person.
I touch his soft head and pray no one will ever hurt him.

I feel that everything will be okay.
I worry how people will treat him.
I cry knowing that he is so innocent.
I am fearful.

I understand that one day he will grow up.
I say to my mother that I will always take care of him.
I dream that his future will be bright.
I hope that he learns not to be hurt by people's harsh comments.
I am his sister.

Mackenzie Gaul, Grade 8
Sanford School, DE

Protector of the Earth

I am a believer
I wonder how I can change the world
I hear a plastic bottle being crushed
I see the man throw it unto the road
I wish he would have recycled the bottle
I am a protector

I pretend I can change everything
I believe the world is dying from pollution
I touch a newspaper with the headline "Global Warming"

I feel defenseless and anxious
I worry what will happen to our resources
I cry out help to every person I see, to "Do Your Part!"
I am aiming for success

I understand that saving the Earth is not easy
I say "GO GREEN" to my peers
I dream of a world beautiful and clean
I hope to see the world in a new way
I am saving the planet

Kelsey Mendell, Grade 8
Sanford School, DE

House

Here I sit every day,
Watching the children play,
Seeing family and friends chat,
Feeling the rubbing against the wall of the cat.
Hearing the thunder crash,
Feeling the heat lash,
Getting a scrape or two,
Along with some splattered paint too.
Hearing the hurt shouts and screams,
Wishing it was only a dream,
Heaving with the sadness of a death,
Springing alive with a new child's birth.
Content with my life,
Through the joy, happiness, the pain and strife,
I'm glad to be me:
The house.

Hannah J. Shearer, Grade 8
Homeschool Plus, VA

Who Is That? What Is That? Why Is It Here?

I stand. I wait with my cat like ears,
just listening to the moaning wind.
My cat like tail swishes back and forth
with the wild wind.
Then with great confusion on my face,
I ask myself…
Who is that? What is that? Why is it here?

I move constantly forward
on the damp, cold sidewalk.
Tip-toe. Tip-toe.
Then I disappear into the night,
and I ask myself again…
Who is that? What is that? Why is it here?

These are the questions I ask myself on dark, damp nights.

Jordan Marsh, Grade 8
Chickahominy Middle School, VA

Lighthouse

The sun sets
The light from the top of the lighthouse barely seen
Guiding in the last boats for the night
The water splashing at the house
The boats sailing in the wind
Kids playing on the shoreline
As the sun shines a warm summer breeze comes about
The light house watches all
Waiting for the night to come to shine its light again

David Tindall, Grade 9
Delaware Military Academy, DE

Watch me

I don't feel safe anywhere
I feel like people is watching me
When I take out the trash people watch
When I'm at school people watch me
When I'm at the store people watch me
People watch me
They watch me
People watch me everywhere
I am not safe from their eyes

Montez Smith, Grade 8
Paul L Dunbar Middle School for Innovation, VA

When I Fall Asleep
When I fall asleep
Into my own world I do creep
No limitations do I keep
When I fall asleep.

I can fly up in the sky
Like a bird just flying by
Or dive into the waters deep
When I fall asleep.

I can travel to the moon
Or be like a crazy baboon
And all the little birds cheep
When I fall asleep.

But when I wake
None of my world do I take
In my world I disintegrate
When I wake.
Casey Morris, Grade 8
Brandywine Springs School, DE

It's That Time Again
I gaze at the glistening white earth
and see the perfection
of all the freshly fallen snow
laying on the still grass.

I stare into my new friend's
vibrant eyes
and realize his is more
than just a lonely creation.

I hear the steady ring of bells
and peer down the street
to see the man
dressed in red.

He is clad in the color
the exact color
of all things
warm and fuzzy.
Adam Lowe, Grade 7
Wicomico Middle School, MD

Never Try, Never Fail
People say, if you don't try,
You won't fail.
But it's like building a ship,
So it will never sail.
Like writing a letter,
That you will never mail.
But by never trying, you can't succeed,
And that is to no avail.
Brittainy Sechler, Grade 7
West Frederick Middle School, MD

I Am a Student
I am a student.
I wonder how many students there are in my class.
I hear pencils and pens, repeatedly touching down on the paper.
I see my teacher standing before the class.
I want to ace the test.
I am a student.

I pretend to understand what the teacher is saying.
I believe I can get this; I just need more practice.
I touch the pencil with my sweating hand, gripping it tightly.

I feel lost.
I worry that I will not do well on the upcoming test.
I cry to myself silently, and without tears.
I am a student.

I understand the material, but I keep getting distracted.
I say, "I know the answer," as I raise my hand.
I dream, and bring the answer out of that cloud in the back of my mind.
I hope that I will get this answer correct.
I am a student.
Claire, Grade 8
Sanford School, DE

Gone
I always wondered what would happen if you weren't here…
I always imagined what it would be like…
It scared me every time I thought about it.
I stopped thinking about my life without you.
You were always happy and alive.
I decided I would stop thinking about the future and live in the present.
That was a mistake…
It hurt so much when I heard what happened and when I saw you in the hospital;
Seeing you there motionless terrified me.
I knew what was coming;
I just didn't want to accept it.
Before I knew it…
You were gone.
Dejubeh Meynard, Grade 9
Gaithersburg High School, MD

Getting Ready for School
My alarm goes off at 6:18 beep beep beep
I hop up hurrying to turn it off
I grab my clothes and tip toe through the hall like a scary ghost
Hoping not to wake a soul
I turn on the shower ready to hop in

I get dress it's 6:59 the clock screaming only 31 mins to spare
I look outside hoping not to see my friend coming down the street
No one's there but the whisper of the wind
I hurry to put all my stuff in bag and doing my hair
I then look outside and see her walking faster then she has ever before
I grab my stuff and jump to the door and on time again
Zamika Bradley, Grade 8
Lafayette Winona Middle School, VA

The Inspiration of Brothers

Brothers are a pain, brothers are obnoxious, brothers are annoying, brothers are over protected, brothers are nosey and never mind their business, brothers are always there for you when you need them, my brothers are all of these things but more. Sometimes it feels as if your brothers either disappoint you, make bad mistakes, or lecture you to the point were you feel as if they would ever shut up and go read a book or something. Growing up all I had surrounding me was my brothers. I look right there they are, I look left there they are, I look up I look down there they are. Even when they grew up and got their own families. For some reason still there they are. When I think about my future, my past, and present I see my brothers. Sometimes I think about the old time saying you can't live with them and you can't live without them. Without my brothers I would be lost and misunderstood. When I watch them make the most terrible mistakes in their life, I love them even more and thank them for making that mistake, because that mistake they made, helps me grow by understanding my brothers did this. So I'm going to do the opposite to achieve. When I watch and see that they always do good deeds and become successful when they put their mind to it, that makes me want to do double than what they did. And live to be as successful as them. I watch, learn, and grow by everything my brothers do. They don't realize that their baby sister is watching them, so they need to be the best they can be so she can live up to those standards. But if my brothers were perfect and never made mistakes, then I wouldn't be able to learn from those mistakes they made to know, ohhh my brothers already did this so why would I put myself in this position, when I know it will lead me to nothing but trouble. Although my brothers tend to be a pain, a bit over protected, super obnoxious, talk too much and always give me lectures, nosey and be all up in my business, I thank them for that because they make me the successful person I will be when I grow up.

Michelle Wilson, Grade 9
William Penn High School, DE

Feelings

Everyone has feelings.
Some are old, some might not have even been discovered yet.
Some decide to hide them while others let them show.
Boys often shove and hide them in a corner.
If you come across their feelings, their guards often yell and scold.
This only makes the ones in the corner feel more alone.
Girls, boys would say, are just an emotional mess.
Are we really? If we let them out, then we don't have a hiding corner of cluttered
feelings with old guards who are cranky and mean.
The only way to free them is by a mother's love.
A woman wise and nurturing will get rid of the guards and throw them away and show her son the way.
Then the true colors show through the constant beating.
What is this beating?
Surely it is not the son.
The beating of a new heart, one strong, one young.

Zoe Walters, Grade 7
Tasker Middle School, MD

The Game

What is the general purpose of playing the game of life?
There may be none, or there may be many.
Life is a game and everyone loses.
Say what you will, everyone eventually dies.
The real idea behind the game isn't how it's played.
It's in what goes on, while you play.
You didn't ask to be born, that I realize, but some people do ask to die.
That's not how you play.
When you only look at the game, and not the things happening within and around it, things change.
You can no longer see the differences between happiness and sadness.
The game has blinded you from the things that matter.
The once defined black lines have become faint and smudged.
The solution is to draw new ones.
You aren't yourself in what you say or do, but it's the combination of the two that defines yourself.

Alyssa Barnett, Grade 9
Norfolk Collegiate School, VA

A Dream Fulfilled

What happens to a dream fulfilled?
Does it shine brightly?
Like the yellow moon?
Or flow like a calm river —
And words in a conversation?
Does it dance like a little girl?
Or soothe a sore throat —
Like a cold strawberry smoothie?

Maybe it soars gently through the sky
Like the soft wind.

Or does it hurt?

Leslie Cabral, Grade 7
Marshall Middle School, VA

A Dream Fulfilled

What happens to a dream fulfilled?
Does it shine
Like a flashlight?
Or flow like a kite —
And soar out of sight?
Does it dance like a tree in the wind?
Or soothe my dream —
Like a fish in the sea?

Maybe it's in the night —
Like a Halloween fright.

Or does it fade in the epic state of mind?

Scott Arrington, Grade 7
Marshall Middle School, VA

Me

When I'm hurt or feeling sad,
when I'm happy or when I'm mad,
there is something that I do,
every time I'm bright or blue.
When I'm excited, it is extra loud,
yes, it's true, even when I'm proud,
confused or stuck in a mess,
or something I must confess.
Helps me through a difficult time,
most of them even rhyme,
this is something that I love,
when I'm feeling all the above.
I sing!

Vanessa DelGizzo, Grade 8
St Augustine School, RI

Fall

Wind blows cool air in.
Blowing leaves from all the trees.
To rake and play in.

Nicholas Jacobus, Grade 7
Marshall Middle School, VA

Dancer

I am a dancer.
I wonder if the judges will appreciate me and my work.
I hear the numbers one through eight repeating over and over in my head.
I see the contented looks on the audience's faces.
I want to succeed.
I am a performer.

I pretend I'm the only one in the room.
I believe I can do what I set my mind to.
I hit all of my moves strongly.
I am a dancer.

I feel my partner lift me off the ground
I worry that I might fall out of his arms.
I cry because I know my team has a great chance of winning.
I am proud.

I understand if I don't get a gold medal, but I know I'm still a winner.
I say to my team, "We won, we won!" as I hear the judges.
I dream of never letting the feeling go.
I hope that this feeling of accomplishment comes again in my near future.
I am proud. I am a performer. I am a dancer.

Katie Moloney, Grade 8
Sanford School, DE

The Ways of the Wasps

I hear them buzz,
They want to go somewhere,
They fly around with all the power
They control the giant honey mine they call home.
They whisper me secrets, so softly but calm.
I feel they are my friends,
My friends who solemnly conquer this world.
I am their queen, my wings so clean
I may not be one of them, but they work for me.
They work for all of us.
They spend all their lives making sweet honey that please our tastes.
It is a swell part to the human race.
No one knows where they go in the night.
They must overcome the speed of light.
They make us whole.

Rachel Satterfield, Grade 8
Capitol Hill Day School, DC

Smiling

Smiling, the boy with AIDS plays with his bright, new balloon.
Smiling, the family with so little welcomes the tired, dirty visitors.
Smiling, the little girl who has lost her father and mother plays with a battered, patched ball.
Smiling, the hard working mother who has nothing to feed her children says, "Thank you"
for a small bag of shriveled red beans.
Frowning, the man with more money than he knows what to do with wants more.
Frowning, the child with everything he ever asked for complains about what he doesn't have.
Frowning, the man who is famous decides that life isn't good enough.
Frowning, the family with more than enough food says, "More."

Peter White, Grade 9
Barrington Christian Academy, RI

Autumn

An autumn day
Colored by the vibrant shades
Of blazing yellows, oranges, and reds.
The leaves fly

Through the air
Like kites in the whistling wind.

You realize how beautiful God's creation really is.
The temperature grows colder
And the days become shorter.

The trees are bare,
And I yearn for the spring.

The autumn will lead to winter,
And the winter will lead to spring,
But, for now, I'll enjoy the fall
Because it's all God's plan.

Olivia Kaiss, Grade 8
St Joseph School-Fullerton, MD

I Like You Just the Way You Are

You don't need to change I like you just the way you are
especially through my troubled times
I know I have you to call.

You don't need to change I like you just the way you are
when I'm lost on my own path
you act as my shining North Star.

You don't need to change I like you just the way you are
Like when we're doing our duets,
singing love songs in the car.

You don't need to change I like you just the way you are
when you need some time away
I know you'll not be far.

You don't need to change I like you just the way you are
It comforts me to know you let me in your heart
and for that, I like you just the way you are…

Victoria Dowling, Grade 9
Delaware Military Academy, DE

Friends Forever

When you are looking down, turn that frown upside down
There's someone who will put together all your broken parts
She definitely has a big, fat heart
This friend is true, dignified, and satisfied with you
She'll be there if you're going through hard times
And be your ringing chime to remind you
You have a true friend

Julia Pitts, Grade 7
St. Jane De Chantal School, MD

Christmas Eve

A lways exciting
B aking cookies
C hristmas caroling
D ark outside
E verybody's happy
F un-filled night
G uessing what you're going to get
H appiness
I love Christmas Eve
J oyful
K in gathered together
L oving one another
M any gifts around the Christmas tree
N ever a sad moment…for me
O pen one present…but I never do
P eople dancing and singing
Q uiet as a mouse when everyone is sleeping
R ipping presents open the next day
S anta Claus stories
T iptoeing to the presents when nobody's watching

Jade Cooper, Grade 8
Lafayette Winona Middle School, VA

Good Morning

5 am says the alarm, but it still looks like night.
It's one of those days where 10 more minutes would be all right.
Crayons, pencils, and paper which I just bought.
Were all over my room in huge distraught.
I run to the bathroom quick as a flash,
And hit the floor with a huge crash.
Shampoo, lather, rinse and repeat.
Don't forget to wash your feet!
Clothes, clothes, so many to wear,
First I'll just go do my hair.
I grab a cute purple shirt,
To match with my brand new skirt.
What to eat? So many things.
Mommy offers me lemon meringue.
"No thanks," I say with a smile.
I grab some cereal, I have a while.
I grab my bag,
And my gym uniform that looks like rags.
Beep beep the bus is near.
Time for school with the bullies I fear.

Chasante Jones, Grade 8
Lafayette Winona Middle School, VA

Color

Rosie red is colorful like the dawn of spring blooming slowly.
Red gives excitement and makes a lot of people smile.
Red reminds the kindness and respect for others.
Red is a lovely color for something to use on Valentine's Day.
Red is for a new day to come.

Justin Williams, Grade 8
Lafayette Winona Middle School, VA

Super Hero

I'm starting to miss you
Even if it hasn't been awhile
I'll try to talk to you
Even if I have to go the extra mile

When you talk to me
I can do nothing but smile
What I'm trying to say is that I'm falling for you
With each and every single thing you do

Always and forever
Our memories will stay
Even if
You're miles away

No matter what happens
Or who denies
You will always be
A Super Hero in my eyes <3

Megan Kramer, Grade 8
St John Catholic School, MD

I Hate Writing Poems

I hate writing poems
They really are a pain
I'd rather do more fun things
Like get run over by a train

I'd rather be outside
With the leaves dancing through the air
Twirling and leaping like ballerinas of the sky
All getting tangled in my hair

The crisp cool air
The rustle of the leaves
Spinning like a tornado
Dancing in the breeze

This poem is going to be hard
And very tricky too
I'd hate to have to write more than one
I'd die if I had to write more than two

Addie Hayes, Grade 7
Kilmer Middle School, VA

Contrast

Brown spectral figments glide from place to place.
Gray sunless clouds a pitch-black fishbowl make.
Wind scattered red and brown leaves fill the air
Ghosts red and tan go storming through the night.
Browns, yellows, reds collide with each fall day.
The daylight comes and I feel safe again.
Night comes and I feel scared, but don't know why.
Light changes from white life into black death
The reds, golds, browns, and greens just fade away.
The gold ball turns, restoring all those hues.
So many questions, no mean thoughts but one:
Are day or night and changes all worthwhile?
The answer's yes, so I will tell you why:
That one gold light can cancel all black death.

Kahlil Epps, Grade 9
St Johns College High School, DC

Half and Half

Every day I walk around
Smiling, laughing like everything's fine
No one knows how much I frown
Even though I have a good heart
Doesn't mean that darkness doesn't squirm
Angry, tired I want to speak my mind
Scared of what those might do who know the truth
It pushes, it pulls
I'm no fool
It might consume me heart and soul
Even when I grow old
I know that only I control
My mind, heart, and soul
Not the other half, but the good half will overrule.

Taniyah Martin, Grade 8
Paul L Dunbar Middle School for Innovation, VA

Tears

I shed the tears one by one and it's all because of you.
Look at me; Do you see what you do?
You've ripped my heart out and showed me what it's like to die.
The only thing I can ask myself is why?
Why do you do these things to make me feel so much pain?
You always make me feel like I'm going insane.
You used to be my everything and all I talked about,
Now you're just that one thing I'm always going to doubt.
You were a waste of my time,
Just this immature guy.
I'm done with you and I'm done with the tears.
I remember when losing you was one of my worst fears,
But now you're out of my life and my happiness is here.

Shelby Charette, Grade 8
Chickahominy Middle School, VA

Different Is the Same

Different is the same!
These days you got to talk the same
You got to dress the same
You got to look the same
You got to smell the same
If you don't people won't treat you the same
You got to be the SAME
But what if I don't want to be the same
What if I want to be different
That's what people hate
Because they know that if one person is different
Everyone wants to be different and then
Different is the same

Bethel Babayemi, Grade 7
Benjamin Tasker Middle School, MD

A Dream Fulfilled

What happens to a dream fulfilled?
Does it shine
Like a shooting star?
Or flow like a leaf in a stream —
And go far?
Does it dance like the fish in the sea?
Or soothe you throughout —
Like warm tea?

Maybe it soars swiftly
Like the breeze.

Or does it sit in trees?

Josie Brown, Grade 7
Marshall Middle School, VA

A Dream Fulfilled

What happens to a dream fulfilled?
Does it shine
Like the burning sun?
Or flow like a rushing river —
And crash down like waves?
Does it dance like a ballerina?
Or soothe the pain —
Like a warm day in the winter?

Maybe it soars to and fro
like a migrating bird.

Or does it just fall?

Derek Santee, Grade 7
Marshall Middle School, VA

Rock Wall

Looming above me
Fifty feet of rock and wood
Stretching to the sky
So intimidating
So, so big
Harnessed up I climb
Placing a foot on each rock
The whole way up
Finally, the top
Look around, enjoy the view
Feel like a flightless bird
Finally, touching the sky
Never wanting to go back to Earth.

Emily Young, Grade 7
St Jane De Chantal School, MD

Fall

Red leaves on a tree
Piling on the ground quickly
Swish, the pile is gone

Preston Helmick, Grade 7
Marshall Middle School, VA

The Performance

I wonder what waits for me beyond the curtain
I hear the crowd, anxious, as they take their seats
I want to get it over with
I am nervous

I pretend I am the only one in the room, alone, and ignore the cheers
I believe all the grueling hours of practicing will pay off
I touch my instrument, ready, willing, and able to put on a show

I feel better, but the performance is now at hand
I worry that everything will go wrong
I cry on the inside with anxiety, yet I must take the stage
I AM ready

I understand the troubles ahead of me, the bumps and the hills, that can get in my way
I say I can do this; so therefore, I will
I dream of a flawless performance
I hope for the best
I am a musician

Chase Rapine, Grade 8
Sanford School, DE

Must Wait

I wake up sun shining
I eat my pancakes, nice and warm
Leave the house and my minutes are numbered.
Slavery will come any minute.
Wacky and tacky swearing kids stomp on the bus.
I hear my
Mobile prison arrive.
At school I walk to my jail cell
The white walls cave in and mock me.
"You will never leave never, never, never, never, never, never, never"
Trapped in a frozen waste land they call school.
My brain spinning tired as a sloth.
School is out.
I race to the door
The school laughs knowing I will be back tomorrow
My bus starts moving toward freedom.
At last
Free from school.

James Pruitt, Grade 7
Blue Ridge Middle School, VA

Six Flags

My favorite amusement park is Six Flags
There are so many scary roller coasters that roar at you
The fake Eiffel Tower is so taller that it looks like a pole way in the sky
The rides at Six Flags are a nightmare of doomsday
Six Flags is larger than the whole state of Rhode Island
I like the way the amusement park plays music when you're walking through it
The sound of the rides getting started is loud
I also like the water park and all the water rides there
That's why Six Flags is my favorite amusement park

Jamik Alexander, Grade 8
Paul L Dunbar Middle School for Innovation, VA

Champion

I am a champion
I wonder what my next accomplishment will be
I hear the fans chanting my name
I see the bright lights shining on me
I want the fame and fortune
I am a champion

I pretend that it's me against everyone
I believe that I can prevail
I touch the sky

I feel my body tense up
I worry about the outcome
I cry about the good things in life
I am a champion

I understand my skills will fade
I say to myself they won't
I dream that I will be the best
I am a champion

Matthew Lupton, Grade 8
Sanford School, DE

Just a Sunrise...

Slowly rising from the ground
All is silent, not a sound
The first ray of light appears
Striking through the sky like spears
So many colors vibrant and bright
Finally the end of night
Light's now leaking through the sky
The breeze blowing slowly by
The gentle warmth from the light
The brightness electrifying the sight
The smell of morning sweet and faint
Giving off a calmness you cannot taint
Beautiful enough to hypnotize
All of this from just a sunrise

Meagan Kenney, Grade 8
Paul L Dunbar Middle School for Innovation, VA

A Dream Fulfilled

What happens to a dream fulfilled?
Does it shine brightly
Like a star in the night sky?
Or flow like a river on a rainy day and wash everything away?
Does it dance like dancing with the stars?
Or soothe sailing on the ocean blue
Like reading a book by Dr. Who?

Maybe it soars in the night sky
Like the wind blows and we say good-bye

Or does it stay and then go away?

Haley Clegg, Grade 7
Marshall Middle School, VA

Money, Money, Money

Money, money, money
Brighter than sunshine, sweeter than honey.
One had money, the other had none.
The one with the money had all the fun.

Money, money, money
Everyone wants it, only a little bit,
Money is good like banana split
I make so much money it's not even funny.

Money, money, money
You have to keep a lot of cash,
So keep it in a stash
Or it will fly by in a flash.

Money, money, money
What I like is money, more than honey, more than fun
Money, money
Money for everyone!

Deja Thompson, Grade 8
Brandywine Springs School, DE

I Took a Walk One Day

I took a walk one day
kicking the ground as I trudged,
I watched the chipmunks play.
I saw a store whose sign was smudged,
and on it sat a bird.
It looked at me and cocked its head,
and never said a word.
The trees were colored red and brown
and rustled in the wind.
The sun barely showed its face, as I turned around the bend.
A wet and glossy raindrop fell gently on my nose,
the water tumbled off a roof and fell upon a rose.
I enjoyed my stroll that day, more than any other before.
I had taken time to notice things, and realize...nature I adore.

Megan Perkins, Grade 9
Home School, VA

Fishing at Smith Pointe with My Dad

When I fish at Smith Pointe,
there is always plenty to catch.
On the end of my line you may find
a fat flounder or tasty trout.
My dad and I spend the weekend camping and fishing,
just Dad and me.

Fishing at Smith Pointe is always a good time.
Out in the middle of the bay, we fish the day away,
just Dad and me.

It is a special day and a special time to remember,
just Dad and me.

Sam Schrier, Grade 8
Chickahominy Middle School, VA

The Blank Page

It lies there and looks at me.
If it had eyes it would be glaring at me…
…waiting to see if I would write.
If it had a mouth it would be yelling at me…
…waiting for me to write upon its blankness.
If it had ears it would be listening to my thoughts…
…waiting to see if I've figured out the topic.
But,
other than that, the page is silent.
I can hear other pencils scratching on the paper,
letting their ideas pour out of their minds.
The crinkle of paper as people hand it in.
But, my paper is blank, a blank paper.
Writers block is definitely not fun…
…until the paper shuts its eyes, closes its mouth,
and stops intruding on my thoughts…
…and I can write.
My pencil then joins the other scratching pencils…
…I guess the blank page isn't so blank anymore.

Taylor Scott, Grade 8
Sacred Heart School, MD

Homework Disaster

Homework! Oh, what could possibly be worse!
It feels like ants are crawling in my skull!
This sonnet strikes me though it were a curse,
Causing me pain and agony not dull.

Flames dancing, children playing merrily,
Their homework done, nothing distracts them now.
They enjoy their freedom so verily.
They snack and digest their sumptuous chow.

I wish I could be as smart as they are,
Finishing the sonnet before it's due.
I guess I just have to work hard and far,
To be super cool, on time, and smart too.

Oh look! My sonnet is awesomely fun,
And what do you know? It's finally done!

Kathryn Molnar, Grade 7
Kilmer Middle School, VA

Writer's Block

Writer's block, writer's block, why must it be
Staring at a blank piece of paper in front of me
I look outside to see what will come to me
A tree, a bird, and a tumbleweed?
Nothing, nothing, nothing at all
Just looking outside seeing the leaves fall
Nothing will come to me,
Until I think of life and family,
You see
And now I start to fill this paper in front of me

Aaron King, Grade 8
Paul L Dunbar Middle School for Innovation, VA

Baseball

He hit the ball so very high
Very far up, into the sky
Like a rocket up in outer space
The batter rounded first base

The batter turned on his jets
He kept on running, past all the Mets
He heard the umpire make the call
Everyone heard him roar, "FAIR BALL!"

Rounding third he felt so proud
Like a giant, with his head in the clouds
Right before he touched home base
He tripped and fell on his shoelace

The fielder saw the batter fall down
He threw the ball, past the mound
The runner got tagged, and they heard a shout
From behind, "THE RUNNER IS OUT!!!"

Kyle Eriksen, Grade 8
Brandywine Springs School, DE

They Say

With a feathery coat I slowly stride
Slowly and steadily I waddle with forlorn
My imposing stature embodies pride
Sadly they say my next of kin will mourn

Soon they say the man with the ax will come
I'm not worried, I don't believe that tale
They try and try to convince me my life is glum
They go through all of this to no avail

They want me to be entranced by fear
I ask myself time and time again why they try
They tell me that Thanksgiving is very near
They say this means I'll soon die

I hope and pray they are just bluffing
Unfortunately I taste good with stuffing

Peter Rohrer, Grade 7
Kilmer Middle School, VA

Keep the Music Alive!

Music is all I want to be a part of.
Everyone is into different kinds of music.
Music is something we all know and love.
If you don't love music, you make me sick.
Music is something we can't live without.
My favorite kind of music is rock-n-roll because it's got soul.
Without music, we all would scream and shout.
This is why we need music.
There's no denying or refusing it.
Keep the music alive!

Joseph Harris-Williams, Grade 8
Chickahominy Middle School, VA

Imagination

Bare and deserted is this place
A place once filled with joy and grace
Not a soul in sight
Nor a bird in flight
It is shrouded in mist forever

There's no wind in the trees
No buzz of the bees
Gray clouds pervade the sky
A lone leaf may float by
But this world remains quiet and still

Then suddenly, a burst of light
The world has been freed from its plight
The sun appears
It casts away all fears
The streams bubble
Buildings emerge from the rubble
But what is responsible for all this creation?
Why it only took a little imagination.

Galen Shen, Grade 8
Paul L Dunbar Middle School for Innovation, VA

While I Wasn't Watching

While I wasn't watching, thoughts leapt into my head,
   Jumping side to side waiting to be heard.

While I wasn't watching my pencil became my sixth finger,
   Writing ideas as naturally as wiggling my pinky.

While I wasn't watching my blank paper evaporated,
   Leaving me with a reunion of words.

While I wasn't watching my eraser became extinct,
   For there would be no mistakes.

While I wasn't watching words became my air,
   I was breathing them while I wrote.

While I wasn't watching my name tiptoed onto the paper
   As the publisher was reading.

While I was watching time passed
   And I had a poem.

Alyssa Edwards, Grade 8
Oak Grove Mennonite School, VA

Bugs Bunny

You are like a big fluffy pillow.
Your crazy teeth are bigger than the moon.
Your eyes are big spot lights.
Your carrots says please don't eat me.
These are some reasons why I love bugs bunny.

Lauren Fitzgerald, Grade 8
Paul L Dunbar Middle School for Innovation, VA

Seasons

Winter, Spring, Summer, and Fall
Those are the seasons and I love them all

Winter is a wonderland covered in snow
Skiing, sledding, off I go!
School is canceled for the day
Should I relax or go out and play?

Spring is the rebirth of flowers, grass, and trees
Birds chirping again and the buzzing of the bees
Baseball season has just begun
Time for players to hit a homerun

Summertime is filled with laughter and fun
Going to the beach, and tanning in the sun
Lemonade, ice cream, and swimming in the pool
All of these things help keep me cool

Fall is here, it's time for Halloween
Ghosts and goblins and witches that are green
Hayrides, pumpkins, and fresh-baked apple pie
Jumping in leaf piles stacked a mile high

Every season has fun things to do
Each of them bringing something new

Nicholas Stanzione, Grade 8
St Rocco School, RI

Happiness

What is happiness?
Happiness is something that can lift your spirits
Something that you can see on someone's face

Happiness…
Happiness can be brought down by anger,
jealousy,
rage.

Happiness…
Happiness can be in me,
in you,
anywhere!
You can make a place fill with happiness by words,
actions,
reactions.

Happiness…
Happiness can be achieved,
has been achieved,
and will continue to be achieved.

Can you help to achieve
Happiness?

Emily Meyerl, Grade 8
St Joseph School-Fullerton, MD

My Loss

Blackness surrounds me
The angel is set free

All colors are a blur
The demon sets his lure

My heart sleeps soundly
They scream loudly

Help me please
Help free me

My breath is last
My beats are gone

I am lost
What is the cost

Death takes me now
To him they will bow

Because one single light
Has turned to the night
Amber Keener, Grade 8
Benjamin Syms Middle School, VA

Take Me Home

I sit on my lonely rock
I gaze into the river
Hope that one day she takes me home
Carries me to the ocean
Where I can be in peace
With the wave's soft rumble
Drifting free with the tides
Like a jellyfish
In and out as I please
A tame wind from the east
Ripples on the calm ocean surface
Like a gentle giant's blow
Take me home
Home to the ocean
Kevin Burkett, Grade 8
Brandywine Springs School, DE

Why??

I sit and try to think of a reason that
he broke up with me.
But for some reason nothing comes
to mind.
People say it's for the best and I say
it's for the worst.
GUESS I
GOT TO
MOVE ON!
Téa Barnett, Grade 8
Benjamin Tasker Middle School, MD

Touchdown!

Down! The word springs through their heads as the quarterback shouts it,
They get down into the stance on the line of scrimmage,
Set! Comes as a warning that the play will start soon so brace for the hit,
They are ready and prepared for the damage.

Hut! Is the call to spring into action,
Two opposing forces meeting in the middle with a thunderous CRACK!
The quarterback fakes the handoff as a distraction,
The ball hits the receiver's hands with a SMACK!

He is running,
Charging for the end zone,
He can hear the defense behind him chasing,
But he holds on to the ball that was thrown.

He sees the end zone,
Not ten yards away,
And he leaps in the air as his body goes prone,
And scored the only touchdown that was scored that day.

The coaches go wild on the sideline in delight,
And gaze in wonder at his marvelous flight,
As he crosses the line they jump for joy,
Hands up in the air,
Like little school boys.
Christopher Sims, Grade 8
Chickahominy Middle School, VA

A Peaceful Night

Snuggled in my pajamas scented with spring, I lie curled up in my bed.
The covers are pulled over me, and my head rests on the stiff pillows.
Walls as purple as plums surround me,
As the lamp casts dancing shadows on them.

I reach for that unfinished book,
Filled with adventure, mystery, and wonder.
As the night wears away, I turn more and more smooth pages.
Each image and event clouds my mind.

The chatter of my cousin playing,
And the whispering of the television,
The smell of leftovers still caught in the air,
And the soft "Hhhaa…" of the dog's steady breathing,
Makes home, home.

My eyes grow sleepy, and my mind slow.
With the stars blinking down at me,
I put the bookmark in its place, and put the book aside.

As I yawn my last yawn,
I fall into a deep sleep,
Dreaming of magic, suspense, horror, and love,
From the adventures I took,
That were only in one little book.
Amanda Ricard, Grade 9
Barrington Christian Academy, RI

The Season of Spring

Baby lambs take their first walk,
One by one, eggs start to crack.
Proud mothers stand by and gaze down at their newborn,
It's the start of new life.

Trees sprout leaves after a winter of bare branches,
The grass turns into a carpet of dark, luscious green.
Willows obediently bow to the wind,
It's the start of new beginnings and the restart of growth.

Farmers take out their dirt-stained plows,
Tractors take their place in the fields.
The weeds are pulled, the soil is fertilized,
The seeds are planted and then watered to grow.
It's the start of hard work.

It's a season of life,
It's a season of beginnings.
It's a season of hard work,
It's a season called spring.

Zeming Zheng, Grade 8
Carson Middle School, VA

Green

Green is the silent spring
Peeking out from winter.
The trees
and the grass,
With the gardens scattered all around.

Green is calm
and serene.
Waking up sleepily.

It's the tennis courts and chalkboards,
the rain forests in the tropics.

The herbs fresh from the garden,
making your taste buds sing.
The sound of the ocean wish — washing lazily,
lulling you into a sweet slumber.

Green is the Earth,
wrapping its welcoming arms around its children.

Sara Warrington, Grade 7
Kilmer Middle School, VA

The Song

Noise fills the room
Beat by beat in sensible time
Creating a lovely chime, for the first time.
The rhythm keeps everything in line
The beat is a heart keeping time
All work together creating what is song.

People stare with amazement
Their eyes open and wide
Music coming in, like a watery tide.
No one could believe this greatness
Not even me!
Too bad I was stuck on stage standing like a tree.

The song went on from night until dawn
People cheering like mad in a clattered mess
But enjoy the peaceful sound they will dearly miss.
People stand up to clap
But the song will not end
In fact, we will just begin.

Garrett Wulbrecht, Grade 8
Brandywine Springs School, DE

Through My Eyes

Am I the only one who can see what's going on all along?
All the things he's doing, they seem so wrong.

I can see it, his cruelty and greed,
It makes me worry, where this life will lead.

I long for the past
I wish I knew how long this will last

Am I the blind one here? Really is that true?!
The only blind one here is you!

I've seen it all, and suffered through the pain
Even if I can't see it, I still feel the rain

So ask yourself who's blind and who's not!
Because I can see your chances are shot!

Because you know I can see through your lies,
When you see it through my eyes.

Essence Anderson, Grade 8
Paul L Dunbar Middle School for Innovation, VA

Friends

Friends are people who are like family
They always keep you laughing
They always have your back
Friends for life or friends for days
They will always be your friend

J'asia Perkins, Grade 8
Paul L Dunbar Middle School for Innovation, VA

Computers

Computer like a brain you are really smart.
You can do a million things at once.
You are a door that leads to a lot of things.
You think of a lot of things.
You are the future.

DeShawn Anderson, Grade 8
Paul L Dunbar Middle School for Innovation, VA

Holocaust

As kids grew up they had a life that was great
Meanwhile being behind bars they must have someone to hate
Kids were being kidnapped and killed
While others didn't have meals
Kids lived desperate and sad
While others were trying so hard not to be mad
It was the sad things in life that kept them that way
Now not having anyone also having nothing to say
Kids were at the end of their life
While others had to deal with a strife
So now you see they tried to have a smile on their face
While others had to deal with a sad grace
It wasn't easy being a captured child
While their life was running around being wild
Maybe that's why they weren't happy some days
Because they knew it shouldn't have been that way
Kids had to deal with so much
None had a parent to hug or even touch

Kayla Venable, Grade 8
Paul L Dunbar Middle School for Innovation, VA

Halloween

Ghosts and goblins knocking on my door
Spiders and bugs crawling on the floor
Vampires hunting in the evening air
Werewolves howling and giving quite the scare
Witches brewing up a grim surprise
Walking around where the hills have eyes
Leaves are still falling out of the trees
While children are walking with shaky knees
Ringing the doorbell yelling trick or treat
While there's something snapping at your feet
It's quite a fright when vampires bite
On this creepy and cold Halloween night!

Max Trent, Grade 8
Sandusky Middle School, VA

Bright Black

Black is the empty feeling you get when it's over
The dark dazzling night around the corner
Black is the loudest sound of silence
The darkness approaches with violence
Black is the when all the colors disappear
And when you begin to feel fear
It's an echo about nothing
And yet it's all something
It's a dark painting of the sky
Where you wouldn't want to fly
Black is the color of everything
When there is no light

Luisa Beltran, Grade 7
Kilmer Middle School, VA

First Boyfriend

He was the love of my life.
He really makes me glad.
But now, it's 2010,
And he really makes me mad.
Now, he's not with me anymore.
He goes to another school.
But I'm in love with another boy.
He's really cool.
Now, that boy is the love of my life.
He really makes me glad.
And now on this beautiful year,
He never makes me mad.

Tamera Edley, Grade 8
Paul L Dunbar Middle School for Innovation, VA

Walking Through the Woods

I walk through the woods.
The birds chirp softly.
The breeze flows through the trees.
The sweet taste of honey lingers in the air.
I smell the fragrance of leaves covered in dew
I see the animals waking from winter's rest…
But I know,
As I know this woods,
That this is my last walk here.
The trees will soon be houses,
And the woods a sweet memory.

Steven Greene, Grade 7
Blue Ridge Middle School, VA

Horses

Riding at night,
    I feel happy to ride them
Even though it is creepy,
    I feel safe.
When I see the trees going past,
    I feel excited.
When I am brushing my horse
    I feel relaxed.

I always got excited to go riding.
Horses make me feel like I am in another universe!

Shelley Germain, Grade 8
Chickahominy Middle School, VA

Shiver

Stepping through many thick
    branches in a place
where their feet were in the sky's light.
A day with him
    in the clear sky,
that the robins and he shivered
    just before branches fell.
It had been unpleasant.

Jackson Chambers, Grade 8
Norfolk Christian Middle School, VA

Trevor, Where Are You?

Trevor where are you?
I haven't seen you since.
That Saturday when I went
To my dad's and left you all alone that day.

Where could you be?
If you're near Virginia,
Could I see you
One last time today.

I don't want to think you died
When I wasn't there.
I want to see you one more time
Before you pass away.

This is all that I can say.
Because I don't know where you are,
I still have stuff to say,
So next time I see you I'll never forget the day.

Steven "Hunter" Burgess, Grade 8
Chickahominy Middle School, VA

Checklist

Love is meant to be used for good.
It's not like a piece of firewood.
Love is suppose to be real.
It doesn't mean you can feel feelings you don't really feel.
Love is something that seems right.
It doesn t end up without a fight.
Love doesn't have to be kind.
It knows that if you really felt it you wouldn't mind.
Love will always be there.
It wants you to know you shouldn't fear.
So the next time you think of this…
remember it is on your life checklist.

Amber Riley, Grade 8
Parkside Middle School, VA

Killing King

As I walk down a path
I hear a hiss-hiss then slash
My leg was bit by a cobra
It is sleek, black, and quick
"Why are you so fast," I moan
As it bites my leg I continue to groan
It smells of dirt and leaves
As it rapidly retreats in the breeze
It slithers soundlessly so I can't track it
"Who made you so mad," I wonder as I start to fade
All I can hear is my heart go boom
Boom, boom, boom, I am doomed!

Nathan R. Thomas, Grade 7
Kilmer Middle School, VA

Singers

The tree whispers a secret song to me.
Its leaves flutter in the wind to the rhythm of the music,
As I crane my neck to hear the birch tree
As it whispers its secret song to me.

The tree sings of prisoners
Rooted to the ground
That cannot move
Or say a sound.

They are bound with ropes made of vines.
Their mouths covered with moss
They try to shout
But their screams are drowned out.

Covered up by the sound of a gurgling stream,
Covered up by an owl's hoot,
Their struggles are not heard
Covered up by the sounds of nature.

Their efforts are futile.
All they can do is wait
For they are trees,
Prisoners of nature.

Shelby Patrick, Grade 7
Glenelg Country School, MD

Different But Amazing

There are certain types of plants
That never ever bloom,
And yet we find them sometimes
Like the gingko or the yew.
Mushrooms, moss, and lichen are plants
But they don't grow from a seed!
They're different but amazing…well, at least they are to me.

There are certain types of marine life
That don't swim around on fins.
But one of those, the octopus,
At hide-and seek it always wins.
The squid is long and jets about,
And eels and shrimp it'll see,
They're all different but amazing…well, at least they are to me.

We people all are a bit different,
Be it in height, in health, in stride.
Our fingerprints, unique by far,
Your voice differs from mine.
It would be boring if we had the same
Personality,
We're different but amazing and that shouldn't be just to me.

Christopher Sáenz, Grade 7
Longfellow Middle School, VA

Seasons Transforming
One starts while another ends
All the withered trees slowly mend
Into green filled trees from naked and brown
When the snow covered it like a crown.
The transformation of seasons
Is beauty I have always seen

The weather gets boiling
The later it gets.
Summer fun is one I can't forget.
But leaves soon fall one by one
And turning autumn colors for some.
Crispy orange, red, and brown too
There is so much to do
During the transformation of seasons

After the trees are stripped of leaves
It's time to close your eyes and believe
That Santa Claus will stop by
As winter snow covers the earth and the sky
The transformation of seasons
Will once more come again
Crystal Dong, Grade 8
St Joseph School-Fullerton, MD

War
1. Black hawks
Metal birds with
Hard core weapons
With wings that
Guide the flying explosive
Toward its other opponent to
Solve its conflict, which solves
Nothing but another conflict to resolve
With this one word called
2. WAR
With soldiers fighting
Like a giant shield
To defend the United States of America
Against terrorism which creates
More conflict for every angry
Person to get back at each other for seeing
WHO IS BETTER?
John Thomas, Grade 8
Paul L Dunbar Middle School for Innovation, VA

I Got the Blues
Sometimes I'm mad
Sometimes I'm blue
And when I'm mad I felt like throwing a shoe
Sometimes I'm naughty
Sometimes I'm nice
Sometimes I just want to say
Goodnight
Amiya Cole, Grade 7
Tasker Middle School, MD

A Bright Bikini
Yellow is a bright bikini,
a golden sunrise or autumn leaves.
It is the color of summer,
filled with happiness and lemonade.
The glaring sun and shining key,
squeaky rain boots or chirping chicks.

Yellow is a lonesome dandelion,
twirling in a frilly tutu.
It is the sweetness of a songbird,
nestling atop the tallest tree.
The playful butterfly dancing on the breeze,
an annoying traffic light about to turn red.

Yellow is like a lemon,
sour yet sweet.
It has a sting like curry and a bee,
and is like a birdhouse on the shivering oak.
The color of beauty,
the color of life.
Yellow.
Sydney Parks, Grade 7
Kilmer Middle School, VA

Hatred Is a Virus
Once there was peace.
Once there was serenity.
Two nations caused it.
It started with uneasiness, then it spread.
Rumors plagued both kingdoms,
like a virus, passed from generations.
It was a volcano. Their hatred boiled like magma.
It erupted.
Innocent villages gone,
the only proof they had existed lay,
Hidden in the ruins.
Even through this,
the nations fought.
Now there is nothing.
Barren ruins lay, lonesome and lifeless.
Hatred is a virus.
Carter Hunt, Grade 7
Blue Ridge Middle School, VA

Love
Love
A very strong word;
Also touching and romantic;
Is what every human being
Should find in this world;
Love is also what I found at
A very young age
Love is so beautiful and wonderful
It makes me cry.
Tianna Arnold, Grade 8
Paul L Dunbar Middle School for Innovation, VA

It's Just One Audition

You get up early in the morning to drive half way across the country, for a chance of being discovered!

People get up to get in line at five or maybe even three or four, hoping just to get a number.

Or, their five hours of waiting has been a total waste.

You and many others have questions like: What are the judges like? Is the person next to me talented?

500 people and only the first 200 will audition and out of that number, not even half will make it.

You practice so hard, you feel you are ready!

You take your seat in the auditorium and study the judges, especially the lady in the green.

"Thank you, don't call us we'll call you." They say to the girl on stage.

Everyone knows that means you didn't make it.

"Next." That's you, give it all you got!

You look out to the audience as the music plays, and you go over every line just as you rehearsed.

The lady in the green says, "I'd like to see you again. Maybe the next audition!"

You don't know if she likes your performance or not.

But hey, it's just one audition, there's plenty more waiting for you.

Caitlin Conn, Grade 8
Benjamin Tasker Middle School, MD

Battlefield

People scream, people die, people kill, and people hate

This is what is happening on the battlefield

Bullets fly by at extremely high speeds carrying pain, death, and sorrow

Grenades are thrown exploding with hate

Explosive devices go off shaking the Earth with fear

Rockets and missiles are launched causing confusion and havoc

These are things happening on the battlefield

Soldiers fall, sorrow spreads, pain attacks, and hatred for the enemy on both sides haunts the air like a virus

Confusion, havoc, and fear occur everywhere

Eventually the battle ends and the results are only some of the many people leaving the battlefield changed forever

Noble Americans, some young, experience this

Enemy soldiers, some young, experience this

Some experience this by choice, force, confusion, hatred, honor, bravery, or patriotism

R. Stephen Estrada, Grade 8
St Rocco School, RI

The Real Jesters

Brava, my jester, yet again you amaze me with your tricks and your flips and quick-witted tongue!

Yet, as I think more and ponder and wonder, indeed, I realize one thing that speaks of one's deeds.

You may be the jester of me and my crew, but who be the one, the only true fool? Is it the man who but gambles, or but the king on his throne demanding, the cardinal perhaps, for they can mislead, my proud, gallant fool.

It is they who make mistakes big or large, noble or common, young or old that are the fools. Mistakes of politics or money, love or hatred. Fools of the court and country and war. We are all fools in our lifetimes.

For those are the real jesters.

Abigail Roberson, Grade 8
Post Oak Middle School, VA

My Roller Coaster

My favorite ride is a roller coaster.

Roller coasters are my favorite because you never know what to expect.

If you just look at it, you think you know what to expect but you really don't.

Whenever I'm about to ride a roller coaster, I always feel like my stomach is going to jump out onto the floor.

When I know that there's going to be a big drop I scream my lungs out of my mouth.

Roller coasters are as fast as race cars; at least that's how I feel while I'm riding them.

Roller coasters are big monsters full of excitement.

They dance on the tracks while I am riding.

Kiyera Randolph, Grade 8
Paul L Dunbar Middle School for Innovation, VA

Be the Difference

Each night I close my eyes thinking, how can I make a difference here?
There's so much judging, so much drama, how can I be different from my peers?
But I look past those things, and think back to this girl from school.
She's not an outcast, but some people wouldn't call her "cool."
But this girl is different from all the rest,
she's known to be confident with herself, which brings out her best.
She stays happy, always has a smile on, even when things get rough and things go wrong.
She stays out of drama, but when rumors come her way,
she doesn't let them bother her, and eventually they fade away.
She stands up for what she believes in,
doesn't let temptation get mixed up with her dreams, chooses good influences too, seems like a perfect kid to me.
But on the inside, she's not. She makes her own mistakes.
But she strives to make things better and do what's right, no matter what it takes.
People respect her greatly, for being optimistic, and always so sweet,
nobody will ever understand, what kind of role model she's turned out to be.
Near the end of her life, she'll look back and say,
"I lived my life to the fullest, without letting the little things get in the way."
If one girl can make such a difference, by showing love or showing she cares,
it will make an impact around you, and eventually everywhere.
Be the difference you want to see, and be the person you want to be.
Because this girl has changed my life, and made me see things completely differently.

Emily Elizabeth Wills, Grade 8
Chickahominy Middle School, VA

The Wedding

pink, pink, pink, I say. everything is pink. gah.
live with it, my cousin tells me. and anyway, those flowers aren't pink. they're orange.
I sigh and look down at my dress. pink. at least I'm not wearing shoes.
pink, pink, pink. everything is pink. gah.
leave it to them to come up with this appalling color scheme.
all the bridesmaids have pink dresses.
there are four of us.
I'm a bridesmaid. yuck.

the bride has a pink-and-white bouquet.
the groom has a pink rose in his lapel.
everyone is wearing something pink.
there's a pink shirt, pink shoes, pink socks.
and these are boys! where do you even find pink socks for boys?

I'm tempted to burn the dress. I will refrain.
at least until after the wedding, when I won't have to wear this thing again.
oh no. I might. my cousin and the guy with pink socks are looking at each other in a way I don't like.
(sigh) here we go again.

Marina Stumpf, Grade 8
Grace Episcopal Day School, MD

Winnie

Winnie was a free, courageous, soulful heart
The passion and love that she brought acted as a fine work of art
As she gallops through the misty forest, unconsciously wondering what would happen now
Her mind blows with imagination that she allows
But as her heart bursts out of her chest and she realizes it's only an impossible dream…
Realizing she is no longer free as a bird and is trembling around four cold walls, no longer feeling what seemed to be so supreme

Aundia MehrRostami, Grade 7
Kilmer Middle School, VA

Student
I am student
I wonder what I will be in the future
I hear my thoughts run wild
I see my grades
I want to make them higher
I am a student

I pretend I am going to get a good grade
I believe in myself
I touch the pencil

I feel scared
I worry that I'm not prepared
I cry as the teacher places the test in front of me
I am a student

I understand some questions
I say to myself, "You'll be okay."
I dream of making my parents proud
I hope I will
I am student.
Aleczandra Bryant, Grade 8
Sanford School, DE

I Am Who I Am
I am who I am
I wonder what I will be
I hear my thoughts circling in my head
I see my hands dancing before me
I want to make my thoughts last
I am who I want to be

I pretend to be someone I am not
I believe I never will be
I touch the necklace around my neck

I feel the familiar silver horse
I worry my memories will fade away
I cry when I think about how fast time is passing by me
I am who I am

I understand the world can't be what I want it to be
I say it's okay that it's not
I dream about the days that have passed
I hope I will remember them forever
I am who I want to be
Ivana Gatica, Grade 8
Sanford School, DE

Gone
I am still and quiet
I wonder why everyone is crazy
I hear shouts of people, echoing through my mind
I see nothing, simply a black space
I want to know what is happening around me, my senses are dulled
I am floating off

I pretend to come back, to wake up
I believe I can
I touch the real world, but I am still moving away

I feel nothing, no pain can touch me, no hurt is near me
I worry about my family, will I see them again?
I cry for those I've lost, myself being one of them
I am drifting away

I understand just barely
I say nothing, I am silent
I dream of calm in all this chaos
I hope it will all end
I am gone
Samantha Stevenson, Grade 8
Sanford School, DE

Scared
I am scared.
I wonder if I will be remembered.
I hear my friend talking.
I see the field in front of us.
I want to run away.
I am scared.

I pretend things will never change.
I believe that my friends will leave.
I touch my horse's reins.

I feel my horse wanting to run.
I worry I will be left behind.
I cry because I know I will be.
I am terrified.

I understand we all grow up.
I say nothing will change.
I dream that we can always gallop through this field.
I hope that someday that dream will again come true.
I am scared.
Rachael Straightiff, Grade 8
Sanford School, DE

Winter
The sky is covered with white clouds; snowflakes are flying by.
The children are laughing and building snowmen very high.
Plows are scraping and pushing the dirty, old snow away.
The yellow sun will be shining brightly later today.
Cari Middlecamp, Grade 7
St Joseph School-Fullerton, MD

Soccer
The teams are getting prepared for the soccer game today,
The players came to the field and they were ready to play.
The ref has blown the whistle and the game has just begun,
And before you even know it, the score is one to one.
Brian McGuire, Grade 7
St Joseph School-Fullerton, MD

The Golden Gate

I sit wondering how I got here
All I heard was everyone say Oh Dear
Hearing the sound of slamming breaks
Not having to deal with all the fakes
Why couldn't it have been another?
Now I've lost all my brothers
The last thing I saw was a gray car
Now all I see is a lot of stars.
I thought it wasn't really close
Now they make a toast
To the end of my name
And all of the fame.
It was coming so fast
Too fast to put me in a cast.
I don't remember much
Only that it was December.
I had different plans
I didn't say goodbye to the fans.
Entering through that golden gate
Why did this have to be my fate?
He must have different ideas than me.

Daniel Bieler, Grade 8
Benjamin Tasker Middle School, MD

My Wonder

The world went on without her.
And in that race, mankind,
Kept the hands of time on running,
Leaving her behind.
She went on standing all alone,
In a world she no longer knew.
Smiles became fairytales,
And happiness, it flew.
No one was to save her,
But she could not save herself.
If she were drowning in her own tears,
There'd be no boat to float her out.

But for all she knew she was not heard.
Invisibility was just a game.
And if the people felt the least bit shamed,
Guilt was not its name.
And as she watched the world go past her,
She began to ponder.
Let me too, spread my wings of life,
And show the world my wonder.

Amber Liu, Grade 7
Kilmer Middle School, VA

Ocean Dreams

The waves were my hopes and dreams,
Thrown upon the sand.
I was drowning in my future,
Looking for dry land.

Anna Gallo, Grade 9
Barrington Christian Academy, RI

Soccer

Soccer is the something I love to do,
I can play mostly when the sky is blue.
Even though it sometimes causes pain,
I can only have myself to blame.

When I play soccer it clears my mind,
Playing for rec was when I mostly shined.
Now Cardiff Bluebirds is the name I bear,
Come and challenge us if you dare.

Our club team is hard to beat,
No matter what Maryland team we meet.
As the tournaments come and go,
We will always win four and oh.

As the outdoor season comes to an end,
Indoor becomes the new trend.
As we enter the field,
The other team's fate will always be sealed.

The bounce of the soccer balls,
Against all the walls,
The noise and cheers,
Will strengthen the fears
Of the other team, who will lose after all.

Connor Donovan, Grade 8
St Joseph School-Fullerton, MD

I Dream

I dream of freedom.
Of laughter and of joy.
No one can destroy
Or alter my world.
Only I, me, and myself.

I dream of angel wings
Appearing upon my back
Glistening, ethereal.

The right is as black as midnight.
While the left is pearly white.
I dream of spreading them,
Far and wide.

I dream of flying, soaring.
Higher, higher, and higher, I go.
I dream of reaching Him.
My Creator, my Father.
Of living in Heaven.
Where no one will die,
But live eternally.
With his guidance.
I dream.

Khrystelle Estrella, Grade 8
St Joseph School-Fullerton, MD

Visiting Europe

i myself have been
to many
countries in *Europe*.
my favorite happens to
be *Luxembourg*!
my family and i go to this *huge*
mall with about 50 floors!
It is so big!
but of course,
i haven't been
to Europe in
a long time.
the next time
that i go to Europe,
i hope to visit
England…

Arnelle Fonlon, Grade 7
St Joseph School-Fullerton, MD

So Much Depends

So much depends
upon
the gray mini
sub
protecting its brave
occupants
from the waters
beyond.
They must accomplish their
mission
to protect the
fleet
before they meet
the
islands of the
Philippines.

Michael Walshe, Grade 8
Highlands School, MD

Life

Miracles
joyful cries of laughter
fill the day and night
kids are jumping
bouncing
with cries of delight
house lights are on
kids out of bed
saying hello and good night
to those all ahead
parents, sibling, grandparents
we love those around
so to bring this to an end
Life is a miracle all is said

Nora Dever, Grade 7
St Jane De Chantal School, MD

Autumn Thoughts
As I walk along a lonely autumn road,
Whilst the breeze flows gently through
My bare scalp,
I stand and ponder the essence of life.

However doth the crisp brown leaf float
Ever so softly to the ground?
How too doth the human mind contain such
Trivial fathoms of what once was.

For just as the leaf falls from the branch
And withers away into the dust from which it came

So does the once meaningful fathom
After a short time.

So children, remember my words today, as they contain
Great meaning to those who heed them.

Do not dwell on the past, but set thine sights toward the future, as better things are sure to come.
But shall these verses be whisked away in some dark corner,
never to be heard from again?
This depends upon the heart of those intelligent enough to comprehend the message

Chantz Taylor, Grade 7
Hampton Christian High School, VA

My Feelings for K.L.
At first I didn't want to be here, but then I saw him.
Couldn't help but wonder if we had the same classes.
Day dreaming about being friends with him.
Every second trying not look at him to much. Feeling nervous inside out.
Getting more nervous every second. Just wanting to talk to him without being weird.
Klinging to my chair, looking with curiosity, muttering inside my head,
Nicknaming him the cute mystery boy.
Opening my mind to staying, pending on what happens.
Questioning his age, resting my head on what to say.
Sitting there with a pen and paper. Thinking I have no chance, underneath my fears I was shy.
Venting my way to talk to him. Excited to talk to him, yesterday and today.
Zero time to spend with each other in school.

Catherin Caparaz, Grade 8
Lafayette Winona Middle School, VA

Living in the Autumn Breeze
The sight of brown, red, and yellow leaves makes you happy inside. You look forward to the smell of the fire as well as the warmth.
The fresh air is extremely refreshing to you. You're living in the autumn breeze.

The deafening screams on Halloween give you chills up your spine. You can hear the doorbells from the trick-or-treaters that night.
The taste of candies as soon as you get home excite you. You're living in the autumn breeze.

The smell of fresh picked apples and pumpkin pie fill the air. After dessert you carve your pumpkin with extraordinary skill,
and you hear the crackle of the fire as the cool air starts to blow. You're living in the autumn breeze.

You taste your potatoes and gravy, and hear the laughter of family and friends.
The smell of the spices of the pumpkin pie overcome you while you wait for the parade to start. You're living in the autumn breeze.

Amanda Finkle, Grade 8
Chickahominy Middle School, VA

All My Fault

I'll miss you.
Even though you're loud; — or stole my socks
I'm sorry,
even though you bit me, — and stole my food when I didn't look.
I yelled, — I wished you were gone.
You were betrayed, — by the ones you love.
I'm sorry.
It's the one intruder you couldn't scare
It waltzed into our lives,
and took you away.
I sat on the stairs, and watched
as they took you.
I'm sorry.
A tear slid down my cheek.
BAM,
the door closed
I'm sorry.
I didn't even try to save you.
I'm sorry,
for everything.
It's all my fault.

Taryn Smith, Grade 7
Blue Ridge Middle School, VA

Giraffe

Standing tall, your head up high,
Silent, calm, and shy.
What does it look like from so tall?
Does the world look small?

Your long neck stretches up to the sun,
Looking for leaves, your meal's begun.
Your design of large brown squares are so distinct,
For only to you this pattern can be linked.

Embarrassment occurs as you try to drink.
Such an awkward position, don't you think?
Wobbly, long legs is how you are built,
Like a circus clown walking on stilts.

What does it look like from so tall?
Does the world look small?

Emma Volanth, Grade 7
Kilmer Middle School, VA

The Darkness

In the morning when I wake up all I feel is darkness. I
sit down and eat breakfast, the soggy cereal floating in
the bowl. I go to school and enter a classroom where I feel
all alone. This darkness is following me everywhere I
go. The darkness brings emptiness inside me. It makes
me feel like everyone is happy and has friends but me. I
now know that darkness is now here to stay and I am
gone forever.

Kira Davis, Grade 8
Benjamin Tasker Middle School, MD

Yellow Cactus Flower

The yellow cactus flower,
Her petals crinkled like a flimsy
Tissue paper bud,
Her color that of the
Dying gold of the setting sun,
The feel of silky, cool
Velvet under my hot fingers

Her sweet fragrance brings me back,
Back to the past —
Summers reduced to nothing but
Dusty memories —
Slurping cherry popsicles, dripping
Sticky crimson juice onto the
Deck just outside the screen door

The yellow cactus flower,
Dancing in the whispering wind,
Reaches in and grabs my brain with nimble fingers, deftly
Twisting the memories back, bringing back a shadow of the
Overwhelming wistfulness that remains.

Angela Ma, Grade 8
Kilmer Middle School, VA

The Night Haunter

It was time to go to sleep,
So I hopped in my bed,
I almost fell asleep,
Until I heard a weird noise,
There were bashes and clashes,
Bangs and clangs,
It came in my room and there it was,
It was big and tall, It climbed on my wall,
It hopped on my bed,
I screamed out of my head,
It growled and howled,
But when daylight came it ran out of my room,
I did not see its face due to the darkness in the room,
But I can assure you that this story is true,
If you see or hear the monster there is nothing that you can do,
But when the sunlight hits the room,
He will hide and decide who he will haunt next.

Alejandro Arriaza, Grade 8
Sacred Heart School, MD

Remember When?

Remember when the boys had cooties,
And the girls were afraid of them?
Remember the times we all had,
When we laughed so hard we cried?
When the school years went by so slow,
And now we don't want to go!
We couldn't wait for the school year to end,
And now we all know that we may never see each other again!

Alexis Mirabile, Grade 8
St Rocco School, RI

Meaningless Me

Sister speaking:
She sings so loudly.
She's always so lazy.
She cries herself to sleep.
She seems so crazy.
Brother speaking:
She can get on my nerves.
And drive me berserk.
But all at once she's still
My favorite little jerk.
Me speaking:
My mom says I'm sweet.
She thinks I'm very neat.
But one thing she wants me to do.
Is one day finally, clean my room.
Dad speaking:
She's great at hunting — much like me.
The big fish she caught drives me crazy.
She's no longer my little baby.
I know it seems crazy, I love her anyway.

Kiersten Ball, Grade 7
Marshall Middle School, VA

Fall

Finally it is fall,
I've been waiting for this day,
When the leaves turn vibrant colors,
And then slowly drift away.

Finally it is fall,
My favorite of the seasons,
Fall is a breath of fresh air,
For so many, many reasons.

Finally it is fall,
The season where colors are plentiful,
Fall is like designer fashions,
Not around long but beautiful.

I guess you could say,
My favorite season is fall,
No prejudice against others,
But fall is the best of all.

Makailea Hidalgo, Grade 8
Brandywine Springs School, DE

Me

I used to think I was a lone wolf,
But now I know I am a dolphin,
Because I am swimming with the crowd.

My days used to be dull
But now they are bright and sunny,
Because of Him.

Krystal Harrell, Grade 9
Homeschool Plus, VA

Martial Arts

I am a martial artist
I wonder how this will turn out
I hear the judges call the name of my next opponent
I see a crowd of people staring at me
I want to win this next fight
I am a martial artist

I pretend that I am the best, even though I know I am far from it
I believe I can win
I touch the hand of my opponent as I wish them a good, clean round

I feel my heart beating faster than I can count
I worry that I might not win
I cry tears of pain when the judges says, "Fight"
I am a martial artist

I understand that I can't win every time
I say to myself that I will win
I dream that I have already won this match
I hope that I will win
I am a martial artist

Cheris Congo, Grade 8
Sanford School, DE

The Pressure of Being Great

I am everything: I am an athlete, a writer, a friend, a sister, and a student.
I wonder what one day I will be because I cannot be everything for long.
I hear voices. Expectations are being made for all the students in the room.
Everyone expects me to be something.
I am scared for what the future brings.

I pretend I am an athlete strong and great.
I believe I can do anything, and make the crowd roar for me.
I touch the field with my cleats, my soccer ball balanced on my foot.

I understand that was a dream, and realize that I am still me.
I say to my friend, "What will you become when you are older?"
I dream that we will all be great one day.
I hope that we will never forget where we come from and who we are.
I am everything and will one day become great at something.

Emily Friedman, Grade 8
Sanford School, DE

That One Moment

I cling to the car door, as if I'm hanging off a cliff.
My family tugs my legs,
trying to make me go to the party.
I budge,
and pout as I trudge from the car.
I collapse when we finally finish walking four billion miles.
Mom and Dad abandon me and my brother.
His smile makes that hard, irritating feeling flow right out of my body.
We start talking.
Before I know it, I forget I don't want to be there.

Lindsey Sweet, Grade 7
Blue Ridge Middle School, VA

Seasons

Summer, calm and peaceful
Fall, colorful and windy
Winter, cold and dreadful
Spring, warm and happy

In summer we play in the sand
In fall we play in the leaves
In winter we play in the snow
And in spring we avoid the trees

Summer is a ball, flying through the air
Fall is a leaf, falling to the ground
Winter is a cave, which holds a sleepy bear
Spring is a four-leaf clover, waiting to be found

Summer is fun and active
Therefore I like it best
Although it's really hot
It's better than the rest

Nathan Mastrangelo, Grade 8
Brandywine Springs School, DE

The Rain

The rain is pouring down
I love the way it sounds
When the rain hits the ground
It wets the whole town

She loves to play in the rain
She wants to keep it the same
The rain opens the flower
She watches them for hours

The pouring rain stops
The flowers start to drop
The sun comes out
And we all shout!

Jade Graves, Grade 8
Paul L Dunbar Middle School for Innovation, VA

Fishes

Fishes are like clouds.
Fishes swim in the ocean and
Clouds swim on the sky.

Fishes are like humans.
They feel, smell, they see,
And eat just like us.

Fishes are useful they are
Food to us and other animals.
Fishes are like humans and
Any other thing in the world.
They are useful no matter what.

Bianca Barba, Grade 8
Paul L Dunbar Middle School for Innovation, VA

My Dog Maggie

My three year-old puppy, Maggie,
Is twelve pounds of love.
She's black and white,
And her eyes are wild since they're different colors.
One is blue and one is brown.
Her tail plumes up like a skunk's.

She loves her bacon treats,
And loves her favorite stuffed toy,
Monkey Boy.

She doesn't like loud noises,
Hates the crashing of thunder.
She loves going for walks and is great on a leash.

Maggie behaves at bath time,
But she'll shake when it's over while she's still wet!
She'll run in circles and is too fun to watch.

When it's snowing outside she's leaping with excitement.
But then, the poor thing gets cold so quickly.
She's so small sometimes we can't find her.

Maggie greets people with a little bark.
She's so glad to see you and her tail wags happily.
She's the best dog and friend in the world!

Jenna Thomas, Grade 8
St Joseph School-Fullerton, MD

Birthday

Every single girl and boy,
Waits for our day that's filled with joy.
We all love our special day, don't you?
It's filled with presents, parties, and piñatas too.

At night we children stay awake,
Thinking of candles, cards, and cake.
We think about all the people we'll meet,
And all our other birthday treats.

Such as families, friends, and presents we'll see,
And what kind of person we'll be.
About our party and what kind of board games to play,
We think: what if it rains on my special day?

Will I feel different after I'm a year older?
would I be much colder or bolder?
Are my friends going to understand,
All the fun games that I've planned?

Oh my, this is stressful,
Will I be successful?
Maybe I better go to bed,
All this thinking is hurting my head.

Caroline McCraw, Grade 7
Linkhorne Middle School, VA

Why Did You Have to Go

After I walked into the room,
I knew it was too good to be true.

My poor baby was on the ground,
The whole house was feeling blue.

All that day was I spent crying,
Morning to night and didn't stop.

None of us knew this would happen,
That he would have a heart attack and drop.

On to the ground and not take another breath,
His heart just had a sudden stop.

I know he is in heaven now,
And that is the best.

I will see him soon,
When I'm laid to rest.

Hailey Layfield, Grade 8
St Clement Mary Hofbauer School, MD

I Am More Than a Rock

I am a rock
Wind and rain have worn me down
I am smooth on the outside
But inside, I am rough
No one looks at me
They think that I am just a pebble by the road
I am much more than that
I am part of the ecosystem
But at least I know
And that's all that matters
Not what they think
But what I think
Because it's
Me

Hanna Holland, Grade 7
Wicomico Middle School, MD

Blue

Blue is the stretched out sky
Pouring tears of sadness onto the earth
Dying by the hands of the evil called man
Trapped with the earth, defending its borders
Blue is the shining sea
Frowning at the stupendous starlit night
Hugging the beaches of Mother Earth
Guarding its children from the beams of the Sun
Blue are the bulging balloons
The dreams of children, floating into the heavens
Reaching out to the sky, calling for help
Crumbling to the deadly atmosphere…POP!

John Matuszewski, Grade 7
Kilmer Middle School, VA

I Am a Volleyball Player

I am an athlete.
I wonder if it will go over the net.
I hear the whistle.
I see the players getting down and ready.
I want to win.
I am determined.

I pretend I am a professional athlete.
I believe I am amazing.
I touch the soft surface of the ball.

I feel the pressure coming down on me.
I worry I will miss this hit.
I cry when I know I could have done better.
I am uncertain.

I understand I cannot be the best.
I say I can be better.
I dream of being greater.
I hope I make it to the top.
I am an athlete that is determined, yet uncertain.

Anneli Wingertz, Grade 8
Sanford School, DE

My Sister

Tall, beautiful, tan and skinny
These are the things that make my sister pretty.
From Abercrombie to Hollister
My sister is a true fashionista.

On her way to a big success
My sister is the best.
She wants so badly to have a pet
I think that she will make a great vet.

Honesty, responsibility and kindness
This is what makes her flawless.

Tall, beautiful, tan and skinny
These are the things that make my sister, pretty.

T.J. Warren, Grade 8
Chickahominy Middle School, VA

Dance

When I dance I feel the world is a better place
Children are smiling
The sun is always shining
A gentle breeze is blowing
No one is suffering
No one is hungry
No one is angry
No one is poor
Everyone is happy
When I dance I feel the world is a better place

Theresa Cotton, Grade 7
St Jane De Chantal School, MD

Make my Day!
When I'm sad or mad
Or even glad
You always make my day

With laughs, hugs,
Or even crap
That seems to last all day…

Happy, sad or
Even mad
I'm glad you're here today

So every day, I will have someone
To wash away my never ending pain

The pain that whispers through my soul
The pain that has a might hold…

It makes me sad to think about
But then your round and about to say hey every day
And make sure that I'm always okay

So there it is out in the open
One too many things have been spoken

But this is just one last thing…
I'm super happy that you made my day
To wash away almost everything
Monica G.L Walton, Grade 7
Tasker Middle School, MD

Fashion Fashion Fashion!
Pink, yellow, blue, green
Those are colors of what fashion means
Silk, wool, cotton, denim
Makes you want to go get 'em
Tyra, Kimora, Channel, Iman

Prada, Guuci, Juicy Louis
I want this, I want that
But I want that skirt in black
50, 60, 100 dollars
Prices that make my mom scream and holler!

You always have to keep up on the latest fashion
Or do as you want, because it's your passion
Ripping shirts, cutting jeans
Making what you want, because it's your dream
Not caring what other people say
Because it's your style, and you'll do it your own way

So that's what fashion means to me
Doing and making your own things
And just hoping people agree with you too
Ashleigh Crockett, Grade 7
Tasker Middle School, MD

Love
Love, love, love…love is above
Cries and tears, love opens our ears
To others' sadness, loveless and lifeless.

Love is not loud love is not proud
Love trusts and protects,
It is better than any helmet

Love is not boastful, but it is useful.
Love cares it chases despair, and all nightmares.

Love is like music but you don't need its lyrics.
Love is kind, gentle, it is even prettier than crystal.

Love is tiny
Love is funny
Love is only a feeling,
It is amazing.

Love is a light, a light brighter, stronger than the night.
Love comes from the heart it never leaves someone apart.

Love is pure and always sure.
Love leads friendship, it curves all hardship.

Love is nice, love is peace it does never decrease.

A world without love
Is a world without hope.
Marguerite de Galbert, Grade 7
St Jane De Chantal School, MD

Snowy Dreams
In this evening, it is freezing
But to my surprise, I am not sneezing

The wind has not died down or stayed still
Yet, I do not feel the slightest chill

There is white all around me
But my breath I do not see

White flakes are forming into clumps
Although on my skin there are no goose bumps

Even without gloves or mittens
Jack Frost has not yet bitten

Kids are sliding
Kids are gliding
Kids are on their sleds and riding

But now it is all beginning to seem
Like this has all been just a dream
Lilly Hollenbeck, Grade 7
St Jane de Chantal School, MD

Streetlight

Illuminating the sidewalk, the street,
helping to guide people on their way
to the amusement park, work, or to meet
with friends they haven't seen since yesterday.
It only shuts down during midday
it also needs to rest, you see.
everything in the world wants to be free.
Oh, the streetlight! What a treat
to see row of lights paving the way!
lining up single-file, so neat
standing like soldiers every day!
Strong and tall, leading the way
Its main mission is to referee
The roads and sidewalks, actually.
It never misses a beat,
persevering day by day,
it is no small feat
to give out those comforting rays.
The lights will stay
in our hearts; we can hold three
from sea to shining sea.

Enxin (Mary) Wan, Grade 8
Carson Middle School, VA

Flashes of Fall

A flash of red, from a leaf so bright,
with a twirl it spins to a lower height.

A flash of yellow, from a streak of sun,
as it warms the earth till the day is done.

A flash of orange from a pumpkin round,
and the pumpkin pies oh how sweet the sound.

A flash of brown from an acorn small,
in the paws of a squirrel "it's mine," is his call.

A flash of blue from the clear, bright sky,
and the puffy, white clouds, that float up on high.

A flash of green from the grass below,
as I run outside in my barefoot toes.

Marcia Yoder, Grade 7
Oak Grove Mennonite School, VA

Friends

Friends are more than what most people think.
Friends are the ones who keep secrets and
who cheer you up when you're down.
Friends are one of the most important things in life.
Friends tell you the truth and don't lie about you behind your back.
Friends are like family, a sister or a brother.
That is what you call a
!FRIEND!

Charisma Matthew, Grade 7
Benjamin Tasker Middle School, MD

Diary of the Deer Hunter

Gone huntin' be back at dark thirty,
get into stand at 0530,
sunlight gleaming on the early morning dew,
soft rustling in the leaves to my right…
just a little chipmunk.
a wheeze to my left,
just a curious little mink sniffing for my scent.
leaves rustling straight ahead…
DEER!
three doe run past with a buck right behind them.
time slows down
grab gun — aim — make fake snort to stop the buck
real time again
waaaah wahhh (buck stops broadside looks right at me)
BAM!!
deer down I got it!
1300 field dress deer…start dragging
dark thirty get to truck load deer head home.
next day take pictures brag about deer
get it mounted to treasure for ever.

Dillon Conway, Grade 9
Delaware Military Academy, DE

Water

Running down the mountainside
And splashing into the sea,
Light dancing on the surface —
What a beautiful sight to see!

Hitting the rocks hard
But no scratch to be found —
Just get back up and going,
Fleeing, without a sound.

Flowing with a careless ease
Overlapping each passing wave;
Not losing any time to spare,
Moving away with hours to save.

Running down the mountainside
So bright and so free.
Without a care in sight,
Crashing against the world with never-ending glee!

Robyn Welborne, Grade 9
Southern Maryland Christian Academy, MD

Spring

O how I love to see you walk in every year
Your warmness is like a blanket after a long winter
The flowers dance at the sign of your presence
The snow is a lion running from you
The sun feels like a thousand times warmer
And looks a thousand times brighter
O please stay for a while

Amber Melton, Grade 8
Paul L Dunbar Middle School for Innovation, VA

In the Spotlight

Don't you love the feeling of being in the spotlight?
You can be the star you were meant to be.
Anyone you want.
Jealous eyes watch your every move.
Envious individuals wish they were you.
Paparazzi and raging fans everywhere.
Personal assistants, maids, and butlers.
You're the one in charge.
You make the rules. You call the shots.
You have everything you could ever wish for.
But then you get the feeling you're missing something.
You can't exactly put your finger on it, but then you realize it.
What you're missing is acting like a real person.
When you're in the spotlight, you can't make mistakes,
Or make a wrong choice.
Every flaw you have weakens you.
The industry owns you.
You can't be yourself.
You can't please everyone.
So next time, instead of dreaming about being in the spotlight,
Think about how great your life already is the way it is.

Lauren Garafano, Grade 8
St Rocco School, RI

Nature

The beautiful falling leaves.
All the different sounds.
Nice warm spring breeze.
Different things all around.

Exciting new insects.
New varieties to find.
The outdoors you must respect.

Stepping on sticks.
Hopefully not getting stung by bees.
Seeing bugs like tics,
And different big trees.

I love the great outdoors.
I wish I could go more!

Lauren Carter, Grade 7
Paul L Dunbar Middle School for Innovation, VA

Saint Patrick's Green

Green is a pleasant day,
Fresh smelling grass and humongous trees,
A nature color that we can't live without.
Dazzling shopping bags and frosting,
Green is the color of a ping-pong table,
The lucky one on St. Patrick's Day.
A money plant with long vines of leaves,
The color of Christmas decorations fills the air,
Green is the brightest color of all!

Rathnam Parthasarathi, Grade 7
Kilmer Middle School, VA

Engineering

I am an engineer.
I wonder if I can solve the problem.
I hear the sizzling of my mind.
I see tools scattered on the floor.
I want to solve the enigma.
I am an engineer.

I pretend I am finished with my work.
I believe my work will come to life.
I touch my tools, working diligently to finish.

I feel like I am going to come out victorious.
I worry about failure.
I cry tears of joy when my creation comes to life.
I am an engineer.

I understand I may fail.
I say to myself "Zero in on the puzzle."
I dream of my contraption working.
I hope to finish it tomorrow.
I am an engineer.

Trevor Schlack, Grade 8
Sanford School, DE

A Walk Somewhere

Walking slowly down the lane,
How jealous I am of the plane
That flies so freely through the air
While I walk on, going somewhere.
Somewhere that I can truly know
What life is like without the woe
That constantly pollutes my mind
With troubles that I left behind.
As I reflect, my pace grows fast
The more I think about my past.
Why can't my walking save me from
The trials and errors yet to come.
In hoping that each step I take
Will keep me from making mistakes.
One thing I learned when I had gone:
Don't run from problems, face them head on.

Noelle Acaso, Grade 8
St Joseph School-Fullerton, MD

My Two Favorite Sports

Basketball, basketball is my favorite
It's fun because you get to shoot it
And you can do crossover with it
And that's the favorite about it.

Football, football is my second favorite
You get to throw it
And tackle people with it
That's why it's my favorite.

Jamel Jennings, Grade 8
Paul L Dunbar Middle School for Innovation, VA

Picture

A thousand words that sting
Like the tale of a fallen king
A hundred phrases told
As if they never grew old
A million simple letters
That didn't make it better
A single fallen tear
That no one thought to hear
A thousand hours that cry
As their duration passes by
A hundred days gone
As if they've been trampled on
A million tiny seconds
That can't be recollected
A single broken moment
That was lost to this poet
In fear, in hope, in rage
In sorrow, in peace, in a page
It was silent, it was lost
And none can compare the cost
Of a picture.

Brittany Crow, Grade 9
Woodbridge Sr High School, VA

Snow

Snow…
Comes in the winter
Floats from the sky
Piles on the ground
Kids come out
Plays…
In the snow
On the snow
With the snow
Snowflakes..
Unique and different
Each and every one
Beautiful
All pile up and
Makes a snow land
Everything…
Covered in white
Sparkles in the sun
Shines the sky
Brightens the day
Snow…

Boxi Chen, Grade 8
Tasker Middle School, MD

Knotty

The slithering snake
Hissed with no delight,
"Please help me" he said
I've tied myself too tight!

Connor Richerson, Grade 8
Homeschool Plus, VA

Mommy

I love my mommy
My mommy loves me

She's always there
She's always the key

I love my mommy
She's pretty and sweet
She's silly and playful
She's just like ME!!!

I LOVE MY MOMMY!
and
MY MOMMY LOVES ME!!!

Deezya Monroe, Grade 7
Benjamin Tasker Middle School, MD

Dealing with Younger Siblings

Dealing with younger siblings is never fair,
And there is no way to prepare,
For you will be trying to act humane,
But they'll find a way to drive you insane.

They'll get you in trouble by a false claim,
And everything you do is in vain,
You'll always try to act your age,
But they'll find a way to make you enraged.

No matter how crazy they may be,
Even if they act like a chimpanzee,
You'll always find a way,
To love them times three.

Devin Poist, Grade 8
St Joseph School-Fullerton, MD

Crazy

I have two Brothers
They are as bad as monkeys
Fighting over a banana,
They pull at my shirt with cheesy fingers,
Yell in my face,
Change the channel as I watch TV

When they ask
For piggy back rides
I cannot resist
Even though they weigh
A ton

They are my life.

Emma Lindemeyer, Grade 7
Blue Ridge Middle School, VA

At the First Glimpse

At first I am shy
At first I may lie
At first I show fear
At first I may pretend you're not here
But that's only at the first glimpse

And then I am fun
We laugh and we run
You may change your mind
About that first glimpse

At first I am mean
At first I show greed
At first I am helpless
At first I may make a mess
But that's only at the first glimpse

Tabitha Meritt, Grade 9
Delaware Military Academy, DE

Every Time You Lie

Every time you lie to me,
I don't know what to think.
Every time you lie to me,
I cry myself to sleep.
Every time you lie to me,
I see it in your eyes.
Then you touch my hand,
and say it's all right.
You lie to me every day.
You lie to me all the time.
And I can't help it,
when I run away and cry.
You seem to think I'll be okay,
but it never turns out that way.
So every time you lie to me,
I can't help but cry.

Arianna Gray, Grade 8
Chickahominy Middle School, VA

In the Summer —

Innocence grows like the grass
Love blooms like flowers
Happiness shines like the sun
Time is cherished like a cool breeze
Road trips are as fanciful as clouds
Kisses are as frequent as raindrops
Hope shines through the darkness like stars
Tragedy can strike like lightning
Friends are like birds
Inspiration is created everywhere
Silence is a loud as thunder
Worries vanish like the wind
Music travels through the humid air
Freedom knocks on your heart's door

Amber Cluesman, Grade 9
Cape Henlopen High School, DE

All About My Feelings for You

I still remember the first time we met,
I loved it and couldn't wait to hang out again.
I went to sleep that night and dreamt about you,
But I don't want to dream about you, I want to be with you.
School seemed so far away, but I know the greatest distance wasn't east and west,
But it's when I'm looking right into your eyes, and you don't know.
When my eyes water up and I speak to you,
You don't seem to realize that I'm tired of crying,
And I'm sick of trying,
On the outside I'm smiling,
And inside I'm dying.
I finally found someone who can make me happy.
Anyone can make you smile or cry, but you make me smile when I already had tears in my eyes.
I come to realize that the only part of my life that seems to make sense,
Is the part of life I share with you.
I promise I will never let you go.
I miss you and love you.
Please don't change.

Amy Field, Grade 9
Gaithersburg High School, MD

Daisies

I feel like an eight year old with a daisy that has half its petals torn off,
In my head chanting he loves me, he loves me not,
Waiting desperately for the final petal to fall,
But dreading the answer.

Now the concept seems silly,
But yet, at whatever age I may be,
I'm still pulling the petals off of daisies and chanting in my head,
Feeling that insecure little girl I was many years ago poking through my stone-hard mask of maturity.

Shelby Butt, Grade 8
Chickahominy Middle School, VA

I Look

It is the day. I look out into the crowd,
looking for my only support. For him.
This loneliness I feel is as if fate itself has cut my heart into an island,
never to be washed over with the waters of love again.
TICK TOCK.
The mischievous clock sticks out its tongue of broken hearts,
collecting mine in the bunch,
as it allows time to go on
when it should stand still with remorse.
They all tell me it will pass
but my mind doesn't register it
because I still look for him
and I will until my eyes lose their light.
I am the shroud of darkness covering this place.
Even though I wore black for him.
Even though I still cry in our bed.
Even though he is now silently singing with the angels
still, I look.

Priscilla Mariam, Grade 7
Kilmer Middle School, VA

Siblings

Overwhelming joy
Sometimes frustration
Still, they're just kids.
Being the role model
For a young boy
And a young girl
Is hard at ties.
They want to be just like me.
Whatever I do, they'll do.
My brother's like a spy,
Quiet by day, energetic by night.
On the other hand,
My sister is a princess.
She's adorable, yet very picky.
One second they could be naughty,
Another and they're nice.
But remember, they're just kids.

Christian Mananghaya, Grade 8
St Joseph School-Fullerton, MD

Life

It lives,
It changes,
Things are born,
Things die,
That's just the cycle.

It's beautiful,
The flowers,
The landscapes,
The animals,
But most of us take advantage of it.
We don't take time to enjoy what
Life gives us.
We should take time to enjoy the goodness
of Life
Life is short
Enjoy It!

Nicole Johnston, Grade 8
Sacred Heart School, MD

Escape

The walls cave in all around me.
I must go, escape.
Running, my legs propelling me forward.
Running, with no destination in mind.
I must go, escape.
My life is not mine anymore,
it belongs to everyone else,
but not me.
I must go, escape.

Kathryn Rappold, Grade 8
Chickahominy Middle School, VA

Fall

Fall brings in the cold
The leaves start to change color
Halloween is here.

Madison Kerns, Grade 7
Marshall Middle School, VA

Who Am I?

I taught everybody how to sleep,
I made the willow tree's all weep,
I make water rush back and fourth,
I make it snow way up north.

I'm the one that makes the sun shine,
I'm the one that can change or stop time.

But what really matter's is who I am
to you...

I am God.

Alexandra Owen, Grade 7
Tasker Middle School, MD

Coming to God

Come one, come all, do not delay.
Tis' the Master's call, come in today.

A broken man that very day.
Received the word, but did not obey.

He'd been a fool, for so many years.
There was no hope getting joy from tears

Down on his knees, he softly said.
"Forgive me Lord, for I've been dead,

To all the teachings, I have heard.
And for not listening, to your word."

The Lord drew near and touched his heart,
A new man rose to do his part.

Ariana Webb, Grade 9
Oak Grove Mennonite School, VA

Silence Is Golden

I've always dreamed
Of having a class
Where there's total
SILENCE
Because silence is golden
I've always wanted
To have a day
Of total silence
Because silence is golden
Silence is...
Golden
Yes, silence is golden

Leneé Hill, Grade 7
Tasker Middle School, MD

Halloween

H ouses looking scary
A wesome costumes
L ots of candy
L ollipops in your bag of candy
O ut loud kids are saying trick or treat
W owing and surprising people
E ating all the goods you got
E ating all different kinds of snacks
N ight time is when you go trick or treating

Alexis Anderson, Grade 8
Lafayette Winona Middle School, VA

Txts!

Texting is fun
When you're on the run
If you send me a text
I'll send you one next
Text language can be cool,
Just not for school.
Did I just hear a beep?
Who might this text be?
Oh wait...that's just me
Fast as a Firefighter
Quick as a cheetah
I text my friend one extra time
For I hope it's not a crime,
But I drop my phone
And it shatters like bones.
What will I do next?
Since I can't text.

Erin Cadden, Grade 8
St Joseph School-Fullerton, MD

Friends

F riends are like your family, we
R un around like crazy and have fun.
I talk to my friends and see them almost
E very day at school. We get on each others
N erves sometimes because we are together
D ay after day, but that doesn't matter.
S o after all, friends make up a big part of your life.

Chrysoula Vasilakopoulos, Grade 7
St Joseph School-Fullerton, MD

Grades 4-5-6 Top Ten Winners

List of Top Ten Winners for Grades 4-6; listed alphabetically

Allen Chen, Grade 4
Highlands Elementary School, IL

Alexander Chojnowski, Grade 6
Immaculate Conception Academy, ID

Kallie Fisher, Grade 4
The Mirman School, CA

Yuna Kim, Grade 5
Edwin Rhodes Elementary School, CA

Jewel Mason, Grade 6
Chester E Dye Elementary School, MO

Andrew McInnis, Grade 5
John G Dinkelmeyer Elementary School, NY

Sam Roberts, Grade 6
St Philip Fine Arts School, AB

Alysa Rogers, Grade 5
Foothill Elementary School, CO

Ashley Workman, Grade 6
Southwest Middle School, AR

John Xue, Grade 6
Chapin Middle School, SC

All Top Ten Poems can be read at www.poeticpower.com

Note: The Top Ten poems were finalized through an online voting system. Creative Communication's judges first picked out the top poems. These poems were then posted online. The final step involved thousands of students and teachers who registered as the online judges and voted for the Top Ten poems. We hope you enjoy these selections.

I Am a Cheerleader

I am a cheerleader when I am at practice
I wonder if I'll be a flyer
I hear the fans cheering for us after the team scored the winning
touchdown in the game
I see people in the stands cheering for the "Knights"
I want to win 1st place in competition, go "Knights" go!!

I am a cheerleader when I'm at practice
I pretend I am a flyer at practice, awesome!
I feel I am warmer up in the air at our home game, look up!
I touch the ground in cheerleading
I worry that I'm going to fall in a stunt, smile!

I am a cheerleader when I'm at practice
I understand that I can't be a flyer
I say I want to win
I dream to win 1st place in competition
I try my best in competition, practice!
I hope my team is 1st this year at my competition
I am a cheerleader when I'm at practice

Desiree Silva, Grade 5
Blackrock School, RI

Gorgeous Green

Leaves on a tree, a big bowl of fresh salad.
A binder on the side of a desk.
A huge Christmas tree, with huge green lights.
Green is a highlighter, the stem of a flower, the color of a name tag.
Green is the color of a car, the color of a turtle.
Green is a poster.
A backpack and lunch box in a cubby.
The land on a map.
Green is the color of a book cover.
Poke-a-dots and stripes on pants and shirts.
Green is a dragon, blazing bright with fire.
Green is a yummy sour apple lollipop.
The color of a dry erase marker.
Green is a colored pencil used for coloring.
Green is an eraser, the color of a snail.
Green is a chameleon.
Green is a caterpillar.
The color of moss that lives in cracks and sidewalks.
Green is a lonely slug finding a leaf.
Green is the color of friendship that me and my teacher share.

Isabelle Lucca, Grade 4
Immaculate Conception Catholic Regional School, RI

The Beach

The beach, the blue water with high rising waves
The sound of water hitting the shore
The sand all over your feet with a smell of sea water all around
The blue sky, the kids running around
The sounds of sea gulls screeching
As I enjoy my day at the beach.

Daniel Gray, Grade 4
Mary Walter Elementary School, VA

Blue Is a Pretty Color

Blue is as clear as the sky.
Blue is my school's color.
Blue is the color of a crayon.
Blue is as clear as the water.
Blue is a color.
Blue shows a lot in the summer.
Blue is the color of rain.
Blue is the color of my uniform.
You can sometimes when you are outside,
When it is not raining out.
Blue is the color on the American Flag.
Sometimes when you write with some pens
The color might come out blue.
I like the color blue.
Blue is many things.
Blue can be the color of a popsicle,
On a hot day.
It's good for a really hot day.

Alexandra Roy, Grade 4
Immaculate Conception Catholic Regional School, RI

Googling Green

Green is the color of a happy leprechaun,
or maybe an old green grasshopper.
Green is the color of nature in the summer,
or possibly even a parrot.
Green is the luck of a four-leaf clover.
Green is the color of Shrek,
or a green dragon.
Green is the color of my shimmering eyes,
on a winter day.
Green can be the color of a scaly snake or lizard.
Green can be the color of an apple or pear,
hanging from a branch.
Green is the color of a turtle in the water,
or maybe even my favorite color.
Green can be a swampy rain forest,
and green is a Christmas color.
If there was no green I would be sad,
and also the globe would be all blue!

Edward Ruggieri, Grade 4
Immaculate Conception Catholic Regional School, RI

Rocks

Dark shadow behind my back
Dust flying with no fear or happiness
I'm always lonely with no others
I have no identity and nothing knows where I am
Until she comes back
And she picks me up
And I get to have a true life
I'm a rock with feelings now.
Now I can roll and do things now
People notice and pick me up too.

G'Angelo Quintin, Grade 5
Rosemont Forest Elementary School, VA

Blue

Blue is skies during the day
Tears in your eyes
Rain
Oceans
Favorite markers
Blue is sad unlike red
Blue is not mad
Blue is school doors,
Walls and backpacks
Blue is cool and cold
It is new and it is old
Blue is the pitter-patter of rain on a window
Fish
Even a glass dish
Blue is water or blue jays flying through the sky
It will never say good-bye
But will stay with you
Blue is some weird goo
My little brother's shoe

John Travis, Grade 5
St Bartholomew School, MD

Beautiful Blue

Blue is the color of the sky.
Blue is the color of a crayon.
Blue is on the American flag.
Blue is the color of shoes.
Blue is a piece of construction paper.
The color blue is on my glasses.
Blue is the color of my hair elastic.
Blue is my school color.
The color blue is very soothing.
The color blue was on some dinosaurs.
Blue is a big juicy blueberry.
Blue is a wave that will gush over your head.
Blue is a cape that will show you're brave.
Blue comes out when you're sad.
Blue could be a snugly stuffed animal.
Blue is on the ground on a rainy day.
Blue is a door to an imaginary world.
Blue is my favorite color.

Madison D'Ambra, Grade 4
Immaculate Conception Catholic Regional School, RI

Unexplored

Nature is unexplored
Like a newborn baby is to walk

Nature is unexplored
Like a picture that is in motion

Learn about it and you can feel the difference in yourself

I did.

Claire Dunham, Grade 4
Riderwood Elementary School, MD

Brown Is...

Brown is the silky hair on a persons head.
Brown is the bricks and wood to build houses.
Brown is the cross that Jesus died on.
Brown is the color of animals
like dogs and rabbits.
Brown is a picnic basket
and the stem of an apple.
Brown is the crust of bread
and the color of cardboard,
but they don't really taste the same.
Brown is the hotness and delicious hot chocolate, coffee and tea.
And brown is the color of a tree with no leaves.

Alexandra Coutu, Grade 4
Immaculate Conception Catholic Regional School, RI

A Friend

A friend is someone who can be fun
A friend is someone who you can hang out with in the rain or sun
A friend is someone who is very giving
A friend is someone who should be forgiving
A friend is someone who is extremely nice
A friend is someone who gives good advice
A friend is someone who is understanding
A friend is someone who isn't demanding
A friend is someone who is sympathetic
A friend is someone who isn't pathetic
A friend is someone who is courageous
A friend's personality can be contagious

Cristin George, Grade 6
St Jane De Chantal School, MD

Dance

I love to dance
It's who I am
It opens up the world
It's who I am,
It's who I'll always be
When it's night, I feel like I'm at a laser show
When it's day, I feel better
I always put my heart on my feet and body
and have emotion and energy
It's who I am,
It's who I'll always be

Madison Grace Jackson, Grade 6
Graham Middle School, VA

Love

The most thing I care about is my parents
I care about them so much
And no body can stop me from loving them
I will fight for them if I have to
That is how much I love them
If somebody pays me to not love my parents I won't do it
Because that is who I am.

Trent Jenkins, Grade 6
Floyd T Binns Middle School, VA

Over Soon

I climb into the car,
waving to my mom standing at the door.
Fear is streaming down my cheeks,
hoping this ride will over soon
next to me are my neighbors.
Irritating, restless, and selfish boys
who want to make you feel,
as miserable as possible.

Their mouths are watering to taunt and tease me.
I am just a 1st grader,
small, shy and scared.
I don't know what is happening.

"Why are you so late Dollie?"
Dollie is not my name.
I am so upset, but there is nothing I can do.

I hope carpool
Won't go on like this.
I hope it will be, over soon.

Dahlia Katz, Grade 6
Charles E Smith Jewish Day School Lower Campus, MD

Ode to Raspberries

I crush you,
You red bumpy berry
Against the roof of my mouth,
And your sweet juice sets in,
Gushing out of each individual little juice pocket,
Flooding through my mouth…
Although it is fall,
Your summer air
Rushes through me,
Making me forget
which season it is
I feel relaxed,
The perfect combination
Of soft
And sweet,
Those quick moments of
Excited,
Content taste buds
Make me relax,
And lose focus,
On life…

Joey Rushfield, Grade 6
Charles E Smith Jewish Day School Lower Campus, MD

Winters

Some hopes shine like precious stones on
Winter's quiet eves. Others glisten small and hopeful.
Yet, none compare to those like twinkling lights, above
Me like stars glee on a winter's eve.

Karrah Large, Grade 6
Graham Middle School, VA

Stream

Life is like a stream,
Not knowing when it is going to end,
Some say that when you're born,
A death date is picked for you,
Or some say it just naturally happens,
A stream doesn't flow forever,
It eventually meets an end with a body of water,
Which is the end,
During the flowing of the water,
There are obstacles to go through,
Somehow it manages through it,
There are harder obstacles than others,
Sometimes a river meets a fork,
You try to go the best way,
Sometimes you run out of time to decide,
And you end up going the worst way,
And not the best,
It does not mean you can't fix it,
But sometimes you can't,
No matter how hard you try,
Life is like a stream.

Angelica Borrero-Sichette, Grade 6
Tilghman Elementary School, MD

Cupcakes

It's the warm, delicious gift from above.
Sweeter than anything, and filled with love!
It's moist on the inside, smooth on the out,
the rich, creamy flavor will make you wanna shout!
Just a couple of eggs,
A splash of milk,
Watch it bake,
Inside you'll melt.
When you take it out,
It's nice 'n' hot,
Savor the flavor,
It'll hit the right spot.
It makes me feel warm and safe,
When I'm eating cupcakes.
They make me want to spring,
They make me want to jump;
To think something so good,
Just started with a lump.
Cupcakes are my favorite food,
And forever will be,
Who will be next to try something so amazing?

Maria Wray, Grade 6
Paul L Dunbar Middle School for Innovation, VA

My Fish

If my fish were a dog I'd train it to sit,
if my fish were a lamp I'd make sure it's lit,
but my fish is a fish not burnt coal,
if my fish were on a plate I'd put him in his bowl!

Gaby McInnes, Grade 5
Pemberton Elementary School, VA

The Stranger in the Night

On Halloween night
I am alone in my house
I'm supposed to be sleeping
But I can't because I hear someone coming
Then I see two feet under my door
I only hear breathing and a loud scratching
And someone calling my name
I hide in my covers
Then I hear my doorknob go click
The dark feet seem to be getting closer and closer
And I'm crawling deeper and deeper into my covers
And then…
It closes
I take a big sigh of relief
The feet and the scratching noise finally go away
Then it is quiet again

Heidi Chu, Grade 4
Tower Hill School, DE

Peculiar Purple

Purple is the juicy taste of grapes.
Purple is the color when you get a bruise.
Purple is a sunset.
Purple is a sweet violet flower.
Purple is crayons and markers too.
Purple is a feeling inside of you.
Purple is a butterfly.
Purple is a juicy sensation.
The color that comes up when the picture didn't get taken.
Purple is a kite that flies high in the sky.
Purple is the color of your heart.
Purple is a midnight sky.
Purple is a book.
Purple is a jellybean.
Purple is sunglasses.
Purple is a crab shell that has a design.

Emma McDonough, Grade 4
Immaculate Conception Catholic Regional School, RI

Cupcakes

Cupcakes are so good
If you want to eat one you should!

The cake is so fluffy it's hard to resist
If you don't eat it, you don't know what you missed!

There are so many different types of icing
So when I look at them it is so enticing!

There are a lot of toppings too
Even red, white and blue!

Cupcakes are so good
If you want to eat one you should!

Anna Cottrell, Grade 4
Mary Walter Elementary School, VA

Imagine

The waves crash against the sand
So calm, quiet, and peaceful
Her long blonde silky hair brushes against her rosy cheek
Like a bunny hopping across a meadow of silk
Her sister sits next to her and they watch the waves together
She smiles and her eyes widen like sunshine
The little girl looks up at the seagulls
And wants to fly
And then she looks down and sees the sand crabs
Digging down below
And wants to dig
She can do anything
If she imagines

Alyssa Queen, Grade 4
Boonsboro Elementary School, MD

Basketball

I dribble down the court.
I feel kinda short.
All the other players are tall.
But I can dribble through them all.
I'm open for the shot.
Sweat is pouring down my body a lot.
The ball is going airborne now, I hope, I pray,
It will be a winning day.
But thanks to my shot,
The momentum we got,
Caused us to be in the winning spot.
Basketball is my favorite sport.
I like to dribble down the court.

Blake Jenkins, Grade 6
Floyd T Binns Middle School, VA

My Brother

I have a brother named Ross
He does not care who is the boss
Ross really likes video games
I bet he could tell you all of their names
A character named Mario has special powers
Ross plays it for hours and hours
All he does is play the Wii
But I love him because he plays it with me!

Sydney Wyant, Grade 4
Mary Walter Elementary School, VA

Fall, Fall, Fall

Watching the fall's sunsets
Will relax you like an egret,
But when you see the sunset disappear
You will wonder where it will reappear,
Even though you may think it's silly
But some people don't like the sunsets really,
I guess they just cannot imagine
How much wonder it can begin.

Brittany Heath, Grade 6
Gildersleeve Middle School, VA

My Family

My family the people I love
Also my dead family I see from above
If I didn't have a family I wouldn't be born
or my heart would be torn
If we didn't have a family no people would exist
so why would we risk the consequence.

Markiece Banks, Grade 6
Floyd T Binns Middle School, VA

Family

A family is like animals
They all love each other in different ways
Animals love each other because of their braveness
People love from kindness
Most important, they love

Brooks Reahl, Grade 4
Riderwood Elementary School, MD

Metal Giants

Big metal giants reach up to the sky
Big metal giants give power to wasteful things.
Big tall metal giants are huge, but do not fly
Big tall metal giants hold up power lines
Big tall ugly giants destroy what nature brings.

Kinsey Kidder, Grade 4
Mary Walter Elementary School, VA

Moms

M oms are awesome and amazing
O ut of this world
M oms go through a lot to make sure that us, kids,
    grow up to become successful adults
S o very nice and sweet

Emily Blackwell, Grade 6
Graham Middle School, VA

Pippin

There once was a hobbit named Pippin
Who often deserved a whippin'
For he liked to explore
And rules he'd ignore.
And his feet they would dance without slippin'.

Ari Stein, Grade 4
Blacksburg New School, VA

Soccer Player

Run run as the wind blows through your hair
you run as fast as you can kicking the ball
everybody counting on you pressure everywhere
you shoot the ball and you make the goal
happiness everywhere

Jonathan Lopez, Grade 6
Floyd T Binns Middle School, VA

Art

Art is a way of life
you live in it every day
it's at your school,
your home, at the stores, open your
eyes and admire it the wonders of art!
Art could be different countries,
places, galore! Art is your shoes.
Art takes patience and time to make art work.
From sculptures to painting art is the world.
Open your eyes and see art!

Hunter Newton, Grade 6
Floyd T Binns Middle School, VA

I Am a Cell Phone

I am a cell phone, ringing away!
Getting text messages day by day!
Oh no! I'm getting dropped to the ground!
I hope they can still hear my sound!
Oh thank heavens, I got repaired!
N-o-o-o, with destructive baby Brian, I will be shared!
I am an iPhone!
I go on an iHome!
I am a cell phone!
Ringing away!

Christina Collins, Grade 6
Homeschool Plus, VA

Love

Love is showing that you care,
Love can take you anywhere.
Love comes from up above,
Love is what makes you!
Like I said before,
Love can take you anywhere.
Love,
When you are loved, and you know that you are loved,
There's always going to be a seam of goodness somewhere in
Your heart.

Madison Spayd, Grade 5
William B Keene Elementary School, DE

Music

It is my everything.
My world, my inspiration.
I hear it when I'm sleeping.
I'll tell all I LOVE through MUSIC!
I hear it miles away, I feel it on my lips before it's there.
MUSIC is in dawn, it's in the moon light.
MUSIC is everywhere you go.
MUSIC is always there, it will never leave.
It is like a ghost, here to stay, here to haunt my heart forever!

Caroline Price, Grade 6
Floyd T Binns Middle School, VA

Cheerleading

I step out on the mat,
Butterflies in my stomach.
Ready to give my all for three whole minutes.

Smile, be loud, never give up.
These are the things my coach has told me all year.
Now its time to put our plan into action,
The music starts to pump in my ear.

Jumps, stunts, tumbling too,
Things I've worked on the whole time through.
My time is almost up,
The team and I have done it,
A first place trophy goes to the team
And that was always our dream.

McKenzie Kaitlyn Lester, Grade 6
Graham Middle School, VA

Good Times

Family spread far and wide,
But when Thanksgiving comes, they all arrive.
The young and the old, we're all glad to see
Those close and far are all welcome by me.
Dinner is cooking, smelling great,
I keep saying, I just can't wait.
When dinner is ready and set on the table,
We all give thanks because God made it able.
We eat and talk while enjoying the dinner,
Our compliments to the cook because the meal is a winner.
No one leaves without tasting all the desserts,
Then we slowly get up, knowing we all ate too much,
Hoping our stomach's don't ache and such.
We make our way to the living room to watch the game,
To complete our evening, before we all go our own way.

Keyshawn Taylor, Grade 5
North Tazewell Elementary School, VA

Buff Blue

Blue is the sky so bright and calm.
Blue is the school's uniforms that stretch out to our palm.
Blue is the color of school bleachers.
Blue is the sea with all the sea creatures.
Blue is the color of school jerseys.
Blue is sometimes the wrapper of chocolate Hershey's.
Blue is the color of water in the pool.
Blue is the rain so cold and cool.
Blue is the color of markers' ink.
Blue is the color of the water we drink.
Blue is the color of nail polish for girls.
Blue is the water that brings pearls.
This is the last one for now.
You make people blue when you bow.

Matthew Lee, Grade 4
Immaculate Conception Catholic Regional School, RI

Vicious Vortex

The tornado is like a great white shark
So dangerous, and bigger than I could ever imagine
The once blue sky is an ugly green and gray brown
Is there shelter for me?

Lightning leaps across the sky and cracks it in half
With its jagged fingers
The thunder is so loud; it makes me drop to my knees
My mind tells me to sprint, I can only jog
Too tired to save myself
Are my parents looking for me?

I fall millions of times
Too scared to stay on my feet
The whirling wind is a dragon, and it destroys everything
My ears, they ring with its terrible roar
Where can I go?

Buildings crumble, they too are weak with fear
I look up to see fire in the distance
The air feels so hot, so sticky, and so humid
Sweat pours from my face, and I run in the last shelter I see
Hearing c-c-c-crack as the building collapses
Will I be crushed and killed? Will I be lost forever?

Cassia Jervier, Grade 6
Dumbarton Middle School, MD

Disasters

People's homes are destroyed
People's families are lost
People's hopes are gone

I see people crying
I see people dying
I see people suffering

You wonder how
You wonder why
You wonder all through the night

Children ask, "Where are my parents?"
Children ask, "Why us?"
Children ask, "Where will we go?"

You don't know what to say
You don't want to lie
You don't want to see the heartbreak in their eye

Everyone is praying
Everyone is silent
Everyone is laughing to keep from crying

Somer Stone, Grade 6
Graham Middle School, VA

Waiting and Waiting
Waiting and waiting,
Where is it?
It's big, it's yellow,
and it's missing.
How long has it been?
My mother says 15 minutes!
School starts at 9:00.
Our driver is nice
And never late.
I don't know what is wrong!
Is she okay?
Is she hurt?
I call my friend
At another stop.
She was there too
Waiting and waiting.
Kathryn Robinson, Grade 5
Clifton Elementary School, VA

Blue Skies
When I'm down I look outside and I see you
blue skies
It's always hot when you're outside
blue skies
You put a smile on my face
blue skies
I play outside when you're out
blue skies
Your best friend is the sun
blue skies
You look the best above the mountains
blue skies
Sparkling on the lake chilling is the
blue skies
You are the best with blue
blue skies
Joe Gearhart, Grade 6
Graham Middle School, VA

Steak
S teak is my favorite food to eat.
T he taste is really neat.
E very type is savory meat.
A t supper time I take a seat.
K nowing that I'll get a treat.

I like mine with a baked potato,
S alad with ranch, no tomato.

G rilling out is really fun.
R ibeyes and sirloins, why pick just one?
E at them medium, rare, or well-done.
A nd, sometimes you can add A-1.
T astebuds get ready for a real home run.
Ridge Patteson, Grade 5
Pemberton Elementary School, VA

The Greatest Mother
My mother loves me
I know because
She's always there for me
She cooks my favorite foods
She bakes white, fluffy sugar cookies
She is always laughing

That makes me feel good
Because
I love to see her happy

She hugs me as soon as she gets
home from work.
And she always remembers
to ask me about my day at school
She gives me kisses before bed

I don't know what I would do without her!
Janiah Ward, Grade 4
Bensley Elementary School, VA

I Love Christmas
"Christmas is coming!"
"Christmas is coming!"
It's snowing outside
Everything is covered with white
Cars, houses, trees
I go outside to play with my friends
We pack the snow into little balls
My hands turn to ice
Snow flies through the air
Hitting my friends
Or missing them by only an inch
The snowballs shatter
Falling slowly to the ground
It's cold
It's white
And that's how I know
Christmas is here.
Erika Ascencio, Grade 4
Bensley Elementary School, VA

Under the Sea
Under the sea life is in action.
The seaweed squirms around
Like a flag in the everlasting wind
Fish swim gracefully
Like a black stallion running in the sunset.
Sharks swim faster than a cheetah.
Swordfish are knights in medieval times
Defending the castle.
The octopuses are gardeners
Planting royal gardens
And that is under the sea.
Nicholas Cofrancesco, Grade 4
Boonsboro Elementary School, MD

Why So Many Questions
Why do waves crash against the shore
Why do we have the number four
Why don't dinosaurs exist anymore
Why
Who said the first insult
Who saw the first lightning bolt
Who fed the first colt
Who
What makes the wind blow
What carved the grand canyon years ago
What makes the flowers grow
What
Why do I have so many questions
Abigael Harwell, Grade 6
Floyd T Binns Middle School, VA

My Dear Friends
My dear friends
short and stout
tall and thin.
Have always been
at my side.
They have done
things for me,
as I have
for them.
They help me
when I am down.
My friends like me and
I like my friends.
Billy McKinnon, Grade 6
St Jane De Chantal School, MD

Christmas Morning
Waking up to a Ding, Ding, Ding
My alarm clock is singing
Telling me it's Christmas morning
Running to my parent's bedroom
I shout
"Wake up! Wake up!
It's Christmas!"
I hurry downstairs
And see all the sparkly presents
Under the tree
I rip them open
All the presents I ever wanted
makes this the best Christmas Ever!
Yajaira Ramirez, Grade 4
Bensley Elementary School, VA

Wonderful Weather
Wind is blowing now
What is nature I hear sounds
Outside here I come
Deondre Clark, Grade 6
Floyd T Binns Middle School, VA

I Am

I am a saxophone and soccer player
I wonder if someday I will win the World Cup
I hear the crowd chanting my name
I see the ball soaring my way
I want to block the ball
I am a saxophone and soccer player

I pretend I'm up on stage playing the sax
I feel the music within me
I touch each button as I play
I worry I will not make the big stage
I cry when I break a reed
I am a saxophone and soccer player

I understand I may get scored on
I say it was a nice shot
I dream of holding that trophy above my head
I try my best to block the shots
I hope to play for Spain or Brazil
I am a saxophone and soccer player

Will Olive, Grade 6
Graham Middle School, VA

An Artist

I am a girl who loves drawing.
I wonder if I'll be an artist.
I hear the art teacher saying to look at our beautiful drawings and
the crayons, pencils breaking.
I see my pencil moving in circles and pencils breaking.
I want to be an artist when I grow up, it's fun.
I am a girl who loves drawing.

I pretend I'm an artist at drawing school.
I feel happy when I draw it is really, really fun doing it alone.
I touch my paper with color pencils.
I worry that I'll not become an artist when I'm older
I am a girl who loves drawing.

I understand if I don't become an artist
I say I love to draw
I dream of being an artist
I try to do my best
I hope to become a wonderful artist when I grow up
I am a girl who loves drawing.

Destiny Hernandez, Grade 5
Blackrock School, RI

Autumn

A lot happens during this season
U nder a pile of leaves, the grass slowly starts to die
T all trees gradually grow bare
U mbrellas are sometimes required for this season
M any different places have certain scents for this time of year
N o one loves autumn more than me!

Emily Carlisle, Grade 6
Graham Middle School, VA

Enemies

Jack Frost is the one who makes ice.
He isn't always nice.
He's also very cold,
but not very old.
He's the enemy of Santa.
Santa's the one who go's down your chimney at night.
when he's done delivering presents he says,
"Merry Christmas to all and to all a goodnight."

Alicia Quinteros, Grade 6
Floyd T Binns Middle School, VA

My Dog Daisy

Daisy makes me laugh.
When she plays with her toys,
her bunny, raccoon and dinosaur.
When she begs, she gives us puppy eyes.
I know that she is special.
I make noises and she moves her head sideways.
I love her with all my heart I know that I will never forget,
My Dog Daisy!

Madilynn Snyder, Grade 5
Rosemont Forest Elementary School, VA

Sitting Where the Mountains Are

Most beautiful thing you have ever seen.
Over the mountain I see a gleam.
Under the mountain it is kinda clean.
Near the mountain where the trees are I
am sitting in the shade with my black blue jeans.
J.T. my brother is in his teens and sitting right beside me.
Me and him are having a picnic with pork and beans.

Kierah Groves, Grade 6
Floyd T Binns Middle School, VA

Autumn Leaves

Descending
Dancing with the wind
Turning into the cover of a rabbit's burrow
Playfully skimming the water's surface
Transforming color with the change of seasons
Blanketing the earth, softly protecting
Sheltering, Dancing, Transforming, Protecting

Meredith Beavers, Grade 6
Midlothian Middle School, VA

Seasons

The seasons change no matter how we feel about them.
Each has it's own personality.
Winter, so cold.
Fall, see the leaves float by.
Spring, zingity-zing, new life.
Summer my favorite, to run and play with glee!
Don't forget we cannot control them, just enjoy them.

Makenzie Anne Novinger, Grade 6
Graham Middle School, VA

The Missing Present

It's Christmas Morning
My parents are snoring
As I sneak to the living room
Tiptoeing all the way
I take a present to my room

Open it silently
As quiet as can be
My dad wakes up
I hide the present

Somehow he soon discovers
"the missing present"
I'm afraid he'll find
it in my closet.
And he does
My dad takes it away
And he hides it under the sink

This was the funniest Christmas morning ever!
Gustavo Medrano, Grade 4
Bensley Elementary School, VA

The Everlasting Circle of Friendship

When I think about friendship
I think of a great heart
If you never got that feeling
I think you should start

Friendship almost never stops
It just keeps going on and on
We could almost say it hops
To arrive into everybody's open hearts

When you have friendship
You feel so great
And just to see your very best friend
You will never ever dare to be late

That is all I can say about everlasting friendship
But as I said before it will always keep showing
And yes it will also
Always keep on growing
Marie Merveilleux du Vignaux, Grade 6
St Jane De Chantal School, MD

Burj-Al-Arab

This building is beautiful.
It's shaped like a big white sail
On which we see the reflection of the clean blue ocean.
When you get close to it, you hear a soothing sound.
It's the sound of lazy waves hitting the golden sandy beach.
This building is beautiful.
Even at night, when soft colored lights shine all over it.
Gabriel Karam, Grade 5
Seven Locks Elementary School, MD

Imagination

Put your wings on
Soar so high you can see the heavens above the sky.
Ride a rainbow
Down, Down, Down, to the pot of gold.
What? The pot of gold cannot be found.
I guess it must be sold.
Oh, well! I'll go to bed with my thoughts inside my head.
Dream a dream about my trip
Hold my teddy bear with a tight grip.
Tomorrow, maybe I'll ride a ship or a train in the rain
Or I might even drive a crane.
If I don't go insane.
If only I could ride a purple horse
Or play golf on a pink golf course.
Mommy would be so happy,
If she could see what I have seen.
Oh, what fun to visit all these places
To see all kind of different faces
In my imagination!
Carrie-Anne Moss, Grade 4
Tazewell Elementary School, VA

Boy Playing Baseball

I am a boy who loves playing baseball.
I wonder will I catch the ball?
I hear people screaming my name and yelling,
"Hit a home run for the team Devin."
I see my mom and my brother in the stands.
I want all the signed baseballs in the world to myself.
I am a boy who loves playing baseball.

I pretend to be the best baseball player ever.
I feel the ball in my glove and me falling to the ground.
I touch the wooden baseball bat.
I worry that I will get out and lose the game.
I am a boy who loves playing baseball.

I understand all of the rules in baseball.
I say I got the ball.
I dream to be the best player.
I try to hit a homer when the bases are loaded.
I am a boy who loves playing baseball.
Devin Correa, Grade 5
Blackrock School, RI

Health

Be healthy and exercise
You want to be smart, healthy and wise
Being healthy isn't a trick
Eat your fruits and vegetables so you don't get sick
Run around, play a sport
Just play outside you don't need an official field or court
Your health should be important to you
Your health depends on you and what you try to do!
Leah Stribling, Grade 5
Mary Walter Elementary School, VA

Our Trip to New York
When my dad and I visited New York
We saw tall buildings and busy sidewalks
People were going to stores
To shop for clothes and shoes
Just like us

We stopped at two stores
One just for my dad
And one just for me

He spent a long time in his store
I spent just a little time in my store

When he tried on his clothes
He looked funny
He chose a shirt that was so big
He looked like a man in a long nightgown

When I tried on my clothes I looked gorgeous
I chose a glittery green top
And looked like a fairy tale princess

It was the most special day
Just me and my dad!
Arryella Thompson, Grade 4
Bensley Elementary School, VA

Music Man
A frozen night.
I wonder why the music man
chooses this blistering cold night
to play his flute.

The sound of joy fills the air.
A sound of new life.
New beginnings.

Sinister people walk by
not paying any attention to the music man
with a crumpled box at his feet.
'Donations' it reads.

But I do.
I place a quarter in the box.
All I have,
but it seems enough for the old man.
He smiles, a twinkle in his eyes.

His smile is captivating.
He's a hawk
glittering,
in the winter twilight.
Elizabeth Paglinauan, Grade 4
Roland Park Elementary-Middle School, MD

Picture This
Photography is my goal
It's something I want to do.
I want to take pictures that are fun and new
I want to take pictures of nature and other things
I want to take pictures of the sea and jellyfish that sting.
Pictures of wild animals and plants
I want to take pictures of creatures like ants
Pictures of flowers and other things too
I want to take pictures of the sky so blue.
Photography is my goal.
Jordan Hadler, Grade 4
Mary Walter Elementary School, VA

Leaves
When I walk outside,
and gaze at all the trees,
I see the beautiful colors of all the leaves.
There's a bright orange
that reminds me of the sun,
and a magnificent yellow
and a majestic red.
As I walk by,
I die
to see all the beautiful leaves on each tree.
Bekah Lemer, Grade 4
Roland Park Elementary-Middle School, MD

School
School is important to me
Just being there fills me with glee
School is where I make friends
I follow the rules and try not to bend
I make mistakes and make amends
They teach me lots of different things
Adding, reading and problem solving
I study and study with all my might
School is your future light
Oh! yes and remember don't ever pick a fight.
Jose Romero, Grade 4
Mary Walter Elementary School, VA

A New Cover
Look around and what do you see?
People working peacefully.
But, how is this so with violence about?
Has the news finally got out?
As we work house by house, place by place,
we soon see smiles on everyone's face.
As we start our new world and work with each other,
our world will soon have a new cover.
Peace and love will be our title;
Our world is sure to be loving, not vile.
Olivia Odeh, Grade 5
Herndon Elementary School, VA

I Wanna Be Famous

I wanna be famous
Maybe an actress and a singer
I'm very dramatic
And talented at singing
I can see me now
Spotlight bright and right on me
I would sign autographs
I can see my name Katie Knight
All over TV.
Biggest kid pop star all over the world
Although I would hate paparazzi
All the flashing lights and lies
It can ruin my life
But I would love and enjoy every moment
This might not happen or maybe so
All I know is if I keep on trying
My dreams will come true
I wanna be famous

Katie Knight, Grade 6
Paul L Dunbar Middle School for Innovation, VA

Blazing Blue

Blue is my favorite color,
Blue is the color of the ocean,
It is as cool as a toy,
It is the color of my favorite sweater,
Blue is the color of the sky, which is light blue,
My iPod's color is blue too,
Water is clear of blue,
Blue is the best color in my opinion.
Shiny and regular blue are possible,
It is the background of the stars on the U.S. flag,
Other people love blue as much as I love blue,
Blue is the color of my school uniform,
Blue is the color of my laptop,
I hope blue gets famous and other people love blue,
I hope it spreads around the world,
Blue is also the color of the background of the cloud-men scene,
In the play: *James and the Giant Peach.*

Kenneth Lee, Grade 4
Immaculate Conception Catholic Regional School, RI

Catching Santa Claus

Christmas is a time for happiness
Family is gathered together
All day we play games and tell stories
There's happiness all through the house
At night I lay in bed
As quiet as a mouse
Thinking Santa might be very hard to catch
But I will still try
Because I'd love to fly
His sleigh
All over the world

Jonnelle Partin, Grade 4
Bensley Elementary School, VA

A Mother from My Heart

She's my handprints
She's my footprints
She's always there for the aftermath
Leading me to the best path
She's a mother that I would never abhor or abominate
All our problems she always alleviates
She's never an also-ran
At many things she's an artisan
She's never abstruse
Because she thinks in many views
When anything is askew
She wants to keep it perfect and in view
She is never a cache in my heart
In fact she is a very special part
When there is a candle out in the dark
Empty and impossible to find a person's mark
She is that one light lit to guide
Always there, bringing me to the end by my side

Siri Doddi, Grade 6
Colvin Run Elementary School, VA

The Joy of the Perfect Strawberry

My eyes may be deceiving
Your ruby red color is ablaze with life
Your fragrance I can almost taste you
The feel of your scruffy sides makes me ticklish

A thought pushes through my mind
take a bite
your juice is memorable
it's the pure joy of sweetness
A small "squish" and chewiness inside
strikes me with surprise

I bite to you with no mercy
until sadly you were all gone
That is how I found out
that some things last for life
but the best things get eaten away
to Nothing

Jared Cooper, Grade 6
Charles E Smith Jewish Day School Lower Campus, MD

Woman with Her Cat

The cat curled up on a woman's arm.
His jade eyes flash at pigeons in the window.
The woman's pretty, pink, painted lips
Form a smile at the cat.
Her emerald ring shines as she strokes the fur, so fine.
The cat's eyes glitter, like the rain's pitter.
His fur is as beautiful as a jewel.
He is as lazy as a bear hibernating.
The woman is almost as tired as the cat!
The cat is in her arm, sleeping like a mighty tiger.

Emma Horne, Grade 4
Boonsboro Elementary School, MD

That Thanksgiving Mood
Hooray, Yippee, Hurrah
Today is Thanksgiving Day
The crunchy turkey is piled high
The delicious creamy pumpkin pie
Happy faces full of food
Putting us all in a cheery mood
Wonderful tales from days past
Wishing that this great feast could last
Everyone is here, no one is late
Happy Thanksgiving from the dinner plate!
Genna Hebert, Grade 5
Mary Walter Elementary School, VA

Basketball
B est
A thletic
S port
K ids
E ver
T o play
B asketball is
A lways
L ots and
L ots of fun
Tyrese Dawayne Ellison, Grade 6
Graham Middle School, VA

Basketball
B asketball is my life.
A ll I wanna do is play basketball.
S lam dunks.
K ickin' butt.
E ven with a broken arm.
T aking it to the hoop.
B all hogging not a chance.
A sk Michael Jordan.
L ove the sport.
L ove the game.
Anias Saunders, Grade 6
Floyd T Binns Middle School, VA

The Woods
The woods at midnight
Become the horror in a movie.
Dogs howling at the moon,
Screaming at the unknown.
The woods are like
A ferris wheel stuck at the top,
Falling down, but when you wake up;
It's gone, faded away in time.
Lost in my brain,
Stuck in the dark.
Michayla Neumann, Grade 4
Boonsboro Elementary School, MD

My Heart
My heart has fought
A war many have not

So my heart is fragile
And hard in letting in
It may go in the wrong direction
My family is for my correction

My heart lost the battle
But not the war
Thank God
Jesse Beavers, Grade 6
Graham Middle School, VA

Nothing to Fear
One terrifying night
There was a huge thud
Checking it out with fear
Seeing an ugly monster shadow
It was only my brother
Then there was tapping on glass
I anxiously walked down to go check it out

It was just my sister.
I should not always be so afraid
I have nothing to fear.
Micah Bell, Grade 5
Rosemont Forest Elementary School, VA

Blue
Blue is the color of the big sky
As it wraps around all people
It's the color of my eyes
The feeling when you're under the weather
The ocean of all oceans
When your tears drip
Wish, wash, splash
Dolphins are playing in the sea
If you like this color you are quite clever
There is no color better
Bridget Brown, Grade 5
St. Bartholomew School, MD

A Boy and a Girl
Girl
Pretty, loving
Likes to party
Has sleepovers
Shop till they drop
Eats like a slob
Is wacky at times
Acts like they are cool
Handsome, rough
Boy
Ella Liefke, Grade 4
Boonsboro Elementary School, MD

My Oreo
He's black and white
And very fat
I love him the most
He is my cat

He doesn't like to hunt
He just lies in the sun
If a mouse ran by
He wouldn't even run

He never leaves his home
He is here every day
When I step out the door
I move him out of the way

I talk to him sometimes
He always listens to me
It doesn't matter if he's a cat
He's part of my family
Hannah Ball, Grade 6
Belfast-Elk Garden Elementary School, VA

Dragons Fly to the Moon
Dragons so big
Dragons flew
Dragons flew high
Up to the Moon.
Their mothers tell them
"Come back real soon!"

They fly back home
They're red, white, and gold
One dragon's name is Marigold
Do you know
what I've been told?
About Dragons that fly to the moon

They like flying
They like flowers
And they like spending lots and lots
of hours
with caring Dragon mothers.
Breon Banks, Grade 4
Bensley Elementary School, VA

Caroline
C aring
A thletic
R espectful
O utgoing
L oving
I nteresting
N ice
E ncouraging
Caroline Wilkinson, Grade 6
Graham Middle School, VA

Movie Ending

Now everything to me seems tragic
Like the world is devoid of magic
Like never again can we be together
I am at the end of life's movie reel
You were the climax
The reason for my existence
No longer will I stay alive with persistence
Now the movie is over
And there is no happy ending

Emma Walker, Grade 6
Floyd T Binns Middle School, VA

Christmas

C hrist's birth
H oly time
R un from Herod
I n the night
S cared to death
T errified
M ary holds Jesus very tight
A ll is scared
S tarting to cry…hope that will not die.

Riley Redden, Grade 4
Angelus Academy, VA

My Old Friend

My old friend
wasn't always nice,
instead he was mean
most of the time.
As I sit and think
under my willow tree,
I find out he means a lot to me.
One day, when he moved away,
I never saw my true old friend again.

Eric Jurkiewicz, Grade 5
St Joseph School-Fullerton, MD

Stars

The stars looked at me
And said come up here with us
It was time to go

Jessica Fanduro, Grade 6
Floyd T Binns Middle School, VA

Blue

Blue is
Water that looks like the sky
A lake of sadness
A river of blue fish
The ocean filled with blue water
My pencil case filled with blue pens
The backpack that is all blue
The sound of the wind blowing hard

Lucas Bautista, Grade 5
St Bartholomew School, MD

Wallpaper

I want to decorate my room
What should I use?
Wallpaper of course!
So many kinds
It makes you unwind
Some of them can be colorful
Or just plain dull
It could also be bright
Just like sunlight
It tells about the owner's personality
If they are gritty or pretty
Wallpaper is great
Because it helps to decorate!

Bethany Mizelle, Grade 5
Mary Walter Elementary School, VA

Virginia Tech

V ery good
I nteresting players
R eally great campus
G reat teamwork
I ndependent students
N ice coaches
I just love it!
A mazing team

T errific skills
E xciting games
C reative jerseys
H okies are awesome

Natalya Curto, Grade 6
Graham Middle School, VA

Rain

Rain
All wet
Like some
One was
Crying and
Never stopped.

All blue like water.

When the rain stopped
A shimmering, and glimmering
Rainbow comes out.
Rain

Jimmy Brinkman, Grade 5
Seven Locks Elementary School, MD

Free Bee

Did you see the bee?
Running amuck in that tree.
Do you think it's free?

Lenna Neely, Grade 6
Floyd T Binns Middle School, VA

White Snow

Snow is here and everywhere else.
Rivers are frozen.
Trees are covered with white glittery snow.
It looks like heaven.
Layers of white puffy clouds.
Covering the sky like a blanket.
The snow falls.
I go into a cabin.
Its warmth comforts me outside,
Hot cocoa gives me internal warmth,
I sit and watch the beautiful scene.
I feel calming.

Zachary Valverde, Grade 5
Rosemont Forest Elementary School, VA

Little Suns

The stars gleam in the night
Shining so bright
Little suns in the dark sky
Are so beautiful I want to cry
You can see them
So can I
As they fly
I wish
"So can I"
As the sun paints pink across the sky
My dream is still alive
As I walk inside

Julia S. Gibson, Grade 5
Pemberton Elementary School, VA

Halloween

Halloween is indeed very scary.
Ghosts, witches, and ghouls vary.
Candy in bags you see.
Tons and tons come before thee.
Halloween's for ghosts and freaks.
Home to people with tricks and treats.
It's no place for us people.
Halloween is coming near.
Now bring your screams,
And your fears.
Now fun for your dear life!
Halloween is near.

Vy Nguyen, Grade 5
St Joseph School-Fullerton, MD

Tigers

T igers are my favorite animal
I ntelligent masters of disguise
G iant cats
E ndangered in some places
R arely spotted before they strike
S ighted swimming in rivers and ponds

Chantel Rios, Grade 6
Floyd T Binns Middle School, VA

My Best Friend
You've been my friend for six years
Ever since the first day of school
I think you are so cool
You are like my missing tool
That makes everything work

Liam is so fun and awesome
He is a ton of fun to be around
Always trying his best
At school or at a test
Liam is the best

Either basketball or soccer
Liam always works his hardest
Always trying to win
Never sighing or giving up
Liam, always better than the rest

Liam will always be my best friend
Always willing to lend a hand
Or making sure I land on my feet
Liam would never be a foe
So that is why Liam is my best friend
Nicholas Pottker, Grade 6
St Jane De Chantal School, MD

New School Year
A new school year is almost here
I can feel it, it's very clear
I'm nervous, but I've got nothing to fear
Even though some kids may be weird
I can't wait to lend my ear
To any teacher I'll have this year
Even though it may be near
I cannot wait until this new school year
Zachary Carlisle, Grade 6
Graham Middle School, VA

Aqua Marine
Aqua Marine is a blue-green mix.
The color of coral.
Calm,
Soothing,
Soft,
Forgiving.
The color of the Pacific ocean.
The color of a clear sky.
Cool,
Friendly,
Meek,
Quiet,
Color of a colored pencil.
Sounds like water dripping.
It is the color of spring.
Colin McLearn, Grade 5
St. Bartholomew School, MD

The Fall
My favorite season is fall.
It is the most wonderful of them all.
I love the color of the leaves,
as I watch them fall from the trees.

It starts to get cool,
so there is no more pool.
I have to rake leaves,
it's one of my pet peeves

I get piles of candy,
which is very dandy.
On Thanksgiving I eat turkey
and also eat beef jerky

But fall will be gone,
at the crack of dawn.
Winter will come,
and now my poem is done.
Jacob Thompson, Grade 5
Pemberton Elementary School, VA

Friendship
Friendship is everything
The most exciting thing
That ever happened
In our life

With it life has more colors
Life is more exciting and beautiful
Friends are joy
Friendship is a part of life

Friends are like trees
They can change color
Friendship grows
And has many branches

Friends are everything
Friends are love
But they can also be sadness
Friendship never ends
Alexandrine Zelenko, Grade 6
St Jane De Chantal School, MD

The Wait
My palms are sweating
Knees are shaking
I can hardly say her name
I open my heart
It seems as if
Every thing falls into place
Then I wait and wait
For the answer I've been waiting for
Jay Stiltner, Grade 6
Graham Middle School, VA

Love Is Just a Fairy Tale
Love is a fairy tale
At first you believe
Everything seems so easy
So perfect, so smooth
Every minute feels like a day
Every day feels like a lifetime
Then reality breaks through,
Creates a storm…
and then you truly realize
…that love is just a fairy tale.
Jeweliana Moore, Grade 6
Dr E A Ricci Middle School, RI

Hurricane…
I wake up to the sound
of rustling trees

I feel the breeze
of shaking trees

I open the door
until a crack

I see a storm forming Black.
Shreya Kurdukar, Grade 4
Little River Elementary School, VA

Rainy Day
I don't want to do my homework today
everything seems so gloomy and gray
I want to go outside and play
that's sure not to happen right away

I wish my homework was all done
maybe then I can have fun
and play under the sun
before my day is done
Anne Kohlroser, Grade 5
Pemberton Elementary School, VA

Nerf Guns
N ot stoppable
E xtra fun
R adical
F iring

G oals
U nited
N erf power
S hoot
Byron Cornelius, Grade 6
Floyd T Binns Middle School, VA

Homework!!

Monday is the worst,
Because it is the first day
Of my homework filled week.
My teacher gave us work,
But I knew it would lurk
In the back of my mind for the day.
Tuesday wasn't much better,
Because we had to write a lengthy letter
To the President of the United States.
Wednesday was another story,
I completed all my homework early,
Only to have it shredded by my dog.
Thursday was such a pain,
My term paper flew off in the rain;
That was the easiest "F" I ever got.
Thanks goodness for Friday,
But my teacher had the last say…
"Write a 15 page theme on Einstein's Theory of Relativity."
Don't worry folks,
this isn't a joke!
Another Monday is only two days away!

Kyler Carl, Grade 6
Bishop Walsh Middle High School, MD

Rain

As I walk
The rain comes down
The droplets bounce
On the sidewalk
They stream down the road
Like streaks of light
Bursting in the heavens
The rain is like a crystal
Millions shattering as they hit
Coldness spreads like a fire
It rolls off my skin
It reminds me of a happier time
I think of the stars
Falling like meteors
Showering us with sadness
Showing us the ways of life
Making peace with the world
The rain stops
The sun beams
All is better
Life is beautiful

Indya Page, Grade 6
Paul L Dunbar Middle School for Innovation, VA

Beach

Warm, sunny
Swimming, riding the waves, building sandcastles
Shells, sand, crabs, umbrellas
Beach

Sophie Remington, Grade 5
Pemberton Elementary School, VA

Cheerleading

The music starts
I look at the crowd
I start counting out the beats in my head
5.6.7.8.1.2.3.4.5.6.7.8
Then suddenly I start my routine
I spring off the floor so high
I feel like I can touch the sky
Then I do a pike then I land gracefully
Next is my stunt I hop onto my base's hands
Then they push me up
I bring one foot to my ankle
Then pull it over my head
The rest of my routine is a breeze
The backhand springs and the splits
The dance and the stunts
Every good thing has to end though
So I smile and wave
To show I love what I do
Furthermore to show team spirit too
Cheerleading is the best
In addition it will put you to the ultimate test

Victoria Edwards, Grade 6
Graham Middle School, VA

I Am a Soccer Player

I am a girl who loves playing soccer
I wonder how my game will go.
I hear coaches telling me to stay where I am
and my team asking me to pass.
I see my team in front of and next to me.
I want to make goals the last second of the game.
I am a girl who loves playing soccer.

I pretend I am being chased by my brother.
I feel good when I pass the ball to my teammates and they score.
I touch the ball with cleats.
I worry that the other team will score on us first.
I am a girl who loves playing soccer.

I understand I will not win every game.
I say, "Pass me the ball."
I dream I'll be professional player.
I try to score a goal.
I hope we will win the championship game and other games.
I am a girl who loves playing soccer.

Sara Fiddes, Grade 5
Blackrock School, RI

Snow Milk

The milk of a Norway Maple is like snow.
It is cold.
It is sour like a blizzard.
When it drips, it is like a winter wonderland falling
from the sky.

Gavin Peters, Grade 4
Riderwood Elementary School, MD

Cheetah

Cheetah, Cheetah
Running in the grass.
Running with a pitter patter
Very fast.
Cheetah very hungry,
Running after prey.
Cheetah not hungry any more.
Riley Place, Grade 5
St Bartholomew School, MD

Free

I am me,
I am free.
See me go,
Or watch me leave.
I believe in my country,
To stay free.
Amber Proffitt, Grade 6
Graham Middle School, VA

Family

F riendly
A musing
M erry
I ntelligent
L oving
Y ou will love my family
Chika Nwakama, Grade 5
St Joseph School-Fullerton, MD

Future

F ar from today
U nder water
T echnology
U nderground
R obots will invade the earth
E verybody will live free
Noah Makhmreh, Grade 5
St Joseph School-Fullerton, MD

I Am a Norway Maple

I give milk that is white like snow.
I am green with no more colors.
I have a little stem and a dot of milk.
I am like a grassy plain green and bright.
The tree I came from is so very perfect.
I am a Norway Maple.
Margot Key, Grade 4
Riderwood Elementary School, MD

Life

Overcome hardships
Reach new heights in our hard lives
The sky's the limit
Sai Samayamanthula, Grade 6
Floyd T Binns Middle School, VA

I Am a Blackbelt

I am a boy who is a blackbelt. I wonder if I will break bricks,
I hear the board cracking and dropping down towards the dojo's
floor with my sweat and foot, I see my foot whipping the big,
fat, heavy bag, I want to achieve my goals including getting my
2nd degree blackbelt, I am a boy who is a blackbelt.

I pretend I am Bruce Lee sparring with my opponents, I
feel my opponent with my foot striking his body with lots of power,
I touch the very sweaty mats, I worry that I am going to lose this
breaking tournament, I am a boy who is a blackbelt.

I understand that I am not the best, I say that there's no limit, I
dream of being a 10th degree, I try to be a role model, I hope my family
comes to my testing so I'm confident, I am a boy who is a blackbelt.
Joshua Leavitt, Grade 5
Blackrock School, RI

But, That's Just Me

My name is Gerika.
Companionable, hardheaded, pleasant, and beloved.
Older sister of Jade and Jaylen, also the daughter of Ria Reynolds and Derrick Helm.
But that's just me…
Who loves to eat Mexican, Chinese, and Filipino food.
Who also loves to watch music videos and Netflix movies (sometimes).
My name is Amber.
But that's just me…
I listen to 102.7 jamming JJS and anything else.
I also want a Pomeranian, a Boxer and also a new laptop.
Who would love to go to Paris, France, the Bahamas or the Philippines.
I'm a resident of Lynchburg with my mom and a resident of Madison Heights with my dad.
I go to Paul Lawrence Dunbar for Innovation, grade 6.
My name is Gerika Amber Moorman.
Gerika Amber Moorman, Grade 6
Paul L Dunbar Middle School for Innovation, VA

Green Is Great

Green is grass beneath your toes on a mild autumn day.
Green is a crisp leaf on a tree in the summer time swaying side to side.
An inch worm crawling across your hand is green.
Green is "Going Green" and helping our environment.
Green is the sick feeling when you eat too much sour apple jolly ranchers on Halloween.
Limes are green before they are squeezed out onto a fresh baked pie.
Green is good luck like on a four-leaf clover.
Green is the Shamrock symbol of the Blessed Trinity.
Also green is the color of Saint Patrick's day.
Green is chlorophyll that makes the leaves on a tree green.
Green is mean ferocious dragons in a fairy tale.
Green is aliens that live on Mars.
Finally, green is Joe, the Statue of Liberty.
Megan Mahoney, Grade 4
Immaculate Conception Catholic Regional School, RI

Windy Little Kitten

The wind is like a kitten
Playing all the day
She bats around her cloudy toys
In a kittish kind of way
Until another sees her toy
And she carries it away

She sleeps upon a gray cloud bed
And her purrs rustle the leaves
You never see her, she's so fast
As she races through the trees

No matter when I meet her
I'll answer as today
She's my windy little kitten
And I will love her always
Claire Fisher, Grade 6
Graham Middle School, VA

Her Lovely Flowers

Flowers make me happy
Roses, sunflowers, and violets
Remind me of my mother's garden

My friend and I
Choose the prettest flowers
To press and dry in a picture frame
To keep
As good memories
Of planting and picking flowers
in my mother's extraordinary garden.

I walk slowly through the garden
Not wanting to ruin even one
Of her soft, sweet, precious
Flowers
Sayra Granados, Grade 4
Bensley Elementary School, VA

An Ode to a Basketball

Oh, Basketball
I love when you go into our basket.

I hope I never make you dizzy
when I dribble or pass you.

I enjoy the feel of your soft leather,
and seeing your glowing color.

When we win the game
it's because of you.

Basketball just make sure
you don't go into the other team's basket.
Lexi Kiser, Grade 6
Graham Middle School, VA

Rain

The rain starts drizzling,
fine and small,
Whispering to you,
Telling you its secrets.

It gets heavier,
Angrier,
Like you aren't listening.

Then it's furious,
Banging at your window,
Threatening to break in and destroy you.

Now it is not telling, it is yelling,
Not its secrets, but insults.

Finally, the rain eases,
Forgiving you, giving you another chance.

It starts again with secrets,
Then it gives up
And leaves you at rest.
Rosa Boehler, Grade 5
Seven Locks Elementary School, MD

Green

Green is silence,
The smell of pine,
Some shirts,
A funny rhyme,
Cucumbers,
Tomatoes,
And other plants.
Green is the color of nature,
Leprechauns on St. Patrick's Day.
Green is reptiles and ecology.
It's the color of biology,
Trees,
Cash, murky water.
Green is this and green is that,
Hissing beasts,
Frankenstein.
Green is jungles,
And forests in the spring.
From grass to good luck,
All is green
And green is all.
Jorge Familiar, Grade 5
St Bartholomew School, MD

Camping

Camping is so fun.
Sleeping in a tent all night.
Eating many S'mores.
Ethan Bower, Grade 5
St Joseph School-Fullerton, MD

Baltimore Ravens

B ig hits
A thletic players
L ong passes
T ouchdown madness
I ntimidating team
M onday Night Football
O h man they're good
R ay Lewis
E xciting plays

R ay Rice
A mazing plays
V ictory is ours
E xhilarating games
N o mercy
S weet stadium
Matthew Maggio, Grade 5
St Joseph School-Fullerton, MD

Friends Are Forever

Friends are wonderful,
Friends are great.
On a scale from one to ten,
I would give it an eight.

If you don't have one,
That is very sad.
But if you do, they are very fun.
But if you are bad,
They will get mad.

Friends are forever,
They always will be.
The first time I saw mine,
I knew we would be.
Grant Connolly, Grade 6
St Jane De Chantal School, MD

It Is Spring

Winter months start to end,
with the warmth of the sun.
Chasing the snow around the bend,
making splashing very fun.

The chickadee calls,
from a tree.
At the seashore the gulls,
scream and holler at me.

The trees are budding,
and the grass is growing.
The mowers start cutting,
but the grass keeps growing.
IT IS SPRING!
Kaitlyn Jantzi, Grade 6
Oak Grove Mennonite School, VA

Friends

Friends are the best.
They're better than the rest.
If you ever need a friend
They will stay with you until the end.

They are there with you when you are mad.
They are there for you when you are sad.
You can always count on them.

If you are having trouble
They will be there on the double.
They're the best thing ever made.

If there is something on your mind
They wont' be rude, they'll be kind.
They will listen to what you say
And say, "Hey, that's O.K."
Jack Hamilton, Grade 6
St Jane De Chantal School, MD

Friendship

Friends are important
To help you grow
They pick you up when you are low

Friends are loyal and
Stick by your side
They make you laugh
With love so wide

A friend is caring and
Shares a turn
Give and take are what you learn

To keep a friend,
You have to be one
And that's the way
To have lots of fun!
Emily Matejik, Grade 6
St Jane De Chantal School, MD

Thinking of You

I had a chance to think of you.
As tears filled my eyes.
The memories we lived and shared.
With no chance to say good-bye
I had a chance to think of you.
Our laughs and times together.
I know one day we'll meet again.
'Cause you've gone to heaven.
So please keep watching over me
Make sure I'm doing right.
To spread the love you shared with me
And don't give up a fight.
Hannah Taylor, Grade 6
Graham Middle School, VA

Snow Day

I stand outside
and see the snow.
It glitters in
the air as it
falls to the ground.
My nose is cold,
but I don't care.
It's a snow day.
My skin is red,
but I don't care.
It's a snow day.
Everything is
perfect because
it's a snow day.
No words can say
how I feel when
I stand outside
on a snow day.
Audrey Burton, Grade 6
Bishop Walsh Middle School, MD

Cerulean Crayon

Color of the sky,
Used as a school supply,
Cerulean in particular,
Three inches tall in exact-made of wax,
Waltzes upon the paper,
Making marks to and fro,
Tinge of the sea,
Shine of the sky,
Left corner of the stars and stripes,
Pigment of my backpack,
Hue of my eyes,
Pastel of peace,
Vividness of serene bliss,
Dye of the robin's egg,
Spectrum of my tranquil dreams,
Blush of bliss,
Peace and dreams,
This is my petite cerulean crayon.
Amelia Dilworth, Grade 4
Home School, DE

Friends

Supportive, calming, caring, respectful
Always visit you when you're sick
Help you up when you're down
Are there for you during loss
Make you laugh about anything
Can be serious when necessary
Make up after fights
Say stupid things
There forever no matter what
Heaven on Earth!
Jenna Doak, Grade 4
Boonsboro Elementary School, MD

Books

Read them anytime anywhere
Picture Books
Books without pictures
Adult books
Kids books
Fantasy
Adventure
And mysteries too
Biography
Science fiction
History
Books are like movies in your mind
Jaayden Thomas, Grade 5
St Bartholomew School, MD

Friends Are Great

Friends are great
My first was when I was eight
I took the bait
It turned out to be great

Friends are fun
Even in the hot summer sun
That's why friends are fun

Friends are bright
They are tight
And ready to put up a fight
Christopher DeMartino, Grade 6
St Jane De Chantal School, MD

Ice Skater

Some like to sing,
Some like to dance,
But I want to be an ice skater,
I love the ice beneath my skates,
Even though I fall,
I still get up and glide!

When I'm on the ice,
I feel like I'm in another world,
The cold, slick ice is home to me,
I love it when I begin to glide on the ice,
I feel like I'm going to fly.
Missy Bolton, Grade 5
Rosemont Forest Elementary School, VA

Match Promise

I feel sweat dripping from my chin,
For every time I'm on the wrestling mat,
I try my hardest for the pin,
And knowing I won't give in,
Till the referee raises my hand,
And says I got the win.
Shane Maryk, Grade 6
Floyd T Binns Middle School, VA

I Am a Basketball Player

I am a female who loves to play basketball
I wonder if I'll fake someone out
I hear people screaming, people cheering, the buzzer being the
loudest of them all while walking by
I see the clock ticking while squaring up to shoot
I want to make the winning basket at the championship game today
I am a female who loves to play basketball

I pretend that I will become a WNBA star
I feel nervous when I raise the ball and jump up into the air
I touch the ball held high
I worry someone will steal the ball as I am dribbling
I am a female who loves to play basketball

I understand that I cannot win every game
I say that we can win
I dream that we'll win the championship
I try my best every game
I hope that we can be the undefeated team every year
I am a female who loves to play basketball

Natalie Gannon, Grade 5
Blackrock School, RI

A Friend

If somebody needs a friend, then be one.
If you see someone fall,
then help them back up.
If someone is not sure about something,
then help them gather up confidence.

If you are nice to people,
then people will be nice to you.
If you make friends everywhere,
then you will be able to find them no matter where you are.

Friendship can be broken,
but it can also be fixed.
Losing a friend is like losing a piece of your life,
but that piece can be brought back.

If you help your friends through hard times,
then they will also help you.
Treat your friends well,
for your friends will treat you how you treat them.

Michael Madden, Grade 6
St Jane De Chantal School, MD

Christmas

Christmas is awesome
Christmas is great
What we ask for is always great
When we see gifts we go nuts
What I want is always tight
And at the end we always say thanks to those we love!

Fabian Miranda, Grade 6
Floyd T Binns Middle School, VA

Skateboarding

I am a boy who loves skateboarding
I wonder if I will become a pro
I hear the wheels ride on the hot
tar down the long street to the other street
I see the long street go by faster than lightning
I want a new skateboard so I can do awesome trick easily

I am a boy who loves skateboarding
I pretend I am at a good skate park
I feel the grip tape wearing down from moving my feet all over it
I touch the very hot wheels
I worry that I will slip and fall off my board

I am a boy who loves skateboarding
I understand I might not be any good
I say I will be good
I dream I will win a competition
I try all day every day
I hope to be sponsored and get my own pro board
I am a boy who loves skateboarding

Cole Laferriere, Grade 5
Blackrock School, RI

I Am a Hockey Player

I am a goal scoring hockey player
I wonder how many goals I'll score
I hear the crowd cheering me on and the sound of
skates gliding along the ice rink
I see the goalie trembling, afraid that I will score
I want to play for the Boston Bruins and become very famous
I am a goal scoring hockey player

I pretend to be Wayne Gretzky "The Great One."
I feel the pressure as I am about to shoot the puck and score
I touch the bench between shifts
I worry that our opponents will have more skill than us
I am a goal scoring hockey player

I understand the coach's words when he talks
I say "Pass the puck Nick"
I dream about living in a mansion
I try to skate very fast
I hope to play hard and hold the Stanley Cup someday
I am a goal scoring hockey player

Evan Amerantes, Grade 5
Blackrock School, RI

My Friends

My friends are very special to me
They pick me up when I'm down in the dumps
They fill me up with glee
They help me get over those rough bumps
We have lots of laughs every single day
Without my friends it would be hard to find my way

Natalie Kane, Grade 5
Pemberton Elementary School, VA

The Light of the Night

The light of the night is not exactly what it seems.
The stars shine brighter than the sun
No, this is not the light I speak of.

The light of the night is not exactly what it seems.
The ripples in the water shine the moon's bright light.
No, this is not the light I speak of.

The light of the night is not exactly what it seems.
The fireflies shine off their fiery glow.
No, this is not the light I speak of.

The light of the night is not exactly what it seems.
The city lights are brilliant, like the Fourth of July.
No, this is not the light I speak of.

The light of the night is not exactly what it seems.
The lighthouse almost makes me go blind.
No, this is not the light I speak of.

The light of the night is not exactly what it seems.
Jesus' undying love for me shines, my light of the night.

Aryana Henson, Grade 6
Floyd T Binns Middle School, VA

Fun in Florida

Vacationing in Florida
Just us girls
My aunt, grandma, sister, mom, and I
It's 2008

We're driving in an old rickety-rackety worn out van
Zooming excitedly down the road
The windows are down
The wind is roaring
I'm excited to arrive
To a water park with slides
That make me scream
All the way down

At the bottom
My throat is a little sore
But I also feel proud
That I went down
The swirly orange slide
Even if…
I was a little scared
at first.

LaDasha Robertson, Grade 4
Bensley Elementary School, VA

Beastly Black

Black is the night
with stars to see.
Black is a cat
so soft and furry.
Black is ink
inside your pen.
Black is smoke
from a camping fire.
Black likes to follow you
Black is space way out there
And black is for you and me to share

Jordan Marot, Grade 4
Immaculate Conception Catholic Regional School, RI

The Storm

I am playing outside with my friend.
It starts to storm.
As he runs in
I stand there.
I let the rain tap my face and go into my mouth.
I look up and see the lightning slice through the sky.
I smell the damp air and soggy wood.
BOOM! BASH! CRACKLE!!! I hear the clash of thunder.
Then the sun appears.
A rainbow spreads across the sky.
The storm is over.

Trevor Willard, Grade 4
Boonsboro Elementary School, MD

Gothic Green

Green is a lime
sour then sweet.
Green is a slime (eeeew!)
gooey and glop.
Sometimes green can be a flip-flop.
Green can be an apple, olive, even a bean
You can be keen when you think of green.
Green is a dragon
fast and furious.
Green is a turtle
slow and steady.
Green is a light that says, "Go!"
But most of all green is an army suit that saves our souls.

Violet Kiekbusch, Grade 4
Immaculate Conception Catholic Regional School, RI

Basic Blue

Blue is the feeling of sadness today.
Blue is a bluebird chirping away.
Blue is the taste of a blueberry pie.
Blue might be a bright blue butterfly.
Blue is the blue on an American Flag!
Blue is the color of the sky nice and bright,
Blue is a color in some peoples' eyes.
Blue is a blue crayon that you use to color.
Blue is a book that I'll read tomorrow.
Blue is the color of justice and peace.
Blue is the color that you'll feel piece by piece.
Blue is a cool breeze of water in your face.
What would you do without blue on your mind?

Alexa Gardner, Grade 4
Immaculate Conception Catholic Regional School, RI

Life's Beauty
Life can be a gift.
It's beauty lies around you.
Do not deny life.
Michael Norman, Grade 6
Floyd T. Binns Middle School, VA

Summertime
I like summertime.
I like summer swimming pools.
I like slip'n slides.
Owen Galloway, Grade 6
Floyd T Binns Middle School, VA

Summer!
It is so hot here.
We are sweating all day long.
Why can't it be cool.
Nick Goyer, Grade 6
Floyd T Binns Middle School, VA

The Whistling Winds
The wind is pretty
It whistles wonder and truth
It must be graceful.
Anthony D. Heflin, Grade 6
Floyd T Binns Middle School, VA

Savannah
Hoof steps draw nearer
The antelope raised its head
I ready my spear
Trevor Cosslett, Grade 6
Floyd T Binns Middle School, VA

My Best Friend
There is a cool dog.
He is a very good sleuth.
He is my best friend.
Tyler Jones, Grade 6
Floyd T Binns Middle School, VA

First Sunburn
I jump in water
I feel the heat on my face
I get a sunburn
Nick Jones, Grade 6
Floyd T Binns Middle School, VA

Halloween
When Halloween comes
The ghosts and ghouls come alive
I feel so frightened!
Brandon Reynolds, Grade 5
St Joseph School-Fullerton, MD

Beach Girl
I am a girl who loves the beach. I wonder what's crawling on my feet.
I hear kids laughing, big noisy waves smacking together, children
digging in the sand making sand castles. I see children
playing in the water with their friends. I want to run across
the beach and find an awesome shell.

I am a girl who loves the beach. I pretend I am a fish in the
water. I feel so excited and scared at the same time in the turbulent
water. I touch the sand and seashells. I worry about the crabs in the
sand biting my toes.

I am a girl who loves the beach. I understand if we have
to leave early. I say can we please stay. I dream to
be a sandcastle princess. I try not to get sun burnt. I
hope I can surf and not go underwater.
I am a girl who loves the beach.
Shyann Gaulien, Grade 5
Blackrock School, RI

My Wonderful Cat
You've been there since the day I was born, always there to love,
your cute green eyes staring up at me,
your soft fur always so soothing to hug and to hold.

You silly little kitty cat running all around, always jumping up and down,
your little paws batting and playing with any string you can find,
playful little kitty cat, it is so cute to watch you play.

Annoying little kitty cat, always following me around,
crying all throughout the night when we are all in bed asleep,
following me onto the couch to watch TV with me.

But still I guess overall you're the best pet anyone could have,
at times I know you are annoying and I don't like it,
but like I said before even then you still always make me smile.
Matt Dimond, Grade 6
St Jane De Chantal School, MD

Kayaking
The smell of the salty water…
The feel of the eel grass…
It's the ocean!
The memory of old times at the beach.
The ocean is hope and excitement from in your soul.
The sea breeze in your face is so strong that it makes you want to cry.
Feel the mud. Squash! Squish! Squash! Squish!
As you walk through the salt marsh.
The smell of salty sea spray on a sunny Sunday.
You feel as if you were a shooting star.
Curplush! Curplush! The water against the boat.
All kids feel as if it were Christmas.
The ducks quack, and suddenly…
Splash!
You fall in!
Sydney Bak, Grade 4
Boonsboro Elementary School, MD

Fall

It's cool and chilly
Leaves are turning all around
Wind is cool and nice
Hailey Fink, Grade 5
St Joseph School-Fullerton, MD

Snowboarding

Snowboarding is fun,
I like to go off jumps,
We go on ski lifts.
Kevin Devine, Grade 6
Floyd T Binns Middle School, VA

Lions

Lions, really dangerous,
Roars loud like a microphone,
Fur soft as cotton
Andy Wilson, Grade 6
Floyd T Binns Middle School, VA

Rain

Vaporized water
clear, cold, blue, falls from the sky.
wet, fun to play in.
Logan Pritchett, Grade 6
Floyd T Binns Middle School, VA

Buzz Bee

Black, yellow, fuzzy
Soars through the sky day and night
Flies high in the sky
Chandler Brown, Grade 6
Floyd T Binns Middle School, VA

Waterfalls

Matchless, flows smoothly.
It is an amazing sight.
Beautiful, peaceful.
Kaitlyn Huff, Grade 6
Floyd T Binns Middle School, VA

Windy Day

Wind blows very hard.
It blows the leaves to the ground.
Wind is very cold.
Sonia Meza, Grade 6
Floyd T Binns Middle School, VA

Fall Is So Cool

Fall is very cool
Fall is when the leaves fall down
Fall is so pretty
Emily McCombs, Grade 6
Floyd T Binns Middle School, VA

Football Player

I am a boy who loves playing football
I wonder what will happen next play
I hear the sound of screaming fans and teammates hitting the other team
and the quarterback yelling hike
I see the backs scrambling in the back field for passes
I want my team to win the much pressured football game

I am a boy who loves playing football
I pretend my team is winning by many many touch downs and points galore
I touch the mud splattered football I worry my team will lose

I am a boy who loves playing football
I understand the plays of the football game
I say my team will win
I dream my team will go to Florida
I try to make a tackle
I hope my team will win the championship to go to Disney
I am a boy who loves playing football
Matthew Foley, Grade 5
Blackrock School, RI

Basketball Love

I am a girl who loves playing basketball.
I wonder if I will play on all-stars.
I hear girls breathing hard playing on the court,
Basketball all night long, and wondering about them.
I see players' faces getting red when they're too tired.
I want to play for a Division two school later on
I am a girl who loves playing basketball
I pretend that I am a player in the WNBA
I feel the wind blowing in my face running up the court, ready shooting
I touch the ball while dribbling
I worry if I will win the championship game this winter
I am a girl who loves playing basketball
I understand I will not win every game
I say, "Let's win the game."
I dream I'll play in division two
I try to do my best
I hope I will win every game on my travel team.
I am a girl who loves playing basketball
Paige Greenwood, Grade 5
Blackrock School, RI

Organized Orange

Orange is the juiciness of a fruit.
Orange is the beauty of a sunset or sunrise.
Orange is the color of paint on a pencil.
Orange is a pumpkin being carved by a black kitten on Halloween night.
Orange is the bright lights of the Theater.
Orange is a sign that says, "Car wash on Route 95!"
Orange is the color of a colored pencil, marker, or crayon.
Orange is a paper thin as bread.
Orange is a notebook written in, then read.
Orange is the color of happiness and love.
Alissa Whitworth, Grade 4
Immaculate Conception Catholic Regional School, RI

Peace

Peace is the color of the autumn sky.
It sounds like water running over pebbles.
It tastes like spring water
And smells like morning dew.
Peace looks like a wild rose,
It makes you feel like you can do anything.
Chloe Grimstead, Grade 6
Homeschool Plus, VA

Fairies

no watch out, don't step there
you missed that fairy by a hair
they run and hop like you and me
but them you barely can see
dressed in petals and leaves so green
now you know what I mean
Angeline Marsh, Grade 5
Ewell School, MD

Change

Gold, red, and orange
Those colors past
Now are brown and white
Brown are the barren trees
White is the snow that covers them
Jordyn Petrie, Grade 5
Rosemont Forest Elementary School, VA

The Ocean

The Ocean, as strong as a hurricane
It takes so many lives
People have gone missing
In the bristling winds
The Ocean, as strong as a hurricane
Andrew Gilland, Grade 4
Riderwood Elementary School, MD

Pinecone

A pinecone is like the top of a house.
Its seed pods are like shingles.
The top of the pinecone is like a chimney.
The bottom is like a satellite dish.
A pinecone is like the top of a house.
Ava Gonglewski, Grade 4
Riderwood Elementary School, MD

Myself

I hate myself
I love myself
I express myself in many ways
I make myself laugh a lot
And I change myself always
Joseph Thomas Eugene Pietras, Grade 6
Graham Middle School, VA

I Am a Softball Player

I am a softball player who's number four.
I wonder if I'll make the team.
I hear my team cheering for me when I am up to bat on the softball field.
I see the pitcher getting ready to throw the pitch.
I want to hit a great home run for my team every game.
I am a softball player who's number four.

I pretend I am Jennie Finch when I'm pitching.
I feel like a great softball player when I strike someone out and win.
I touch a softball in games.
I worry if the ball will hit me when I'm up.
I am a softball player who's number four.

I understand school comes first but softball's fun.
I say I can do this.
I dream of being like Jennie Finch.
I try to hit very hard.
I hope I will be a professional softball player someday.
I am a softball player who's number four.
Lindsey Rugg, Grade 5
Blackrock School, RI

I Am a Basketball Player

I am a girl who likes to play basketball.
I wonder if I can make the winning shot.
I hear the people on the bleachers counting down by ten as the ball goes in the net.
I see my team running towards me as I look at my family.

I am a girl who likes to play basketball.
I pretend that it's no big deal, but it is.
I feel like a superstar plus I feel like there are a million bolts in me.
I touch the trophies for next week.
I worry that my team will not win the championship game.

I am a girl who likes to play basketball.
I understand that the game is a fun thing to do.
I say let's go team hurricanes.
I dream that my team doesn't win.
I try my best in basketball.
I hope my team wins the championship game.
I am a girl who likes to play basketball.
Larryn McGee, Grade 5
Blackrock School, RI

My Speed

My speed is like an asteroid zooming through the night going through anything in its sight.

My speed is like wind dodging some trees as leaves fall off and get caught in the breeze.

My speed is like a peregrine falcon striking its prey.

My speed makes me feel powerful.
Jonah Zang, Grade 4
Riderwood Elementary School, MD

Books

Books are filled with stories you may read
It may also help you do a good deed.
There are many stories you can read about.
But all books are enjoyable, there's no doubt.

Read about someone who is your age,
Then just focus on that page.
About anyone, I don't care,
Join the club, it's time to share.

Raden Pak, Grade 5
Seven Locks Elementary School, MD

Fabulous Yellow

Yellow is the color of the hot sun.
Yellow is the color of your yellow pencil.
Yellow is the color of the O's for Googling.
Maybe yellow is the color of a hot desert day.
Could the taco shell you are making be yellow?
Yellow is the color of a pineapple.
Didn't you know?
We see yellow a lot in one day,
But can you imagine living without it?

Shannon DiIorio, Grade 4
Immaculate Conception Catholic Regional School, RI

Soccer

As I go along the soccer field,
I am wide open.
Ten seconds on the game clock remain.
I shoot, I score the game winning goal.
The final score is 1-0.
As my crowd is shouting,
"MVP!" "MVP!"
"Trey is the MVP!"
Then, coach yells, "We won the championship!"

Trey Miller, Grade 6
Graham Middle School, VA

Cheese

Cheese cheese I love cheese.
Any kind, it all does please.
The more cheddar the better.
Gouda and blue I like those too.
I'm a moron for parmesan and a sandwich with
Swiss I just can't miss.

Morgan D. Martin, Grade 5
Pemberton Elementary School, VA

New City

The sun is gleaming on me.
As I move through a new city,
It's so strange in this new town.
That's why I act so down.
It's all a part of the fall season that's the main reason.

Shawna Roark, Grade 6
Graham Middle School, VA

Lucky, My Loyal Friend

Lucky, just a dog to you but to me, a friend
He's there when I wake up, and when I go to bed.
And all the minutes in between.

Lucky, a Saint Patrick's Day puppy, so we named him Lucky Patrick.
He joined our family like he belonged.
He is more like a brother than a pet.

Lucky and I communicate with each other.
A wag of the tail says, "I'm happy," a low growl says, "I'm sad,"
A nudge of his water bowl says, "I'm thirsty."

Lucky never wants to be alone. He sits on my bed or my lap.
He seems to smile and I smile back.
We get cozy together, very content.

You can tell Lucky cares, when you're down, he brings you up.
When you're hurt, he licks your wound.
When you're lonely, he stays close.

Where would I be without Lucky?
Alone? Sad? Scared? Bored?
Lucky, my faithful friend, with me from day's beginning to end.

Chloe Blomquist, Grade 6
St Jane De Chantal School, MD

House in the Woods

The night, spreading across the sky,
The variety of colors, blue, green and so much more,
The house in the woods creaking upon your ears,
The animals whispering to each other,
The ghosts chatter "Sh, sh!" as they come and go,
The leaves fighting in the night,
The woods creep you out with the scary noises,
The crows rattling sticks to scare you,
Bats squealing unseen in the dark,
The trees move with horror,
The house in the woods dies of the fear.

Ashley Conway, Grade 4
Boonsboro Elementary School, MD

Piano

Pianos are wonderful things,
think of the joy it brings.
I love to play.
The music it makes is beautiful,
that's why I love it.
When I play my music,
people come from all around,
To hear its wonderful sound.
The books of music have their own language.
That once you learn to read,
you really understand.
People love to listen from all over the land.

Alisa Myers, Grade 6
Floyd T Binns Middle School, VA

Best Friends

My best friends are Nick and Matthew.
They are really neat
They like to eat meat
They like to beat me at video games.

Matthew is really nice
He is afraid of mice
And he likes to play with dice
Matthew loves ice.

Nick is funny
He is afraid of bunnies
Nick has a lot of money
Nick and Matthew are my best friends.
Liam Morris, Grade 6
St. Jane DeChantal School, MD

My Sister

My sister has a bunny
Her bunny is funny
My sister would look cute
Flying in a parachute
Her name is Abigail
And she never turns pale
She likes to play school
Because she thinks it is cool
She likes cold water
Just like an otter
She takes good care
Of her long, long hair
My sister would miss me
If I moved near the sea!
Hannah Perkins, Grade 4
Mary Walter Elementary School, VA

Me

C reative
A musing
M any friends
E nergy
R eally loud
O rganized
N ever too lazy

S miles a lot
A ll for it
R ides a bike
V ery talkative
E ager to dance
R eads a lot
Cameron Paige Sarver, Grade 6
Graham Middle School, VA

The Best Dinner You Will Ever Have

It's 6 o'clock at night
My stomach growls so light.

I don't know what we are having to eat
I hope it is some warm juicy meat.

Dad opens the freezer door
Shuts it and says "we have no more."

The drawer of the carryout menus is so big
He looks at them without having to dig.

Next thing I see are eggs, butter and bacon
I finally ask "what are you making?"

What he responds is "you will see?"

All of a sudden a plate is before me.
It smells like the kitchen in the morning.

This meal is such a winner
I just finished having breakfast for dinner.
Tyler Frazier, Grade 6
St Jane De Chantal School, MD

I'm Leaving So…

Sea, calm down and feel the breeze.
Stones, stop being so hardheaded.
Stars, show me the big dipper.
Moon, light up and smile.
Sun, quit being so hot headed.
Night, why so droopy?
Trees, take care of the birds.
Milky Way, keep the planets moving.
Caitlyn Razo, Grade 4
Boonsboro Elementary School, MD

A True Friend

A friendship is like a circle
Because a circle has no end
A friend is always there for you
No matter what you do

A true friend loves you for you
And your faults too
Friends will always have your back
In the toughest times
When you are down
They will turn your frown upside down

They help you be grateful
When you are hopeless
A friendship grows in time and
They will be your friend for a lifetime
Nora McCarthy, Grade 6
St Jane De Chantal School, MD

I Am

C aring
E xciting
A rtistic
I ntelligent
R esponsible
A wesome

B rave or bad when needed to
R espectful
O rganized
W eirdly wonderful
N ice

I am me!!
Ceaira Laur'nae Brown, Grade 6
Graham Middle School, VA

A Friend

A friend is someone who is always there
Who will with your problems share
They are not mean to you
Or they don't make fun of you
They show you how much they really care

They will not get mad at you
When you play and win
These are the signs of a good friend.

If you see someone in need
And you help them too
You are a friend that is really true.
Austin Byrd, Grade 6
Graham Middle School, VA

Life

Life
Wonderful, exhilarating
Continuing, breathing, experiencing
It marches on forever
Existence
Angela Estavillo, Grade 5
St Joseph School-Fullerton, MD

Silence

My voice is a shadow
It lingers in thin air
You never hear a thing because
You don't really care
You guess it's just the wind
You think it's a mouse
You never look behind you
when I really am there
you never really know who I am
and the sad thing is you never will
Hayley DeWitt, Grade 5
Rosemont Forest Elementary School, VA

Springtime
Springtime is here now!
and flowers are beautiful
dancing in the wind.
Taylor Rayburn, Grade 6
Floyd T Binns Middle School, VA

The Beauty of Nature
Clouds sit still above
Mountains stir a placid sea
Nature's beauty glows
Camille Harrah, Grade 4
Boonsboro Elementary School, MD

A Fall Day
As the leaves fall down.
I just sit watching them fall.
I sit enjoying.
Zachariah Moss, Grade 6
Floyd T Binns Middle School, VA

Frogs and Toads
The frogs and the toads croak
They eat bugs and sleep in mud
They are really cool
Chase Dillon, Grade 6
Floyd T Binns Middle School, VA

The Windy Day
The wind was blowing.
It was very cold today.
It is December.
Deandre Yates, Grade 6
Floyd T Binns Middle School, VA

Frozen River
Once was wild and free
Then, winter came, and now, all,
Motion is halted
Chiara Head, Grade 6
Floyd T Binns Middle School, VA

Wolf
Aggressive, agile.
Protectors of the forest.
Swift, strong, aggressive
Sasha Samoilenka, Grade 6
Floyd T Binns Middle School, VA

The Thunderstorm
Millions of droplets
Bright flash lighting up the sky
Roll of thunder sound
Emma Wood, Grade 6
Floyd T Binns Middle School, VA

Gymnastics Star
I am a…girl who is a gymnast.
I wonder…if I'll be an Olympian.
I hear…the fans shouting and cheering me on as I flip through the air on bars.
I see…myself on vault doing a front handspring off.
I want…to win a gold medal in the Olympics someday.
I am a…girl who is a gymnast.

I pretend…I am a professional in the Olympics.
I feel…proud when I finish a flip and I stick the landing perfectly.
I touch…all the balance beams.
I worry…I will get hurt while flipping off the vault.
I am a…girl who is a gymnast.

I understand…if I don't win a medal.
I say…I can make it.
I dream…of being a professional gymnast.
I try…new turns and flips.
I hope…I will one day make Hot Shots in gymnastics.
I am a…girl who is a gymnast.
Brianna Angelone, Grade 5
Blackrock School, RI

Me and My Dog
I am a 5th grader with a dog
I wonder if my dog is sleeping
I hear him bark and sneeze a lot
I see him wag his tail and look at me
I want another cute and adorable Cocker Spaniel like my dog Balie
I am a 5th grader with a dog

I pretend that I can take care of him.
I feel very special to have a cute and adorable dog just like mine
I touch my dogs fluffy fur and ragged ears also his small nub of a tail
I worry if he will be there when I get home
I am a 5th grader with a dog

I understand I will not have him forever
I say "I love you Balie,"
I dream of us playing all day
I try to be with him
I hope my dog will not die for a long time
I am a 5th grader with a dog

Gena Anika, Grade 5
Blackrock School, RI

Running Free
I wish I were a Mustang horse. My hair flowing freely as I gallop across the prairie.
My hooves beating down on the earth as I gallop with all my might.
My heart beating fast with every step I take.
Knowing that I'm wild and free and no one can every truly tame me.
My strength and stamina will allow me to keep running and feeling free for a long time.
Running wild and free will forever keep me happy and glad to be alive.
Many may try to catch me but I will run with all my might so that I am never caught.
I will always remain free even it it's only in my spirit.
Stephanie Neal, Grade 6
Graham Middle School, VA

My Teacher's Shoes

My teacher's shoes are sometimes furry like her pet Miles that is her putty cat.
Or they are flip flops in the 95 degree weather that are very comfortable probably like her slippers at home.
Sometimes she complains that her feet are cold and she blames the weather man.
She was a variety of colorful shoes that who knows what is on them!

Most of the time she has little tiny bows or with fancy ribbons with Rhinestones on them.
Of course every teacher has to have a few boring ones also known as sneakers.
They have very vivid colors of maybe the logo with heels in the back to make her look taller than Abe Lincoln when she's not.

If you ask me, she has a shoe for every hour of the month!

Maria Shapiro, Grade 5
Seven Locks Elementary School, MD

An Everlasting Melody

A song that is played throughout one's life shall be called an everlasting melody. Though it continues on, its never ending pattern is pure lyrics. A sign of gratitude could be hinted to one's ear heeding this diverse ballad. Yes when the hands touch this glistening sound of a continuing tune, he should melt in passion.

When the lips say the words from pure integrity, they shall mean nothing less. They can only taste, the true genius twisted and tangled inside, as if one's secrets. When the eyes see this distinct layout of uncommon notes creatively combined, they can only imagine the beautiful harmony these perfect symbols can make.

So when the ear heeds, the hands touch, the lips taste and the eyes see the perfect symbols, you should have an everlasting melody.

Karina Poulos, Grade 5
Pemberton Elementary School, VA

What Happened?

I may only be eleven, but I have something to say.
What happened to this world? Where's the love not the hate.
What happened to marching together, hand in hand and sharing the love, God's creation of man.
Why can't we get along? From white to black. When someone has a disagreement do we have to talk back?
Can we walk out of the house without having to worry?
When don't we have to say "It was a red handed burglary?"
Can we relive the good ol' days when mama said go play?
Can we go out for Halloween knowing that we'll be ok?
Come stand with me and let people know. What happened to the world? Where did it go?

Alexis Adams, Grade 6
Deal Middle School, DC

Waves

A white sandy beach shimmering in the hot sun.
A crystal clear wave smacks on the beach and recoils back into the ocean as white foam
just as easily as it crashes in it slides right out into the ocean.
They bring in shells for stores to sell and for collectors to keep.
Waves may also carry fish, sharks and jellyfish all around and in and out.
They get big and small by the moons command. Waves can create fun or havoc for whoever plays in them or stays in them.
They give surfers rides and swimmers obstacles.
They can do anything you want them to do when you need them to do it.

Jimmy Rubino, Grade 5
Seven Locks Elementary School, MD

Halloween Night
Halloween is here.
Put up your decorations.
Dress up, have fun. BOO!
Gabrielle Christy, Grade 5
St Joseph School-Fullerton, MD

Ravens
The Ravens are great.
The Ravens beat the Steelers.
Now it's time for the Colts.
Emmanuel Sagisi, Grade 5
St Joseph School-Fullerton, MD

Animals
Animals are cool!!
Short or tall I love them all,
Animals are neat!!
Makenzie Bowers, Grade 6
Floyd T Binns Middle School, VA

Winter
Snow comes down slowly.
Burr! It's cold, but I don't care.
It's everywhere!
Sarah Noer, Grade 6
Homeschool Plus, VA

Halloween
Halloween is fun.
Trick or treat fill my bag.
I like spooky songs.
Kayla Szczybor, Grade 5
St Joseph School-Fullerton, MD

Hunting
Hunting time is here.
Shoot and load the guns. BOOM! BOOM!
Down goes the large buck.
Daniel Baxley, Grade 5
St Joseph School-Fullerton, MD

Why Abuse?
Animals are life,
So why abuse them so much?
I think they are great.
Derrick Ahrens, Grade 6
Floyd T Binns Middle School, VA

Halloween Time
Halloween is here.
Ghouls and ghosts have come this year.
Time has come to cheer!
Joseph Cecchino, Grade 5
St Joseph School-Fullerton, MD

Gymnastics
I am a gymnast who loves to flip.
I wonder if I'll bend in half.
I hear lots of girls yelling and screaming and floors pouncing and fans squeaking in the air.
I see girls and boys flipping into the foam pit.
I want to do a back layout into the foam pit.
I am a gymnast who loves to flip.

I pretend to do my over split at gymnastics.
I feel soft floors bouncing up and down, and floors trembling when people bounce.
I touch the very chalky bar.
I wonder if I'll fall on my head and get hurt.
I am a gymnast who loves to flip.

I understand when my coach talks to me.
I dream to be in the Olympics.
I say, "Coach I'll do it."
I try to do the flip.
I hope I will not land on my head without spotters.
I am a gymnast who loves to flip.
Isabelle Branchaud, Grade 5
Blackrock School, RI

I Am a Horseback Rider
I am a smart, awesome, intelligent horseback rider
I wonder how high I can jump
I hear hoses neigh, colts fall into a bed of hay, and a barn that's never peaceful
I see horses playing in the pasture, their silly games
I want a horse, to be able to call it my own
I am a smart, awesome, intelligent horseback rider

I pretend I am in the Kentucky Derby, finally
I feel graceful and fast shooting through the air, just me and the horses
I touch a horse's smooth body
I worry I will come in last in my jumping competition
I am a smart, awesome, intelligent horseback rider

I understand horses are a lot of work
I say my horse is awesome
I dream about owning an awesome horse
I try to be the best
I hope I own a smart, intelligent horse of my own
I am a smart, awesome, intelligent horseback rider
Abigale Reynolds, Grade 5
Blackrock School, RI

Stolen Moments
You gaze into my eyes and think of taking me away.
You trick me so I want to stay with dreams and nightmares, fade into me.
You trick me into believing you with all your hope is going through.
I inspire you with my words although what I say is never heard.
My soul is gone forever, but you take me and we go together.
Through the woods and by a river, you take my life through a sliver.
With love and death combined together you take my soul, yes, forever.
Aeron Spencer, Grade 6
Floyd T Binns Middle School, VA

My True Best Friend
Everyone thinks
That their best friend
Is who they hang out with at school.

They think
That who they talk to
Decides if they are cool.

But I know who
My best friend is,
We may not talk a lot.

But when we get home,
We talk and we talk,
And soon, we just can't stop!

My BFF
Will be my friend forever,

Because she is my sister,
And sisters stick together.
Zoe Westrick, Grade 6
St. Jane de Chantal School, MD

Canoeing on the Ocean
Wind battering
Rain splattering
Crick in my back.

Hard wood
Paddles no good
Crick in my back.

Very dark
Rough bark
Crick in my back.

Stomach grumbling
Waves mumbling
Crick in my back.

Dolphins singing
Dawn coming
Crick in my back.

Oh, oh man, I got a crick in my back!
Mitch Palmer, Grade 6
Chickahominy Middle School, VA

Friendship
Friendship is a two-way street.
Friendship is one special person you meet
It can go up and down
They can turn your frown upside down
Alexis Andrew, Grade 5
Pasadena Elementary School, MD

Culture Is Everywhere
Culture is everywhere.
Culture is in our house,
Culture is in our religion,
Culture is in our everyday lives,
We see it with our eyes,
We look left to right and it is there,
It could be in the smallest object
But, it would be there,
Culture is everywhere.
Christell Azuaje, Grade 6
Midlothian Middle School, VA

Kobe Bryant
As he steps on the court the fans scream
And behind him his invincible team
His silky gold jersey and shorts
Taking air he charges all over the court
They root and he winks an eye and waves
The opposite team goodbye
We call him the invincible king
Cause he has four rings
But we also call him Kobe
Nick Morgan, Grade 6
Graham Middle School, VA

Character
C ourage
H onesty
A dmirable
R esponsibility
A dvisable
C hivalry
T ruthfulness
E thical
R espectful
Kurt Wolford, Grade 6
Graham Middle School, VA

Cheese?
It's a yellow ball
Is that cheese in the night sky
No it is the moon
Ashten Souder, Grade 6
Floyd T Binns Middle School, VA

Werewolf
W hiny
E erie
R unning
E verywhere
W ith
O gres
L ate at night
F rightening everyone
Michael Pierorazio, Grade 5
St Joseph School-Fullerton, MD

The Army of Peace
Stomp, stomp, feet are marching,
The army of peace is marching.
The people look black,
The pink, orange, and blue sky,
Is like a painting.
They think of Martin Luther King Jr.,
He is confidence.
They are chanting for civil rights,
But more importantly,
Peace.
They wave those truce flags,
They hope to make the world peaceful.
They pay no mind to their weary feet.
Martin Luther King is up in the sky.
His lips curled in the barest hint of a smile.
The rocks roll as the men trudge on.
Stomp, stomp feet are marching
Beautiful baby blue sky, stretching silently,
The army of peace.
Gabriel Juedemann, Grade 4
Boonsboro Elementary School, MD

Worth the Wait
Is it worth the wait?
I seem to contemplate.
Do I wish to wait?
I seem to hesitate.

Will I become more keen?
So it may often seem.
Do I want a house?
Do I want a spouse?

Will I still like to play with toys?
Will I still feel like a boy?
All these questions I have.
Yet no answers, too bad.

But if you do, please tell.
When I try, I fail.
Yet I wish to prevail.
Is it worth the wait?
Jackie Michael Whitehead III, Grade 6
Graham Middle School, VA

Hamsters
H amsters are cute.
A re rodents.
M any are kept as pets.
S illy sometimes.
T hey have whiskers.
E ach one has its own color.
R eally chubby.
S leep all day.
Jana Mae Tan, Grade 5
St Joseph School-Fullerton, MD

Easter Eggs
Easter eggs are round
Every different color
pink, purple, green, and red
Some are big
And some are small
Some are solid
And some are hollow
Some parts are edible
And some parts are simply
IN-DI-GESTIBLE!
You can't eat the shell
Or the plastic
But you can always eat the center
Whether it's boiled yolk
Or sweet tarts inside
Either way
An Easter egg is a treasure to any child
Austin Bew, Grade 4
Bensley Elementary School, VA

Fishing Days
My dad and I
Go fishing on Saturdays
Sometimes the fish swim away
If we catch any fish
We go home and grill them
In the backyard
We invite my mom and sister
To eat fish with us

Later on
In the afternoon
We invite my mom and sister
To go fishing with us
My little sister catches a tiny catfish
Then we travel back home
In our big red van
Tomorrow we'll eat fish again.
Marcos Mastache, Grade 4
Bensley Elementary School, VA

The Meanings of Color
Blue means you are calm,
wise, and gentle.

Red means you are mad
and full of rage.

Green means you are
envious and want revenge.

Everyone has these feelings
and there is always someone
feeling either blue, red, or green.
Chris Beinkampen, Grade 5
Rosemont Forest Elementary School, VA

All Alone
Every day I walk this earth with silence.
No one in my world except my family.
Pavement stained with the past history.
Sadness follows my spirit like a dog.
I walk behind…my own shadow
Not to be revealed to the world
Will I ever stop walking in shadows
Will I ever be happy again
Kim Howard, Grade 5
Rosemont Forest Elementary School, VA

Monster
The monster in my dream is big and green.
He growls and snarls but he's not mean.
He helps me sleep most every night.
He goes away when it's daylight.
He makes me happy day and night.
I lay in my bed with no fright.
He keeps me safe all night long.
My monster is big and oh so strong.
Ashley Woodring, Grade 5
Pemberton Elementary School, VA

Drawing
When I'm drawing
Everything is exciting
I feel creative and sometimes confused
Unsure what to draw
So many thoughts, not enough time
Once a masterpiece is created
I enjoy others observations, reflections
and appreciation
Kevin Newbern, Grade 5
Rosemont Forest Elementary School, VA

Beneath the Pretty Sky
Green grass to play in
White clouds to look at
Buildings to explore
Fast cars to ride in
Music to listen to
Churches to pray in
No matter who you are
Just be you!
Angel Smith, Grade 4
Bensley Elementary School, VA

Autumn
Leaves are blowing in the wind
Oh, how great fall has been
Soon winter snow will fall
It's fun to watch people have a ball
Next year it will come again
Then we will start all over again.
Matthew Fulp, Grade 6
Graham Middle School, VA

My Friends
On a plane,
On the ground,
In a car,
Under a tree,
In my heart my friends will be,
Four brown,
One red,
Four blonde to top,
These are my friends,
And I love them a lot!
Caroline Kammer, Grade 6
Graham Middle School, VA

Candy Bags
C olorful
A ddictive
N uts
D reamy
Y ummy

B unches of candy
A roma of chocolate
G ood grief that's a lot of candy!
S weet treat to eat. Mmm!
Nathaniel Heasley, Grade 5
St Joseph School-Fullerton, MD

Green
Green is a frog
Green eggs and ham
Grasshoppers in the grass
Plants and
Food coloring
Markers
Pencils and pencil cases
Books and folders
Sweatshirts to keep us warm
My glasses are green too
Santiago Vesperoni, Grade 5
St Bartholomew School, MD

Turtle Tide
The yellow glow is from the soothing sun
The blue depth is like an aqua aquarium
The green heads gleam like glitter
Underwater beauty has coral and seaweed
Happy turtles swim successfully
You can hear the sound of waves
The dancing water tickles your body
The swaying coral slaps you
The spinning seaweed touches your hair
Turtle tide!
Noah Cook, Grade 4
Boonsboro Elementary School, MD

Veteran's Day Rock and Roll

On Veteran's Day you're so sweet because it's a holiday to honor the troops that served and risked their lives during war time.
We honor people that can never be replaced.
Thank you troops who served and still serve.
It must be hard to leave your families and say goodbye for now.
We wish you good luck.

Cameron Sabel, Grade 5
Pemberton Elementary School, VA

Ode to My Dog, Peppi

When I got you,
You were small.
So was I.
Three years old for both of us.

I think of you as a brother,
Not as a dog.
Your hair is curly,
My hair is straight.

Your puppy years were probably horrible,
Being abused.
Good thing we rescued you.

You never listen to my commands,
You only listen to mom's.
I guess you know who's in charge.

Now you're getting old.
11 years,
That's pretty good.

I don't know where you came from,
Or know what you were like when you were born.
But I know one thing,
You are my dog and I love you.

Noah Green, Grade 6
Charles E Smith Jewish Day School Lower Campus, MD

Equality

Why does mankind fight?
Disaster only comes from it
Soon there will be no friendliness in sight.

Mankind's anger is like a bomb, ready to explode
Why can't we stop?
The world is already full of woe.

We all need to be friends
Everyone should want peace
We need to stay together until the end.

Our love should be as bright as a rose
Not as dark as night
Everyone should be treated equally, as most people know.

Claire Fetgatter, Grade 4
Mary Walter Elementary School, VA

My Best Friends

My friends are very special to me
Sharing fun times and laughing together is key
They are all unique in their own way
Their may be some ups and downs but things always turn out okay

Having sleepovers and going to the mall is fun
We sometimes go to the pool and lay in the sun
Seeing each other at school is not enough
When we aren't with each other things can be rough

Being on the same sports team is the best
Seeing each other on the sports field is better than the rest
We play soccer, softball and other sports together
This is only one reason why we are best friends forever!

We share the same likes
And ignore our dislikes
We share our secrets
Knowing each other will keep it

Just knowing they are there
Really shows how much they care
My friends are the best they can be
This is why they are so special to me!

Ally Edwards, Grade 6
St Jane De Chantal School, MD

Friends

On a cold winter day,
a hot chocolate may warm you up,
but a friend does more than just cheer you up,
a friend makes you feel like you're a magnificent person.

A friend may help you when you're upset
and don't know what to do.
Friends spend good times with you
and bring back the best memories of your life.
Even if you're in a good or bad situation,
friends may always be on your side.

Friends always give you very good advice.
Without friends,
life wouldn't be as joyful and enjoying.
Without enjoying those times,
we would not have our big memories made by friends.

Isa Hoyos, Grade 6
St Jane De Chantal School, MD

I'm a Turtle
I am a turtle
Green and round
I live in a place
Where beauty abounds.
Annie Ponsi, Grade 4
Riderwood Elementary School, MD

Stars
I lay under the stars so happy and light.
It seems as though the sun has rows.
I feel it again so sparkly and white.
I lay under the stars with such delight.
Emily Woodring, Grade 5
Pemberton Elementary School, VA

Dance
Graceful, beautiful
Point, tap, jump
Freedom, floating, pain, victory
Lyrical
Sophie Wyatt, Grade 6
Graham Middle School, VA

Grampa
Wonderful guy
I miss him so, I cry
At least I know he's God's angel
"Papa"
Naomi Pearson, Grade 5
St Bartholomew School, MD

Wind
You think the wind is just air
But I think it is special.
It is God's sign of peace
After a troubled day.
Selena Voodre, Grade 5
Rosemont Forest Elementary School, VA

Soccer
Intimidating, Freedom
Kicking, Scoring, Running
Makes me feel great
Futbol
Logan Surface, Grade 6
Graham Middle School, VA

Life
L ove
I nteresting
F un
E asy
Brooke Menikheim, Grade 5
St Joseph School-Fullerton, MD

Life Takes Baseball
The pitcher's mound is my favorite place to be.
There is nothing I'd rather be doing than facing the best hitter in the league.

It's me against him for the last out of the game.
Both of us want the other to go down in shame.

I know the crowd is going crazy, but I hear nothing at all.
Except for the faint whiz of the ball.

"Strike one!" the umpire said.
I know I just knocked the crowd dead.

I threw a change-up low and away.
"Strike two!" I knew the umpire would say.

For the final pitch I threw the fast ball right down the pipe.
The umpire said, "Strike three!" Man that was a really good fight.
Logan Cox, Grade 5
Pemberton Elementary School, VA

Finding a Friend
When I first saw you, you were all alone.
You were at the table, you were on your own.

I asked you to come on over, and join our little game,
and when I had asked you some questions, our personalities were the same!

From that time on, we never were apart.
We've formed a bond, we're true sisters at heart.

Ten years later, you're still my best friend,
we share endless laughs, our fun doesn't end!

We're getting older, we're growing up now.
I can't believe we're parting, but we have to somehow.

It's time to say goodbye now, I wish that this could last,
we must move on, but never forget the past.
Rebecca Arce, Grade 6
St Jane de Chantal School, MD

A True Friend Is Someone Who...
Cake and candy are wonderful things but friends are even better.
They stick with you in good and bad weather.

They talk and play in the cold, cold rain, because that is what friends do.
Don't you wish you had that great of a friend too?

Having fun and laughing out loud,
Even with a stormy cloud

Right above you,
Because that is what friends do!
Sarah Mattingly, Grade 6
St Jane De Chantal School, MD

Costume

C overing my body is a funky outfit.
O ver my face is a mask.
S cary outfits is what everyone wears.
T rick-or-Treating is fun on Halloween night.
U nder the scary costume is a real person.
M y friends and I dress alike.
E veryone dresses up for Halloween.

Maddie Morgan, Grade 6
Graham Middle School, VA

Blazing Blue

The sky is blue and so are you.
The poster is blue but all I see is a picture of you.
Backpacks are blue and sweater's are too.
Jackets are blue it always reminds me of you.
I love the color blue but most of all it reminds me of you.
Puzzle pieces, blocks, all go together to make the color blue.
Jackets are blue so is the number one hundred and twenty two.

Kenneth Alexander, Grade 4
Immaculate Conception Catholic Regional School, RI

Butterflies

Butterflies fly so high way up in the sky.
Their wings flutter up and down as the clouds go by.
Finding a comfy flower he will land.
A butterfly is so small it can fit in my hand.
With wings the color of golden light.
you rule as monarch butterflies with all your might.

Isabella Wilder, Grade 5
Pemberton Elementary School, VA

Grades

First you're at an A then you're at B.
It's like the alphabet ABC.
It's like you try and try but then you start to cry.
But inside my heart is saying don't be a failure and cry.
So get back up and try, try, try.
That's the reason I know I care about my grades all the time.

Tyra Hackley, Grade 6
Floyd T Binns Middle School, VA

Balsam Fur

Balsam fur trees are as soft as a fur coat.
Caribou live under balsam fur trees.
Balsam fur feels soft when you rub it down, and it will feel spiky
When you rub it up.
What balsam fur and a fur coat have in common is that they both
feel soft.

Cooper Albright, Grade 4
Riderwood Elementary School, MD

The Kangaroo from Kalamazoo

One day when I was walking through the zoo,
I saw a kangaroo from Kalamazoo.
As I continued my walk through the zoo,
the kangaroo from Kalamazoo came up to me and said…Boo!

Molly Kramer, Grade 4
Sligo Creek Elementary School, MD

The Beach

Looking out the window
of our red Expedition
On the way to Myrtle Beach
A sky full of beautiful birds flying high

Once we arrive
We roll out our towels
Put up umbrellas
Trying to hide from the sun

Waves blue and curvy
I see three bright red crabs
Surfing confidently

"Mommy! Mommy!"
Is the sound of a little girl
searching for her mother.

Children are tossing a beach ball
Tiny fish are playing peak-a-boo
Dolphins are jumping out of the
Deep, blue ocean

I hear the sound of love everywhere
As families talk and laugh together

Taiye Johnson, Grade 4
Bensley Elementary School, VA

The Night

As the sun goes down, and the day fades,
the night stirs and comes alive.

The stars dance; the fairies prance,
while the fireflies light up the sky.

The moon gleams; the people dream,
and owls call to the wind.

The streetlights glow; as it starts to snow,
and the moon begins to descend.

The sun gives chase; the night erased,
fun for now must end.

But not for long, soon day will be done,
And the night will come alive again.

Chloe Burnette, Grade 6
Parkside Middle School, VA

Brown

Brown is a burnt pie crust
A little brown bird in a high branch
A shoe in mud
Or your best friends hair color
The color of dead grass
You just mowed
The dirt you and your dad
Just put down
The leaves in the fall
That you put in a pile
Jump in for fun
The old pages of a book
You get from a library
The wood from a tree in your backyard
Brown is the cardboard that you
Make for your Halloween costume
The desk that you sit in a school
Brown is tired, angry and annoyed
Madison Gentilo, Grade 5
St Bartholomew School, MD

Thanksgiving Break

T he day has come
H appy Thanksgiving
A nd Thanksgiving break is here
N o school for five days
K indergarten to twelfth grade
S tuffing
G ravy
I like it a lot
V ery best of is the turkey
I t's all so fun
N ot going to school
G ames and plays

B ut the best of all is the fun
R eady for the next day of school
E ven though we're back at school
A nd no more Thanksgiving
K ind of not that bad at all.
Samantha Marie Eastridge, Grade 6
Graham Middle School, VA

Halloweens

H orrifying
A lways
L aughing
L ooking
O utstanding
W icked
E ven
E xciting
N ight
S cary
Corinne Leubecker, Grade 5
St Joseph School-Fullerton, MD

Winter Snow

Winter snow is beautiful.
I will show you why,
Snow dances right down from the sky
Like a ballerina.

Snow covers the world
Like a white blanket.
Snow is a bare tree's winter clothes.

Snow is like a rabbit's tail,
Soft and fluffy,
White as can be.

Snow also
Glimmers like a diamond,
And is cold as well.

Now don't you see?
Winter snow is its own beauty!!!
Ruth Renberg, Grade 5
Seven Locks Elementary School, MD

Thanksgiving

The leaves are falling
the trees are yellow
it is fall
so don't be so mellow

The temperature is chilly
thanksgiving is near
take out the turkey
the holiday is here

So gather around the fire
and say thank you
to all that we have
especially you!

We had a lot of fun this summer
the sun has went away
the trees are bare
I wish the leaves would stay
Andrea Abell, Grade 6
Midlothian Middle School, VA

Softball

S uper awesome
O ut in the sun
F antastic fun
T he rush of the run
B atting the ball
A way from us all
L oving it all…
L eaving the ball
Kristen Renee Elmore, Grade 6
Graham Middle School, VA

Always Friends

Friends are always
There for you.
Friends are the ones
You call with news.

Friends are always
There to care.
Friends are the ones
With whom you share.

Friends will always
Watch your back.
Friends are the ones
Who keep you on the right track.

Friends are always
Loving you for you.
Friends are the ones
Who you love too.
Julia Kane, Grade 6
St Jane De Chantal School, MD

Dark

Into the pitch-black darkness
of your soul
where everything is between
just you
and God
your darkest secrets
your worst moments
deep sorrow
It's all your fault.
No…
Is it?
No…
Was it?
Well…yes…
I did it.
It was me.
Forgive me?
Yes.
I'm forgiven!
Courtney Bauserman, Grade 6
Warwick River Christian School, VA

Hummingbird

What a small wonder flying by.
Dancing from flower to flower,
Only a blur they seem to be,
A little bundle of nothing but power,
Away they fly in search of one more,
Another sweet drop of liquid awaits,
So away in the blink of an eye,
The beautiful rose bloom serves as bait
Nicki Russell, Grade 6
Graham Middle School, VA

Summer

The summer is hot
It's good to drink lemonade
Yum, yum it's so good
Samantha Chavez, Grade 6
Floyd T Binns Middle School, VA

The Water

The water glistened
Reflecting everything seen
I love the water
Caroline Dwyer, Grade 6
Floyd T Binns Middle School, VA

Nighttime

Nighttime is so still
So bright from the stars' twinkle
Lanterns in the sky
Madison Bannister, Grade 6
Floyd T Binns Middle School, VA

Sledding

Sliding down the hill
into a big pile of snow
I laugh joyfully
Cyndee Croft, Grade 6
Floyd T Binns Middle School, VA

My Mom as an Angel

Mom is an angel
Who watches me in the sky
Loves me all the time
Kyra Weldon, Grade 6
Floyd T Binns Middle School, VA

Fall

The leaves are falling
Today it will get darker
For today is fall
James Jorgensen, Grade 6
Floyd T Binns Middle School, VA

Snow

We go out to play,
It's a winter wonderland,
So we stayed all day.
Danielle Hockman, Grade 6
Floyd T Binns Middle School, VA

The Night

It creeps in swiftly
The day has gone so quickly
Surprising us all
Hannah Thompson, Grade 6
Floyd T Binns Middle School, VA

I Am a Basketball Enthusiast

I am a girl who enjoys playing basketball
I wonder if I'll score a point
I hear the ball pounding to the ground and the crowd cheering
and screaming like frightened people
I see tons of players fighting for the ball everywhere
I want to win the game and prove that we're the best
I am a girl who enjoys playing basketball

I pretend that I'm amazing and dominate the league
I feel sweaty arms, hair all over my face, and a rough textured basketball
I touch the team on offensive
I worry that my team will lose and get really depressed
I am a girl who enjoys playing basketball

I understand that we may lose some games
I say "Play so hard, Cara"
I dream that I'm a threat to everyone
I try to play my hardest
I hope my team will win, every game in the season
I am a girl who enjoys playing basketball

Cara Turner, Grade 5
Blackrock School, RI

The Devil

I met the devil in a world with black days and red nights
Where the dead come out to play every red night
Where fire is the closest thing to light
Where tears are the closest thing to water
With red horns and red eyes
Black hair a black heart
Fire in his eyes and fire every where
I met the devil
He told me that this land of fire
With black days and red nights
Where the dead come out to play every red night
Where tears are the closest thing to water could all be mine
But all for one simple price my essence
I met the devil
I was left as the devil
But I'm not the one he was looking for
I don't have red horns, red eyes, black hair or a black heart
Or was this all just another trick of the devil
I know that somewhere he was looking at me with a wicked grin on his face
Because I fell for another one of the devil's tricks

Ariana Epstein, Grade 6
Charles E Smith Jewish Day School Lower Campus, MD

Whistling Creekside

The whistling creek side is a beautiful place,
No war, no hustling, nor a fast race,
Wake up and breathe the fresh wintry cold air,
To see a scene this beautiful is very much something rare,
Some say it is not fair,
The whistling creek side is a frozen tundra lying there, cold and bare.
Andrew C. Meredith, Grade 6
Graham Middle School, VA

Winter Night

The wind blows in winter
Nights are cold
Stay under a blanket
Be warm
Xiomania Payton, Grade 5
Rosemont Forest Elementary School, VA

Love

L ots of love,
O h my gosh,
V alue the person you love the most.
E very second is worth the wait…
Jessica Carr, Grade 6
Floyd T Binns Middle School, VA

Shadows

Lurking behind you.
Having no true identity.
I watch you day after day.
Every time you turn to look, I disappear.
Owen Sipes, Grade 5
Rosemont Forest Elementary School, VA

Earth

Earth
Wind, water, and air
Ah, earth is all around us.
I love planet earth.
Bonfilia Singh, Grade 5
St Joseph School-Fullerton, MD

Spring

Flowers are blooming
They are so so beautiful
Spring is their Heaven
Heather Ringler, Grade 6
Floyd T Binns Middle School, VA

Snowy Winter

The snow is blowing.
Christmas trees are going up.
It must be winter!
Ryan Warstler, Grade 6
Floyd T Binns Middle School, VA

Windy Day

Wind is very strong
Many birds fly in the wind
Swooping down to feed
Hunter Zwerner, Grade 6
Floyd T Binns Middle School, VA

Change

The wind whispers, as colors fall from the trees.
The earth is covered in red, orange, and yellow.
Fall!
The birds know it, they're already up there in the sky flying South.
The trees know it, they know they need to drop their colors on the ground.
The people know it, there are rakes on the ground along with piles of leaves.
You'll see children jumping in piles of color,
laughing and having fun.
Soon, you'll see pure white covering the branches and still silence everywhere.
We know…Yes we Know
the world knows
We all know
yes.
We all wonder how we know
that our winter is going to come!
Ella Shulgan, Grade 6
Home School, VA

Saying "Goodbye"

Saying "goodbye" will be the hardest part
We used to sit together and enjoy a strawberry tart
We would play hopscotch and jump rope
Now I walk around trying not to mope

Now she has to move away
It will be the worst day
I will miss her beyond comprehension
And the fact that she'll be gone I just don't like to mention

I don't get to see her until next year
And as I look down through the window I see a tear
I also see her family packing the cart
I walk down to see them and realize that saying "goodbye" will be the hardest part
Grace McCrery, Grade 6
St Jane De Chantal School, MD

My Dog, Mindy

I met you enclosed in a damp, dark crate,
scared, whimpering
When we got home you ran like a cheetah around the house,
hopping, pouncing
When we went outside, you noticed the rocky, moist terrain was different,
confused, confined
But now you're feeling enveloped in our family's cocoon,
sheltered, loved
You play with a bright orange ball,
scampering, catching
When I go off to school, you wonder when I will return,
waiting, hoping
My dog, Mindy, will always warm my heart,
cherished, treasured
Teddy Rinaldi, Grade 6
St Jane De Chantal School, MD

Harry Potter

Lives in Gryffindor Tower
Ron and Hermoine are his friends
Draco Malfoy is Harry's rival
Dumbledore is headmaster of Hogwarts
Voldermort is always after Harry
Harry has a scar on his forehead
Hagrid is gamekeeper of Hogwarts
Harry plays a sport called Quidditch
Harry is Gryffindor's seeker
Harry has to catch the golden snitch
A golden snitch is a gold little ball with wings
This is Harry Potter

Hunter Anderson, Grade 4
Mary Walter Elementary School, VA

Autumn

Autumn spreads many different colors around
In autumn most of the trees' leaves fall to the ground
In autumn the leaves come in different sizes
In autumn there are many surprises
In autumn children go to school
In autumn people cover up their pools
In autumn we go trick-or-treating on Hallows' Eve
In autumn children jump in piles of leaves
In autumn the weather begins to get colder
In autumn you should cover your shoulders
In autumn most of the trees' leaves fall to the ground
Autumn spreads many different colors around

Drew Walthall, Grade 6
Paul L Dunbar Middle School for Innovation, VA

Weekday

I jump on the large golden dragon
I sit on the front spine with the other followers.
We see the black castle ahead.
The masters are sitting with their spells.
I am last off.
We are pushed to our chambers.
We do all of their hard work
Suddenly the headmaster comes in
He is about to cast a spell when the bell rings.
I am at school.
I see my friends run to the buses.
An uneventful day.

Kate Rarey, Grade 5
Kensington Parkwood Elementary School, MD

My Family

Fun to play with and be around.
Always loving, giving, and the best.
My family loves me with all of their hearts.
I'll love them always, and I'll never love anyone more.
Love is the best thing a person can have.
Your family is the most important thing in life.

Nathan Smith, Grade 6
Floyd T Binns Middle School, VA

Baseball

Baseball is fun
I like it a ton
When I pitch the ball it's like a bullet coming out of a gun.

I like baseball a lot
When I go to play a game the sun is very hot,
I like the game a lot.

Baseball is my favorite sport,
although the games feel really short.

I'll stick with baseball 'til the end,
baseball is my best friend.

Zack Evans, Grade 6
Floyd T Binns Middle School, VA

Friends

Friends are good
Friends are great
Friends get mad but never hate

I love friends
They love you even when they're mad at you
Friends forgive
Friends forget

Friends are respective
Friends have a good perspective
Friends love you
And you love them

Ryan Myers, Grade 6
St Jane de Chantal School, MD

The Run

I was running down the street,
all of a sudden I stumble,
I fall on my hands and knees,
I look up to find my older brother,
He's standing over me,
He runs and yells come on,
I can't help but looking at Ellagrace running
How graceful she is,
My brother, yelling again
I look in front of me the shadow of my bus
— I say "Oh no!"
It's The Run.

Kaitlynn Lane, Grade 5
Clara Byrd Baker Elementary School, VA

Black and Blue Skies Are Coming

Here come the black and blue skies.
Coming for you, the big, bad, bang.
The angry mob that wants the black and blue.
Black and blue skies make you feel like you're a big ball of angry.

Zoe Etherton, Grade 4
Weyanoke Elementary School, VA

The Best Mother

My mom is beautiful
Her eyes are shiny and bright
Her voice is sometimes
Soft and sweet
Other times
It is hard and firm
She makes me laugh
When she tells me jokes and stories
She buys me clothes and shoes
And anything I need
She makes me happy
She is the most beautiful mother
that anyone could have.

Yessenia Martinez, Grade 4
Bensley Elementary School, VA

The Return

The people go by.
They are like sleek sly foxes.
Why are they so sad?
The flags waving in the air.
A force field of gold surrounds them!
The horses, pounding their feet.
Wind whipping wildly!
Chomp, what was that?
My, oh my, it's just a horse.
The landscape so green.
What a dazzling delight!
Now I am home, and I am free!!!

Daniel Lacey, Grade 4
Boonsboro Elementary School, MD

Thanksgiving

T alking with family
H aving the blessing
A round the table
N ot enough room on my plate
K indly pass me the butter
S et platters of turkey and ham on the table
G et the pumpkin and apple pies
I n my belly I am stuffed
V isiting cousins
I ndian corn decorations
N ow it is time to clear the table
G iving thanks for all I have

Michael Franklin, Grade 6
Graham Middle School, VA

What Is Blue?

Blue is the tears that fall when we are sad
It is water
Rivers
Birds in the sky
And flowers in the garden

Gabriel Polglase, Grade 5
St Bartholomew School, MD

Leaves

Leaves have fallen off the trees
And are raked up in a pile
I am jumping into them
And having fun for a long while

We are building up leaf forts
And having a leaf fight
I'm really enjoying myself
That's what fall leaves are meant for

Rachel Kilby, Grade 4
Mary Walter Elementary School, VA

Christmas

C hildren around the trees
H ere to open their gifts
R ising North Star
I mmanuel
S now
T insel
M usic playing
A pple cider simmering in a pot
S leds going down the hills

Alisha Gray, Grade 6
Graham Middle School, VA

Wonders of Life

The Nature is Beautiful
The Sky, Water and Flower
The Brain is like a Pearl,
Make you shine.
Wherever you go,
My Heart beats.
Life comes; Life goes —
That's the wonder of life.

Bhanu Sharma, Grade 5
Rosemont Forest Elementary School, VA

Apples

Some apples are sour, saucy, or sweet
They can be a tasty treat
Apples are delicious
Also very nutritious
When you take a bite
You get an awesome site
Apples are yummy
They fill my tummy

Madison Bradshaw, Grade 4
Boonsboro Elementary School, MD

Rain

When the rain drops on our faces
you may think it's just water but I
see these drops as God's tears that are
full of love and friendship.

Alyiah Howell, Grade 5
Rosemont Forest Elementary School, VA

Winter

In the Winter
The thought of
Snow falling
Going sledding
Shoveling the driveway
Having fun
Playing with friends
Having snowball fights
The dream of Christmas night

Timothy McCann, Grade 5
St Bartholomew School, MD

Christmas

Opening gifts,
Coming together as a family,
Celebrating Jesus' birthday,
Children smiling and laughing,
Paper and ribbon everywhere,
Stockings overflowing,
Mom trying to clean up,
Dad having fun,
Everyone celebrating.

Joanna Courtis, Grade 5
St. Bartholomew School, MD

Halloween

H alloween is fun.
A ll of us trick or treat.
L ots of pumpkins on the front steps.
L ots of candy for us to eat.
O ur parents just want one piece.
W e see people in costumes.
E laine is a pumpkin.
E van is a rock star.
N ow we are done with our Halloween.

Meagan Smith, Grade 5
St Joseph School-Fullerton, MD

When It Rains

When it starts to rain
I start to feel relaxed soon
I really love rains

Ashley Nicole Williams, Grade 6
Floyd T Binns Middle School, VA

Basketball

My heart is pounding
The ball is bouncing
I stop, take a look and shoot
The ball flies out of my hands, swirling
Toward the basket
All eyes fixed on the ball
Suddenly, the whole crowd springs up,
In joy, screaming and chanting my name.

Christina Mounzer, Grade 6
Graham Middle School, VA

Friendship

From out in the snow
You come in very weary
A mug of hot chocolate waiting
You're so grateful, you're teary

The gratitude you feel is overwhelming
A small thing goes a very long way
But friendship can provide more comfort
Than warmth on a cold winter's day

The memories you make together
Just you and your friend
Are truly eternal
They last 'til the end

They're great memories, too
You'll laugh when you recall
The wonderful things you've done together
Whether in the spring or the fall

With your friend you tell secrets
Feeling a sense that you belong
You can't go wrong with friendships
They will last and stay strong
Emma Eder, Grade 6
St Jane De Chantal School, MD

9-11

September the eleventh I will never forget.
I remember that day very well.
So many people lost their lives
The day the Twin Towers fell.

A bunch of men from Iraq
hijacked four of our planes.
One hit each tower
and blew up in flames

I watched it all happen on the news
so many of us asked why.
The rest of us just stood there
so helpless and cried

There now stands a monument
with thousands of names.
Of victims and heroes
Iraqi bombers are to blame.

The pain and sorrow will never end
to the families we send our love.
We pray for healing and strength
from heaven above.
David Brannan, Grade 6
Graham Middle School, VA

Christmas Time

C hrist
H appy
R eady
I cicle
S now
T ime to open presents
M ass time
A wesome
S tockings
Lillian Tran, Grade 4
Angelus Academy, VA

The Scary Nights and Days

As the nights go by I am alone,
In bed fast asleep by myself.
In my aunt's house afraid
Without a mom or dad with me.
As the days go by, I am in isolation
on my couch, outside solo.
Alarmed that my brothers and I
Single-handed without parents,
We hold onto each other
Jazmyne Lambert, Grade 5
Rosemont Forest Elementary School, VA

Christmas Fun

C old
H at and glove
R eally great
I cy
S uper cold
T otally cool
M ajor snow
A mazing
S uper fun
Noah Morales, Grade 4
Angelus Academy, VA

The Acorn

An acorn is like a Canadian soldier
It looks like it wears a fluffy helmet
The shell is like an army protecting the seed
The seed is as small as an ant.
Timothy Vaikness, Grade 4
Riderwood Elementary School, MD

Caitlin

C lever
A good friend
I maginative
T otally fun
L oving and caring
I ncredible
N ot mean
Caitlin Nalda, Grade 4
Angelus Academy, VA

Winter

Winter is coming
Kids go outside as the snow falls down
Having snowman fun
Bells ring
You feel joy and cheer
Children laughing in the snow
Winter Is Here!
Ana Hernandez, Grade 5
Rosemont Forest Elementary School, VA

Falling Sun

A shade of orange and purple,
Falls straight down like a shimmering star,
It's time for the day to end,
Like a pencil out of lead,
Like a book with no pages left,
It's time for the day to end,
It's time for the Falling Sun.
Will Hyland, Grade 5
Seven Locks Elementary School, MD

My Life

My life is great.
My life is sweet.
I have everything I could possibly want.
I have my family.
I have my style.
My life is my life and it will never change.
I love my life the way it is.
Chase Jenkins, Grade 6
Floyd T Binns Middle School, VA

Color Sounds

Purple yells at me in the darkness
Orange whispers to me on the street
Green is giggling on my sweatshirt
"It's hot!" complains black on my flip-flop
"I look cool!" brags neon green
"But I look cooler!" says neon pink
"We all look cool!" exclaimed neon orange
Meaghan Dal Collo, Grade 4
Boonsboro Elementary School, MD

Rasckle

R estful
A ctive
S leepy
C uddly
K itten
L oving
E xciting
Taylor Cover, Grade 5
St Joseph School-Fullerton, MD

Polar Bear's Grace
White furry dense coats,
They lumber across the ice,
Making dens of snow.
Sylvie Hoy, Grade 6
Floyd T Binns Middle School, VA

Flowers
Dances in the rain
Tans in the hot, melting sun
Dies in the winter
Brianna Watts, Grade 6
Floyd T Binns Middle School, VA

Bears
Black or brown, big, strong.
Walk on four legs, eat too much.
Climb trees, and furry.
Scott Bothum II, Grade 6
Floyd T Binns Middle School, VA

The Wind
The wind is blowing
It is raining very hard
The trees are blowing
Wesley Hoffman, Grade 6
Floyd T Binns Middle School, VA

Basketball
Round, light
Dribbling, shooting, scoring
Basketball is the best sport!
Jia Coppola, Grade 6
Graham Middle School, VA

A Day in Japan
Starting with haikus,
And making origami,
And eating sushi.
Peter Hoang, Grade 6
Floyd T Binns Middle School, VA

Horses
The horse came to play,
he neighed and whinnied all day,
then he ate his hay!
Sarah Humphreys, Grade 6
Floyd T Binns Middle School, VA

sunset
cool colors in sky
night comes after sunset calm
very bright pretty
Gabby Coburn, Grade 6
Floyd T Binns Middle School, VA

Being a Raindrop
Being a raindrop is tough.
It's simply not enough.

When falling through the sky,
We soar in the air and fly.

We see all the cities, so to us it's a pity,
Because we do it again, and again and we're not in the raindrop committee.

We would love to be, love to be.
It would be better than just falling to sea.

When we hit the ocean's depth,
We see water's last breath…

It brings joy! I tell you, joy!
But we wait, and wait, to go again and sometimes it annoys.

So as you can see,
It's tough to be a raindrop.
Waiting in the rain cycle just to plop…to earth.
Joe Beatty, Grade 6
Parkside Middle School, VA

I Am Birthday Excitement!
I am a girl who loves her birthday!
I wonder what presents I will get.
I hear kids cheering, paper ripping, people talking, music playing,
balloons popping, people singing Happy Birthday songs.
I see shimmering wrapping paper, bagged presents, and colorful ribbon.
I want the most quality birthday presents from my friends and family.

I am a girl who loves her birthday!
I pretend I love presents that I really don't.
I feel very happy and excited on my birthday because I'm one year older.
I touch the glossy wrapping paper.
I worry that I will get something that I already own.

I am a girl who loves her birthday!
I understand people who aren't able to attend.
I say, "Thank you for coming!"
I dream I'll get everything I want.
I try to help clean up.
I hope I will get the bike I always wanted.
I am a girl who loves her birthday!
Julia Reed, Grade 5
Blackrock School, RI

Autumn
I walk along in the lively woods letting the crisp wind turn my face a light magenta;
The colors around me brighten my soul and make my heart feel warm;
I wait for the time when all the world seems to lull itself, just to let nature sing us a tune;
Tiny feet rustle the new fallen leaves as if they are dancing along;
My eyes capture the charm and beauty, making me hope it will never go away.
Caroline Brooks, Grade 5
Pemberton Elementary School, VA

Volcano

The mighty volcano,
From below, it gurgles, rumbles, bubbles.

Then, it rushes to the top,
There is a pop, boom and bang.
Spew, shake, sizzle,
That is what it does.

Into the rock and wood,
Its carving is great,
It can burn, scar, and damage.

It travels toward the ocean big and blue,
And slowly cools,
Now, it is rock.

Ryon Warner, Grade 6
Trinity School, MD

My Dog, Sugar

She's white and light brown
She's hyper and playful
Seven years old in dog years,
Forty-nine in people years

A Pit-bull with a huge personality
Some people run away
When she goes by
Some people whistle
To bring her closer

Sugar is special to me
She's my first dog
My first real
Responsibility

Rahkeam Baskerville, Grade 4
Bensley Elementary School, VA

My Three Chums

A good best friend
I want to be…
I have three friends
I'd like to be.

We look at each other
With trusting eyes…
What I see them do
I also try.

I'm very excited
for the years to come…
For my BFFs
The Three Musketeers, my three chums.

Madison Bryant, Grade 6
St Jane De Chantal School, MD

Why I Love Summer

Summer is so very fun
Summer is so hot
Summer is just really cool
Spring is really not
Summer is the time to play
In summer you can also swim
In a big, chilly pool
Summer's not the season
We have to be in school
That's why I love summer
Spring is such a bummer

Mike Hernandez, Grade 4
Bensley Elementary School, VA

Toby

Sitting,
Watching,
Purring in the sun.

Leaping,
Jumping,
Meowing for his food.

Loving,
Caring,
Being my friend!

Carolyn Palmer, Grade 5
Pemberton Elementary School, VA

Fire

Fire burning trees and houses
Embers floating all over the place
Weeping birds watching their nest burn
Fire expanding farther and farther
Destroying everything in its path
Spreading like a virus
The light almost blinds you
Mother Earth is almost dead
Water is its weakness
Burning out the fire
Mother Earth grows again

Michael Ayala, Grade 5
Rosemont Forest Elementary School, VA

Halloween

H alloween is so much fun.
A ll of us trick or treat.
L ots of fun for everyone.
L ots of candy to eat.
O utside are pumpkins round and orange.
W e love Halloween.
E at all the candy!
E at all of it!
N o more candy until next year.

Benjamin Stitz, Grade 5
St Joseph School-Fullerton, MD

Dreams

Dreams, Dreams
Dreams big and small
Dreams, Dreams
We have them all.

Dreams, Dreams
Dreams here and there
Dreams, Dreams
Are everywhere.

Dreams, Dreams
Dreams can reach the sky
so,
Dream your Dreams until the
Day you die.

Victoria Corner, Grade 6
Graham Middle School, VA

Space

I dream of a place,
A place far in space,
A place way afar,
On a distant star.

The star I see,
Has a gas sea,
Where aliens roam free,
That is what I see.

There is a place in the galaxy
Where I long to be,
A place right out there for me.

Space, the final frontier.

Clay Webb, Grade 6
Graham Middle School, VA

My Brother

My brother and I always play together
When we play soccer, we care for each other
I give him company when he sleeps
And make sure I'm by his side
When he gets hurt my feelings grow sad
Whenever he needs me I'll always be there
It took us two years to meet
He's sometimes a pain, sometimes we fight
But when we have fun
We get teary from laughing!
My brother has a loving heart
And always cares for others
I will love him forever
And wish him the best in life.
This is my brother!

Sebastian Villagomez, Grade 4
Mary Walter Elementary School, VA

Pandas

Pandas are cuddly, cute, and soft
They climb trees to gather bamboo
Playing is fun to them
Peek-a-boo, hiding behind thickets
They make an impact on our Earth

Jacob Rush, Grade 5
Rosemont Forest Elementary School, VA

Midnight

The gentle quiet,
the sound of wild animals outside,
the soft snoring of family,
the stars are out,
and the moon is in full blaze.

Zeb Armstrong, Grade 6
Floyd T Binns Middle School, VA

Skate

S kating is what I do.
K ick-flips and ollies are the best
A fter that I do a move called shove it west
T ake my skateboard into the air
E agerly spinning in midair

Kaden Woodward, Grade 6
Floyd T Binns Middle School, VA

Candy

C runch bars
A wesome Kit-Kat
N ever ending chocolate
D elicious Reese's
Y ummy Hershey's

Jordyn Hurley, Grade 4
Angelus Academy, VA

Germs

G reen
E ew
R idiculous
M ean
S ickness

Solana Cokenour, Grade 4
Angelus Academy, VA

Dogs Are There for You

Dogs are sweet like a piece of candy
Dogs are playful like a little brother
Dogs care for you like family does
And dogs are there for you like a best friend

Victoria Cox, Grade 4
Riderwood Elementary School, MD

S t. Patrick's Day
P urple and pink flowers
R abbits for Easter
I ris, daffodils and tulips
N ew birth for trees
G reen, green grass

S wimming
U nder the flaming sun
M iles along the shore
M onths off of school
E xtra cold lemonade
R oasting hot dogs

Seasons

F ootball
A utumn
L eaves changing
L owering temperatures

W hite wonderlands
I cicles hanging from roofs
N ever ending cocoa
T winkling lights
E xtra clothes for warmth
R acing on sleds

Rachel Richmond, Grade 6
Graham Middle School, VA

First Day

Summer was very exciting, although the mosquitoes kept biting.
Then all of a sudden it became colder and the days became shorter.
So I put on my backpack, and went off to school.
I was starting 6th grade, I thought it was cool.
At first I was nervous and felt somewhat queasy,
but as the day went by it became more and more easy.
I joined cross country, I kept a good pace.
Before I knew it I ran my first race.
I was given my first project; I had two maps to make.
I thought of drawing them on paper, but instead I baked it on a cake!
I switched to viola from violin, now I can play tremendous hymns.
I've met many new friends, and look forward to a fabulous year,
because now I have nothing to fear.

Emma Wray, Grade 6
Paul L Dunbar Middle School for Innovation, VA

Men on a Boat

Men on a boat relaxed and calm
One man playing the violin softly
The paddle is splashing loudly in the greenish-blue water
All the trees, talking to the mountains
The wet sand with the heavy logs on top
The bluish-yellow sky watching the boy waving the bright cloth
The men show joy when they see the mountains
All of the clouds whispering to the mountains, "What's up with them?"
"There will never be men like that ever again," said the bushes.
The men sailed home, and the land and sky said, "Goodbye."

Zachary Crampton, Grade 4
Boonsboro Elementary School, MD

My Dad

M akes us all happy
Y es, he does all the cooking

D onald is his name
A wesome things he does for his family
D efinitely the best dad in the world

Josh Sutherland, Grade 5
Pasadena Elementary School, MD

The Costume Contest

I won the greatest costume contest
I really wanted to protest
They shrieked at the suit I had
But this is really really sad,

I wasn't even wearing one

Jackson Walsh, Grade 6
Norfolk Christian Middle School, VA

I Am a Dancer

I am one whose heart yearns for dance
I wonder if I will dance worldwide
I hear the tapping of tap shoes, the music is loud and clear from the echoing, surround sound near
I see my reflection watching me perfect my dance steps
I want my own dance studio so I can teach my dance steps
I am the one whose heart yearns for dance.

I pretend that I am a famous dance teacher
I feel graceful, light on my toes, preparing to put on a great show
I touch hearts of many audiences, I worry that I will fall during an important dance recital
I am one whose heart yearns for dance

I understand to get better, practicing is key
I say dance is my soul, I dream I'll be a dance teacher
I try to improve in dance, I hope that I will be an inspiration for someone else
I am the one whose heart yearns for dance

Kyla Gauvin, Grade 5
Blackrock School, RI

Snowflake

So tiny and perfect, a work of art, but the warmth of your touch makes it fall apart.
Floating gently on the air, twirling and spinning without a care.
So delicate and pristine but what does it mean?
Infinite possibilities in design, no two are a like at any time. A dropping temperature can only mean
soon enough snowflakes will be seen,
purest white replaces green.

Lara Payne, Grade 6
Graham Middle School, VA

My Day at the Beach!

I am, a girl who enjoys the beach.
I wonder if the waves are crashing.
I hear…the waves crashing. I hear people running
In the sand and children splashing each other.
I see, the light house guiding the boats at night.
I want, to relax on a chair and play in the sand.
I am a girl who enjoys the beach.

I pretend, I am sleeping on a sunny beach.
I feel crabs pinching me in the sand. I also feel
The warm water.
I touch the slimy brown seaweed.
I worry I am afraid I will drown in the water.
I am a girl who enjoys the beach.

I understand, there are big waves coming tonight.
I say, the water is cold.
I dream, I am a good swimmer.
I try to ride the waves.
I hope, I can catch some big waves today
Or someday.
I am, a girl who enjoys the beach.

Aryssa Hunt, Grade 5
Blackrock School, RI

New Year's Dawn

I look through the window.
It is almost midnight.
Soon this year will be over
And a new one will commence.
I gaze up at the stars
Reminiscing the past.
One star winks
And disappears into the darkness.
I glance at the clock — 12:00

I watch all the other young orphans
Unaware of the meaning of life.
I take a glimpse at the moon.
It smiles as if to tell me it's time.
I look at the clock — 12:01
I think about some parents
Looking for children.
I hope they are thinking about us right now.

"Happy New Year," I whisper.
I blow out my candle and crawl into bed
Waiting for a new dawn.

Pallavi Bhave, Grade 6
Westminster School, VA

Nothing Lasts Forever

Trapped inside a box,
Calling my name,
Out of many different beautiful pencils,
I choose You

Yellow as the sun on an early Sunday morning,
Nice pink eraser,
Pink as my cheeks on a chilly fall day,
I get relieved just to see you again,
Your wood is Comforting

You glide on the surface of the paper,
You're just like a voice
That could go on forever
Until it breaks,
And it's gone
But only,
Until you meet it again

You slowly run out,
I think about you,
And it gets to me,
You are MY pencil

Your marks are memories.

Noy Dahan, Grade 6
Charles E Smith Jewish Day School Lower Campus, MD

An Ode to Rosie, My Dog

Oh, Rosie
You're so cute. When you come sit next to me I think
you're the best of the best. Your soft fur its like
I'm touching a stuffed animal.
Without you my world would collapse. I would
never trade you for anything. Not even the best
thing in the world. You remind me of a puffball
with your brown spots and smushed face.
You're like an angel to me, always by my side, and you
never leave me.

Christopher Mounzer, Grade 6
Graham Middle School, VA

Friendship

When I first saw you, Rocky, in the 3rd grade,
I knew we would be friends when I stole your Powerade.

You yelled and scratched and hissed and screeched
but all I said was "GET OVER IT GEEZ!"

Then one day you came up to me and said
"Do you want to try my trampoline?"
Then we were friends up to the 5th grade
then I left for sixth grade at a new school.

Jack Scanlon, Grade 6
St Jane De Chantal School, MD

Puppy Love

I first met you at a neighbor's house.
I thought I wanted a kitten,
but you were as cute as a button
and felt like a pair of mittens.

I came to your house as you were waiting for me.
"Oh goodness," I said, "It's a surprise for me!"
You jumped into my arms,
though I wasn't harmed.

You barked and begged and licked my leg,
but now you are older and slow.
You should always know
that you are the best, Snow.

Kayla Tiller, Grade 6
St Jane De Chantal School, MD

Invincible and Indivisible Yet Invisible

It is not something you are born with,
It is something taught from man to son, from son to grandson,
From generation, to generation,
It never dies, but it kills.

It is like a tree, except, it never stops growing.
It is there, always in use,
It is the food of the devil, the dream of Hitler,
And the item of an evil spirit,

It can't be put out by water, stopped by guns,
Or even destroyed by a bomb,
All forms of it will never die.
For it is hate.

Sam Strickberger, Grade 6
Charles E Smith Jewish Day School Lower Campus, MD

The Summer Days Are Good

It must be summer,
Flowers dance in the hot wind,
Don't you like summer?

Alicia Reyes, Grade 6
Floyd T Binns Middle School, VA

Index

Author Autograph Page

Drew Walthall
loves you
-11

EMMA
=11

EMMA
3

Marinmy
11

Gerika Moorman
11

Emma was here!!

Author Autograph Page

Author Autograph Page

Author Autograph Page

Author Autograph Page

Author Autograph Page

Author Autograph Page

Author Autograph Page

Author Autograph Page

Author Autograph Page

Author Autograph Page

Author Autograph Page